At the Crossroads

Special Educational Needs and Teacher Education

Edited by

John Dwyfor Davies and Philip Garner

David Fulton Publishers

London

David Fulton Publishers Ltd
Ormond House, 26–27 Boswell Street, London WC1N 3JD

First published in Great Britain by David Fulton Publishers 1997

British Library Cataloguing in Publication Data
A catalogue record for this book is available from the British Library

ISBN 1–85346–447–3

Typeset by Textype Typesetters, Cambridge
Printed in Great Britain by BPC Books and Journals, Exeter

Contents

Contributors

Mel Ainscow is Professor and Head of Centre for Special Educational Needs at the University of Manchester.

Christopher Blake is Assistant Professor in the Department of Secondary Education, Towson University, USA.

Morag Bowden is General Inspector (Special Educational Needs) in the London Borough of Ealing.

David Coulby is Professor of Education and Dean of the Faculty of Education and Human Sciences at Bath College of Higher Education.

Pat Dodds is Lecturer in Education in the School of Education, Brunel University.

John Dwyfor Davies is Director of Studies (CPD) in the Faculty of Education, University of the West of England, Bristol.

Juliet Edmonds is Lecturer in the School of Education, Brunel University.

Diane Fidler is Deputy Headteacher at Brislington School, City of Bristol.

Malcolm Garner is Head of Service for Hearing Impaired, Visually Impaired and Physically Disabled for Staffordshire. He is also Honorary Secretary of the Special Educational Needs Training Consortium.

Philip Garner is Senior Lecturer in Special Education in the School of Education, Brunel University.

Viv Hinchcliffe is Headteacher of Rectory Paddock Special School, London Borough of Bromley.

Olga Miller is Lecturer at the Institute of Education, London University.

Jim Moon teaches science at Brislington School, City of Bristol.

Sarah Sandow was, until recently, Reader in Education in the School of Education, Brunel University.

Anne Sinclair Taylor is Lecturer in Education at the University of Warwick.

Jane Tarr is Senior Lecturer in Education in the Faculty of Education, University of the West of England, Bristol.

Alexis Taylor is Lecturer in Education in the School of Education, Brunel University.

Gary Thomas is Professor of Education in the Faculty of Education, University of the West of England, Bristol.

Linda Thomas is Professor and Head of the School of Education, Brunel University.

Lynne Thorogood is Lecturer in Education in the School of Education, Brunel University.

Abbreviations

ACSET	Advisory Council for the Supply and Education of Teachers
ADHD	Attention Deficit and/or Hyperactivity Disorder
APEL	Accreditation of Prior Experiential Learning
ARR	Assessment, Recording and Reporting
BEd	Bachelor of Education
CATE	Council for the Accreditation of Teacher Education
CSE	Certificate of Secondary Education
CNAA	Council for National Academic Awards
CoP	Code of Practice on the Identification and Assessment of Special Educational Needs
CPD	Continuing Professional Development
DES	Department of Education and Science
DfEE	Department for Education and Employment
EBD	Emotional and Behavioural Difficulties
ESN(M)	Educationally Sub-normal (moderate)
ESN(S)	Educationally Sub-normal (severe)
INSET	In-service Education and Training
GCSE	General Certificate of Secondary Education
GEST	Grants for Education Support and Training
GMS	Grant Maintained School
HEFC	Higher Education Funding Council
HEI	Higher Education Institution
HI	Hearing Impaired
HMI	Her Majesty's Inspectors/Inspectorate
IDP	Institutional Development Plan
IEP	Individual Education Plan
ITE	Initial Teacher Education
IIP	Investors in People
KS	Key Stage
LSAs	Learning Support Assistant
LEA	Local Education Authority
LMS	Local Management of Schools
MEd	Master of Education
MLD	Moderate Learning Difficulties
NSPCC	National Society for the Protection of Children
NCC	National Curriculum Council

NQT	Newly Qualified Teacher
OFSTED	Office for Standards in Education
PSE	Personal and Social Education
PH	Physically Handicapped
PCFC	Polytechnics and Colleges Funding Council
PGCE	Post-Graduate Certificate in Education
PMLD	Profound and Multiple Learning Difficulties
PoS	Programme of Study
QTS	Qualified Teacher Status
SCAA	Schools Curriculum and Assessment Authority
SEN	Special Educational Needs
SENCo	Special Educational Needs Coordinator
SENTC	Special Educational Needs Training Consortium
SENTAG	Special Educational Needs Training and Advisory Group
SLD	Severe Learning Difficulties
TTA	Teacher Training Agency
VI	Visually Impaired

CHAPTER ONE

Introduction

In planning this book we have asked each of our contributing authors to emphasise the positive aspects of present and future practice relating to special educational needs (SEN) in both initial teacher education (ITE) and continuing professional development (CPD). We acknowledge that it can sometimes be difficult to discount Garrett's (1996) rather chilling contemporary observation on teacher education and SEN that 'half a century after the 1944 Education Act many children with special educational needs still do not have access to an appropriately trained teacher and, with so many of those early pioneering campaigners reaching the age of retirement, as well as financial cutbacks and the closing of special education courses in colleges and institutions of higher education, the future looks even bleaker' (p.23). Nevertheless, it is our belief that opportunities do exist, and our contributors have sought to illustrate some of these in their writing.

We have adopted the term *teacher education* throughout this book, rather than the officially preferred *teacher training*. This, we believe, correctly recognises the status of teaching as a profession. The reader will note, however, that the terms 'teacher training' and 'in-service training' are used from time to time, usually when applied to a particular context or to denote a specific orientation. At various points, also, the phrases 'SEN pupils' or 'pupils with SEN' are used by individual contributors. It is not our intention, or theirs, that these expressions be interpreted to mean that our authors are locating SEN as a 'within-child' phenomenon. Rather, the terms are used for the sake of brevity. Whilst individual institutions are named within the text, pseudonyms have been used for all pupils and teachers named in case studies.

In early discussions concerning the format of this book we had envisaged a volume comprising discrete sections on ITE and CPD. Subsequently, however, we have recognised that, by so doing, we would be advocating a segregation of pre- and in-service professional development. What we have sought to offer, on the contrary, is a sense that teacher development in SEN *should* be an ongoing, lifelong process. What happens in ITE, therefore, will have a bearing on subsequent approaches in CPD; and, as ITE courses are now substantially school-based, professional development initiatives for serving teachers are likely to have a reciprocal effect on that provision.

The first three chapters of this book provide both a contextual analysis of recent and current practices in both ITE and CPD, as a basis for subsequent contributions from individual authors, and an exploration of some of the philosophical issues underpinning current provision. David Coulby's challenging chapter advocates a radical reformulation of current approaches and thinking in ITE courses. Our interpretation of disability, he maintains, is predicated by unchallenged knowledge systems and knowledge protocols: both need to be critically examined if ITE providers are to promote an experience for student teachers which will equip them to meet the diverse needs of the school population and to secure their inclusion. Linda Thomas then examines the values perspective in relation to current approaches in teacher education, and, in so doing, argues that new teachers, irrespective of their subject or age orientation, need to acknowledge the importance of 'individual needs' as a central component in their period of qualification. All three introductory chapters, whilst variously referring to ITE and CPD, provide an underpinning rationale for teacher development in SEN as a whole, and refer to themes to which all our contributing authors frequently return.

The next group of chapters focuses on ITE, and reflects the ongoing struggle of practitioners (HEI tutors, school-mentors, individual teachers and students) to meet the increasing demands made upon them in the mid-1990s. As an indication of the dilemmas and difficulties facing all of those involved in ITE provision, the views of students in training can provide a useful illustration of current concerns: John Dwyfor Davies and Philip Garner thus examine data from a recent study of the views of NQTs about their SEN experiences whilst qualifying. These early experiences in SEN indicate the range of issues which students have to be aware of on entering the teaching profession. The chapter then proceeds to offer some examples of approaches which have provided more effective coverage of SEN within ITE.

'Partnership' has become an over-used, even bowdlerised, term to describe the arrangements that represent current ITE practice. Teachers in schools and tutors in HEIs have, over the last few years, been required to enter into formal training relationships, which are based mainly in schools. Little recognition has been given, in making this mandatory, that most school-and-HEI working relationships have long recognised the importance of the ongoing school experience of ITE students. That many 'partnership' arrangements have been successful is indicative more of this tradition, and the sound professional relationships that have been developed, rather than of the official requirement for schools and HEIs to work in this way. As an illustration of contemporary practice, Pat Dodds, Alexis Taylor and Lynne Thorogood outline a focused partnership approach in three case studies, where ITE providers and school colleagues have collaborated to provide intensive intervention programmes for under-achievers.

A major dilemma facing ITE providers has been the huge range of SEN issues which need to be introduced to NQTs, including some which appear at first glance to be only tangentially linked to children's learning difficulties. One of these is child protection, which is of critical importance in SEN given that the security and wellbeing of children is essential to their learning and emotional development. Anne Sinclair Taylor argues that this area of work should be an ongoing consideration within teacher education, and provides an illustration of a discrete course which has run successfully at this level. Christopher Blake, in the following chapter, provides a comparative dimension. He describes the experiences of a student teacher from the United States who undertakes a school placement in an English comprehensive school. In doing so Blake challenges some of the basic premises on which school-based teacher education, and its treatment of SEN, are based.

The next series of chapters moves the focus on to CPD, where a 'modular' approach to providing CPD has become a salient feature. Sarah Sandow's chapter discusses the origins of this way of operating. She suggests that, whilst from a pragmatic viewpoint, modularisation was essential for the survival of many award-bearing professional development courses in HEIs, such arrangements were largely beneficial to teachers. They brought flexibility, an increased choice of providers, and a recognition, via APEL, of a teacher's previous professional experience. Modular courses assume many forms, and an example is described in chapters by Diane Fidler and Jim Moon. The authors consider a school-based modular programme, developed in collaboration with an HEI, from two different perspectives. Fidler looks at the whole-school impact of the initiative, whilst Moon gives an account of an individual module within the programme, dealing with the 'problem behaviour' of pupils and their relationship to learning difficulties.

Since the mid-1980s concern has been expressed about the notable decline in professional development opportunities in the field of SLD; this has been most recently voiced by SENTC (1996). In his chapter on this subject, Viv Hinchcliffe offers a critique of CPD developments in this area and presents a version of how matters might be improved, not simply for those teachers already in service but also to ensure a continuous supply of new entrants to this important area of SEN.

Two chapters on subject-based work, adopting different forms of CPD delivery, then provide the reader with insights into current and alternative ways of staff development. Firstly, Juliet Edmonds examines recent approaches in science and SEN in order to illustrate the potential available of all subject-based teachers to contribute towards meeting individual needs. In the succeeding chapter, Jane Tarr shows the benefits of linking mainstream and special schools in a CPD programme, which also involves ITE students, in partnership with an HEI. This involves both teachers and children working together using the performing arts as a focus.

The work of LEAs in providing CPD is acknowledged in the contribution of Morag Bowden who writes from the perspective of an LEA officer. She suggests that, in spite of the gradual emasculation of LEAs after the 1988 Education Act, there is still evidence of much innovative CPD work going on. Given the rapid changes that have taken place within LEAs following legislation, such initiatives are not only to be applauded but should also be seen as an essential part of the CPD landscape. Again, the term 'partnership' springs to mind when summarising these developments.

The Special Educational Needs Training Consortium (SENTC) submitted its report to the DfEE in 1996. This marked a major contribution to the debate concerning the current levels of effectiveness of both ITE and CPD provision in SEN. Malcolm Garner and Olga Miller, two members of the SENTC committee, provide an overview and critique of its report to the DfEE, in which a range of recommendations were made regarding the ongoing professional development of teachers working in SEN, whether in mainstream or special schools.

The concluding chapters examine future directions for teacher development in SEN. Mel Ainscow's chapter, building on his research and professional development activity in various countries, considers the implications of the findings of a recent project involving teachers and teacher-educators in over fifty countries. Using the ITE and CPD experiences of colleagues in other countries has important benefits, as Mittler, Conti-Ramsden and Daunt (1995) emphasised: 'It appears that we have different strengths in different countries, deeply rooted in history and culture.' Acknowledgement of this situation can provide an important platform upon which European teacher educators can learn from one another. Ainscow suggests that international experiences can provide an important basis for moves towards inclusive education.

Finally, Gary Thomas, in the summary chapter, maps a vision for ITE and CPD activity in SEN. Thomas was reticent to provide the requested 'blueprint' for the future, arguing that this implies prescription. Indeed, the range of initiatives, and the differential interpretations of teacher development in SEN described by the various contributors to this book, suggest that this was an unwise editorial request at the outset. SEN provision is at a critical stage in its development; the ongoing changes that have taken place as a result of legislation and official guidance require that any projection about the future should retain flexibility at its heart. Bearing this in mind, therefore, the suggestion is made that the future will be characterised by a continued, vigorous debate about our personal and professional beliefs and the ways in which they are translated into actions which enable 'special' education to become 'inclusive'.

This book has a number of important predecessors, and we wish to acknowledge our debt to them. Influential to us in our conceptualisation of both the volume as a whole and our own individual interpretations of SEN and teacher education have been books by Sayer and Jones (1985), Hinson (1991), Upton (1991), Vulliamy and Webb (1992) and Mittler and Daunt (1995). The reader is referred to these volumes as indicative of a rapid growth of interest in staff development (in the widest sense) in SEN over the last ten years. In considering what they have had to say, however, little doubt will remain that we have arrived at a point in the development of ITE and CPD for SEN which, as both threat and opportunity are presenting themselves in equal measure, can be interpreted as a crossroads. Effectively meeting the needs of those children and young people with learning difficulties in the future will require good route-finding – and some brave decisions.

References

Garrett, J. (1996) 'Expanding opportunities: 1944 to 1970', in P. Mittler and V. Sinason (eds.) *Changing Policy and Practice for People with Learning Disabilities*. London: Cassell.

Hinson, M. (1991) *Teachers and Special Educational Needs*. Harlow: Longman.

McClelland, V. and Varma, V. (1996) *The Needs of Teachers*. London: Cassell.

Mittler, P. (1995) 'Special needs education in England and Wales', in P. Mittler and P. Daunt (eds.) *Teacher Education for Special Needs in Europe*. London: Cassell.

Mittler, P. and Daunt, P. (1995) (eds.) *Teacher Education for Special Needs in Europe*. London: Cassell.

Mittler, P., Conti-Ramsden, G. and Daunt, P. (1995) 'Foreword', in P. Mittler and P. Daunt (eds.) *Teacher Education for Special Needs in Europe*. London: Cassell.

Sayer, J. and Jones, N. (eds.) (1985) *Teacher Training and Special Educational Needs*. London: Croom Helm.

SENTC (1996) *Professional Development to Meet Special Educational Needs: Report to the DFEE*. Stafford: SENTC.

Times Higher Education Supplement (1996) 'Whitehall to run teacher training', June 14.

Upton, G. (ed.) (1991) *Staff Training and Special Educational Needs*. London: David Fulton.

Vulliamy, G. and Webb, R. (ed.) (1992) *Teacher Research and Special Education Needs*. London: David Fulton.

CHAPTER TWO

A Context for Teacher Education and Special Educational Needs

John Dwyfor Davies and Philip Garner

Introduction

Thirty years ago Tansley and Gulliford (1967), commenting upon provision for what were then regarded as 'backward children', noted that 'There is a need for all teachers during training to have some instruction in methods of teaching the early stages of reading and number, and to be made aware of the methods of helping children who cannot keep up with their age group' (p.11). A few years later, Galloway and Goodwin (1979) continued this plea for enhanced initial and continuing professional preparation, calling for an 'extension of present in-service education facilities' and recommending that, at ITE level, 'the aim should not be to give factual information about handicap, so much as to reduce the fog of emotion and misunderstanding that surrounds it' (p.130). By the mid-1980s analyses of the shortcomings of existing provision for SEN in ITE and CPD had become a litany. Thus, in 1985, Croll and Moses found that most of the junior school teachers in their national survey had little or no training in teaching children with SEN, whilst Gipps *et al.* (1987) found that there were still many serving teachers with no training whatsoever in SEN. There is consequently a predictable tone to Mittler's recent request that 'those who teach should also have access to additional training to equip and support them in this task. This calls for a radical reappraisal of the whole of initial and post-experience training for all teachers but particularly those with specific responsibilities for working with pupils with special educational needs' (Mittler, 1995, p.128).

The above authors, and their comments on ITE and CPD in the field of SEN, have been selected at random from books in our personal libraries. It was neither a planned nor an exhaustive exercise, and for each illustration we have included perhaps a further dozen remained unused. The activity, however superficial, was instructive in that it allowed us to think with greater clarity (if not less cynicism) about the official advice and legislation which paralleled the work of these researchers. In 1967 the Plowden Report, in recommending a detailed enquiry into the needs of 'handicapped' children, including slow learners, sought an increase in in-service courses and for a review of ITE provision. The Warnock Report (1978) made an explicit and hard-hitting point that there needed to be considerable advances in teacher training to ensure improvements in SEN provision. Not only did the Report call for the mandatory inclusion of SEN within all ITE courses, but that a range of recognised teaching qualifications in SEN should be made available. The Report recommended that 'all teachers with defined responsibilities for children with special educational needs, wherever they are receiving education, should have an additional qualification in special education' (para.12.27, p.234). More recently, the Elton Report (1989), although not SEN-specific, did nevertheless refer to those children whose learning difficulties were connected with their emotional and behavioural functioning. Elton recommended that ITE courses incorporate management of pupil behaviour and relationship-building as central components. Finally, although the Code of Practice (DfE, 1994) made no specific mention of provision of SEN experiences within ITE courses, it provided a substantive recommendation for in-service training (*sic*) of staff, stating that 'The school's SEN policy should describe plans for the in-service training and professional development of staff to help them work effectively with pupils with special educational needs' (p.12).

It is apparent, from the foregoing, that both practitioners and policy-makers are joined in asserting the need for (a) more emphasis on SEN in ITE courses and (b) continuing development of expertise throughout a teacher's career. It is our view that, although official emphasis has been placed on the need for both of these over the last thirty years, in reality teacher education in SEN (whether in ITE or CPD) has not kept pace with the reorientation in thinking and the notable developments in provision for children with SEN subsequent to the 1981 Education Act and reinforced by the 1994 Code of Practice. This discrepancy may seriously impair any chances of maintaining the progress made thus far, not least in respect of inclusivity and the individual rights of children with learning difficulties.

It is our contention, to coin a phrase used some years ago in the same context, that teacher education in SEN is at a crossroads (Mittler, 1993). Many, often complex, tensions currently pervade teacher education in SEN. In our own overview in the present chapter we are keen to emphasise that, whilst matters may be less than perfect, a number of opportunities do exist, for teacher educators, school-mentors and the students and teachers they work with, to enhance the knowledge base, critical thinking and awareness of all concerned. Such a view is supported by the contributions contained in this book.

For many working in the field of SEN the rationale for this book may appear to be self-evident, especially given the complexity of the present situation in teacher education. It could even be argued that there is an element of self-interest on the part of teachers and teacher-educators involved in SEN work in demanding a higher profile for this aspect of teacher development. There is, within all of this, a danger of making assumptions about the nature and extent of the needs of teachers in general, a matter recently explored by McClelland and Varma (1996). In SEN, the catalytic effect of the SENTC Report (1996) should be acknowledged, given that it has provided central government with both up-to-date information concerning the state of teacher education and professional development in SEN and a set of helpful suggestions to move things forward, based on a preliminary outline of teacher competencies (however wary some might be of their implications). The chapters which comprise this book are intended to provide some further contributions to a debate which has, in the last few years of the 20th century, reached a point of critical importance, given the impending adoption of a new 'national curriculum' for teacher training (TTA, 1997).

Our first task, in this introductory chapter, is to map the context of SEN in both ITE and CPD. In doing this we will air some of our own concerns, our fears and, notwithstanding these, seek to communicate our sense of hope that there may yet be a substantial shift within this crucial component of teacher education. What follows, therefore, is a composite of our personal beliefs, informed by both research and practice, and by the observations and interventions of our teacher-colleagues. What we are not seeking to do, here, is to provide an exhaustive treatment of the historical context of teacher education itself. Much has been written in analytical vein on this subject, and we refer the reader to this literature (see, for example, Elliott, 1991; Furlong, 1992; and Elliott, 1993). But it should not pass without comment that much of this literature contains little reference to SEN, a regrettable situation given the large proportion of schoolchildren involved. Reference will, nevertheless, be made to the period following the 1988 Education Act, given that the descent of teacher education into the currently favoured market-orientation began to materialise in this period. Nor do we seek to provide a detailed historical view of the role of SEN in ITE or CPD, an issue which is dealt with in some substance by Sayer and Jones (1985), Upton (1991) and Mittler and Daunt (1995). What we have done, however, is to identify a set of current themes which we believe, as teacher educators, provide for a critical underpinning of the various contributions to this book.

The current context: Initial Teacher Education

ITE in England and Wales has witnessed a significant shift in recent years, both in the way it is organised and in its underpinning ideology. It has, according to Furlong (1992), been 'transformed from that quiet backwater into a major site of ideological struggle between the government and other groups with an interest in education.' This transformation has been summarised by Jordan and Powell (1995) as being marked by a move 'away from the conceptual understandings of the educational process that were provided by the four underpinning disciplines (psychology, history, philosophy and sociology) towards a skills-based model based on an analysis of teacher competencies' (p.120). Given that it is the stated intention of central government to establish a 'national curriculum' for teacher training (TTA, *op. cit.*) – it is vital that a case is made for a significant increase in SEN experience for students undertaking ITE courses. The evidence presented thus far suggests that an important NQT need is currently being marginalised.

Three themes dominate ITE at the present time: the impact of the National Curriculum (NC), the significant shift towards school-based training and the adoption of 'permeated' models of content delivery for SEN within HEI courses. Each has either developed following, or been reinforced by, the 1988 Education Act. There is certainly justification for suggesting that, of all the post-1988 initiatives, those directed towards supposed 'reform' in teacher education are the most heavily predicated by the rhetoric of politicians and by the malevolent intent of the 'New Right'. Both groups have expressed a view, verging on the hysterical, that teacher education remains dominated by 'modish educational theory' (Lawlor, 1990) and a preoccupation with what Furlong (*op.cit.*) has referred to as their view of teacher educators having a 'fetishism with pedagogy at the expense of subject knowledge'. Moreover, each of these themes has had a widespread, negative impact on the ability of teacher-educators to provide insights into the nature and practices of SEN in schools (Jordan and Powell, *op. cit.*).

Firstly, then, there is the question of the impact of the NC on teacher education courses. Considerable adjustment had to be made to the nature of course content to accommodate the demands for more substantial coverage of NC subjects. This followed the advice of self-appointed 'experts' who argued that the key to effective training is to be found in providing students with a firm grasp of the academic disciplines (Lawlor, *op.cit.*). As a result there has been a diminution of the amount of time available for reflection, based upon a critical and humanistic tradition. The principles of technical rationalism, which emphasises competencies in subject knowledge, and control, have been seen as the panacea for perceived shortcomings and a means of meeting the needs of capitalism at the expense of individual democracy (Hartley, 1991). Put another way, a technical-rationalist approach views an understanding of the needs of the child as secondary to an understanding of a body of knowledge to be 'delivered'. The status of this approach has been officially confirmed by the Department for Education (DfE), which indicates that 'the focus of ITT should be on the subject knowledge and the practical skills required by newly qualified teachers, which equip them to teach effectively and are the foundation for further professional development' (DfE, 1993, p.5). This preoccupation, as many of those involved in SEN work recognise, is likely to sustain what has been caricatured as the 'empty bucket' approach to those with learning difficulty.

The shift towards school-based training marks a second area of concern. Prior to 1988 a student's school experience was obtained alongside con-siderable practice-related study within university and college departments of education. This was supported by a series of informally (from a contractual point of view) arranged school placements. Circular 14/93 (DfE, 1993), for example, stated that 'schools should play a much larger and more influential role in course design and delivery' and that 'The Secretary of State intends that the increased contribution of schools to teacher-training courses offered by higher education institutions should be reflected in the transfer of resources from the institutions to their partner schools' (p.12). The effects of such a move, towards what will effectively be an 'apprenticeship model' of 'on-the-job training', will be keenly felt both by students and by newly qualified teachers (NQTs) in terms of the SEN dimension. They will have even less time for a consideration of the important conceptual issues in SEN; and, moreover, as the data presented in this chapter suggests, they will receive only nominal direct input on practical matters relating to such important SEN issues as legislation, identification, assessment and behaviour management.

The move towards school-based training needs also to be seen in the context of recent surveys of special needs coordinators (SENCos), who have reported a massive increase in workload since the adoption of the Code of Practice (DfE, 1994a), and, in consequence, a lack of availability to act as mentors to either students or to NQTs (Garner, 1996; Lewis, 1995). Consideration also needs to be given to the fact that, as OFSTED inspectors are given to noting apparent wide variations in the quality of teaching and learning in schools, students may commensurately face a lottery as to the quality of their school experience of SEN.

The final theme is that of 'permeation', a process by which SEN matters are subsumed within each element of an ITE course and become the responsibility of all tutors within the teaching team. Whilst this approach encourages all tutors to be involved more directly in SEN, there are huge difficulties of quality control. Mittler (1992), for example, noted that 'permeation is by its very nature invisible and therefore difficult to monitor' whilst an official view has been that permeation has an 'insufficient foundation by way of specific course content' (DES, 1990).

The potentially damaging effect of each of these developments has been noted most recently by the Special Educational Needs Training Consortium. In their Report to the DfEE (SENTC, 1996) this group warned that 'Pressures to design training that is school-based; to develop effective partnership schemes with schools; to introduce the competencies required by the DfEE with guidance from the former Council for the Accreditation of Teacher Education and latterly the Teacher Training Agency *and* to deliver courses that cover all aspects of the National Curriculum, mean that time for SEN issues is minimal' (p.19). The Report goes on to state that 'Much therefore depends on the quality of SEN policy and practice in the partnership schools in which the student is placed. Yet HMI/OFSTED reports have in the past been critical of SEN practice in mainstream schools. . .' (p.19). On permeation, too, SENTC expresses reservations, indicating that 'subsequent evaluations by HMI have indicated that this approach is often less than successful' (p.19). Finally, the Report expresses no surprise that 'many newly qualified teachers entering the teaching profession are unfamiliar with their formal responsibilities regarding SEN and are not equipped with a range of teaching strategies that would enable them to deliver an effective education to pupils with SEN' (pp.19–20).

The concerns outlined by SENTC have been brought into sharp focus by the recent news that a 'national curriculum' for teacher training is to be established (THES, 1996). Given that Circulars 9/92 and 14/93 contained only one 'competence' which related directly to SEN (that NQTs should be able to 'identify and respond appropriately to relevant individual differences between pupils') it is hard to be optimistic about future initiatives aimed at an imposed uniformity of practice, in spite of the initiatives undertaken by the TTA as this volume goes to press.

The current context: Continuing Professional Development

CPD refers to all aspects of teacher education as they relate to teachers once in-post. It ranges from the induction phase, for NQTs, to courses for more experienced teachers. This covers a wide range of specialisms and formats offered by an increased range of providers since the marketisation of education from 1988 onwards. Our interpretation of CPD is in close agreement with that provided by Dean (1991), who viewed it as 'a matter of [the] personal development which enables a person to tackle new tasks, relate well to others, see important issues and so on. Part of this development is the acquisition of specific skills, knowledge and understanding. . .[which] gradually needs to become internalised and refined so that it becomes part of the teacher's *professional personality*' (original italics) (p.19).

In a volume edited by Upton (1991), entitled *Staff Training and Special Educational Needs*, attention is drawn to worrying data generated by the Advisory Committee on the Supply and Education of Teachers (ACSET). In 1984 it was estimated that 'less than 30% of the qualified teachers in special schools have a recognised additional qualification specifically related to special educational needs' (ACSET, 1984). Five years later SENTC (1996) noted that, in respect of teachers working with children with SLD, 46% had received no specialist training. Our additional, largely anecdotal evidence gathered whilst working with teachers on professional development courses in SEN, suggests that this percentage may well be higher in the field of EBD, which represents a numerically significant proportion of SEN children in schools. It is partly against this background that CPD in SEN has to be considered.

In addition, the largely deleterious impact on CPD in SEN of other changes in education following the 1988 Education Act has to be acknowledged. Thomas (1993) viewed these developments in jaundiced terms: 'Surveying this particular landscape is to see the absence of clearly marked routes and staging posts. The professional experiences of teachers in the last few years have been in the nature of emergency rescue packs, survival kits on assessment at Key Stage 1, curriculum planning in Science Key Stages 1 and 2, reporting to parents etc' (p.117). He also points to evidence that, post-1988, more serious matters are arising, which threaten the integrity and level of competence of teachers working in the field. These relate to the dangers of having entirely school-based CPD programmes, of an increasing emphasis on cost-effective skills-related training, and to the financial burden being placed on any teacher who wishes to pursue courses of a more flexible, developmental character. The first of these concerns is about what Thomas (*op. cit.*) refers to as 'the danger of incestuous school-based in-service with its danger of recycled bad practice', together with the argument that such arrangements will do little to extend good practice by collaboration between different schools, HEIs or other organisations. Secondly, recognition has to be given to the fact that, in a market-governed education system, some schools will consider CPD in SEN-related matters to be a low-priority staff development need. Consequently CPD, in these contexts, will be a lottery.

In a report entitled *The Implementation of the Code of Practice for pupils with Special Educational Needs* (OFSTED, 1996b), the Chief Inspector for Schools identified certain key areas of focus in the INSET of serving teachers. Whilst OFSTED retained a depressing adherence to 'training', as opposed to professional development, the recommendations in the report neatly summarise the areas of ongoing concern in CPD provision. The body of the report is critical of INSET provision concerning the implementation of the Code – this is especially the case in grant-maintained schools, with the report indicating that 'Attendance at Code INSET provided by LEAs has been poor in grant-maintained schools. It is difficult to know whether GM schools have not availed themselves of LEA Code training because they have not known about, do not choose to provide funds for, or do not wish to attend this training. Those schools that have not attended LEA INSET have not gone elsewhere for Code of Practice training' (p.13).

Such an observation contrasts starkly with Circular 6/94 (DfE, 1994b), which summarises the SEN measures pursuant to the 1993 Education Act. Within the circular there is explicit mention of the role of INSET for SEN. Thus, there should be a clear statement within the school's SEN policy of its 'plans for the in-service training and professional development of staff' and these plans 'should cover the needs of non-teaching assistants' (para.50, p.17).

The recommendation, contained in the Chief Inspector's report, that the DfEE should recognise 'a continuing need to support INSET for SENCos, other teachers, senior managers and governors in implementing the Code of Practice' (p.40) begs certain questions relating to CPD. Firstly, the comment is itself suggestive of an ongoing and healthy level of financial support for serving teachers' professional development in SEN. This interpretation of the recent or current situation is plainly fanciful. As Sarah Sandow points out elsewhere in this book, most reasonable opportunities for relevant and focused award-bearing courses have long since evaporated. The level of 'support' can be assessed by the high number of serving teachers paying their own course fees for professional development courses at HEIs – currently running in excess of 60% in some institutions. This represents a worrying erosion of equality of opportunity for CPD amongst serving teachers. At the present time it is largely those teachers who are in a position to pay who can therefore benefit from this kind of CPD. It represents a situation which would not be tolerated in most other professions or commercial organisations.

The Chief Inspector's report goes on to recommend that headteachers should ensure that 'Priority. . . be given to ensuring that all teaching and support staff are provided with in-service training on the Code to enable them to understand their responsibilities and to help deliver the Code across the whole school' (p.39). There is a certain amount of naiveté in this request. Increasingly, since 1988, the CPD budget of schools has been under severe pressure, caused by conflicting demands on a relatively small resource. SEN has to compete with claims for CPD in such high-status (and politically sensitive) areas as assessment and Key Stage testing, behaviour and discipline, and (NC) subject-related professional development. Based on our first-hand evidence of working closely with a wide range of schools, it seems that OFSTED's recommendation that headteachers should enable all staff to 'be acquainted with the contents of the Code' is a long way from realisation. There are still teachers working in schools at the present time who are unaware of the content and importance of the 1981 Education Act. Given that fifteen years have elapsed since its enactment, this state of affairs does not augur well for future refinements in the implementation of the Code.

The same OFSTED report, displaying considerable ignorance of the widespread attempts by ITE and CPD providers to at least give a basic grounding in the content of the Code of Practice to students on their courses, suggests that 'It would be particularly helpful if an introduction to the Code were included as part of the induction of new staff' (p.39). Maybe, however, the perverse agenda underpinning this statement was that by appearing to demonstrate, however superficially, that ITE providers are incompetent, central government could rid itself of university-based teacher education, which is largely seen as oppositional to the education policy of the Tory Right.

From 1996 the TTA has assumed responsibility for the disbursement of INSET funds. Given the official preoccupation with 'outputs' and of measurements of 'quality' which are firmly located in indicators of academic achievement (as represented by league tables of schools), it is hard to see professional development in SEN being given a priority commensurate with the numbers of children it involves (variously estimated at between 20 and 40%). The absence of an appropriate level of resource to meet staff development needs in SEN may ensure the TTA's agreed principle that 'funds should be targeted at the long-term development of the profession and in particular (they) should form an investment in the experts of the future' (TTA, 1996) remains nothing more than a pious incantation. Smith (1996), in particular, has been highly critical of this situation, stating that 'The Teacher Training Agency's *Proposals Paper on the Future of TTA INSET Funds* appears to have been written without thought for INSET for special education' and that, apart from mentioning SEN coordination as a priority area, the Paper makes 'no mention of training for teachers of pupils with SEN; not even of those with "behavioural problems" about whom we hear so much'. Such a state of affairs is far removed from the 'different version' of SEN proposed by the Institute for Public Policy Research (1993), which stated that 'We wish all staff to be professionally developed to high levels'.

Contextual summary

We noted, in our overview of ITE, that new modes of delivery of such courses do not appear to offer much realistic hope that significant SEN input will be forthcoming. As a result NQTs are not well placed to meet the needs of a large numbers of children. If this analysis is accepted a coherent, well-managed and properly funded range of professional development opportunities for teachers assumes even greater importance. Nowhere is this more pressing than in the case of teachers of children with SLD, for teachers working in the area of low-incidence SEN and for those working with children with EBD. Moreover, we would argue that professional development coherence should be sought across all stages of a teacher's career. Whilst there is undoubtedly much good work going on, in both ITE and CPD (evidence of which forms a substantial part of this book), there is sadly little continuity of approach. The expressed needs of SEN teachers, or students on ITE courses, are mostly marginalised and there is an air of 'quick-fix' about many recent initiatives – some of the GEST provision is a case in point. So, whilst we would give a cautious welcome to the moves towards a 'national teacher training curriculum', we would hope that continuity can be ensured by establishing a formal set of specified professional development objectives in SEN for all teachers, irrespective of their subject specialism or stage of career development.

At the crossroads, looking for direction

At various points in this chapter we have made reference to what needs to be done in order to secure a situation nearer to the ideal in both ITE and CPD in SEN, and individual contributors offer some practical ways in which this is, or can, be done. From our own perspective, working with both ITE students and serving teachers on CPD programmes, there are a number of points that can be made about the prevailing situation. These can be targets for future development.

It would appear that ITE and CPD provision for SEN in England and Wales is somewhat out of step with what is happening in both mainland Europe and North America. Centralised control of what, for shorthand, we will call the training agenda in these countries is conspicuous by its absence. Individual providers are largely left to negotiate their programmes and styles of delivery, with a minimum of prescription. This allows them to be far more responsive to local needs. But there is something more significant about the difference: it appears that many of our European partners have been more whole-hearted in their adoption of the Salamanca Statement (UNESCO, 1994) which argues that mainstream schools which adopt an 'inclusive' approach for all children are the best placed to combat discrimination. These sentiments have been echoed in the Declaration on Education for All (EASE, 1995), which affirmed that 'Teacher training should be more comprehensive and include the basic principles of the education of children with SEN in order to allow inclusive education.' Closer adherence to these fundamental principles is marked in real terms by making resources (human, financial and temporal) available so that both ITE and CPD courses are able, as a matter of course, to include a far more substantial element of both practical experience and theoretical input within both areas of teacher education. It is with these thoughts in mind that we cast a somewhat envious eye towards colleagues in many Central and East European countries where, notwithstanding an often medicalised view of SEN and a largely non-inclusive practice, a five-year period of special education training is mandatory prior to qualification.

We believe that the recent move towards a 'national curriculum' for ITE, and for its counterpart in CPD, should be seen by all educators, and by special educators in particular, as an opportunity to debate the SEN content of future courses. There will clearly be differences of opinion, as interest groups representing different strands of SEN work fight their own corners. But, at this critical time, with SEN very much on the agenda in respect of teacher education as a whole, we would hope that self-interest is suppressed and that some common principles and parameters for professional development are identified and fought for with a single voice.

The emphasis on 'partnership' between schools and HEIs, currently being promoted, could provide a useful vehicle for these developments. For example, NQTs during their first years of teaching should have some mechanism available to them to return to their ITE provider (or, by some form of national agreement, one local to their new place of work) in order to refine or extend specific SEN skills. These are often only apparent to students, as well as induction mentors in schools, once they begin teaching. The process could act as a 'learning guarantee' and could provide a useful way of assessing quality provision. Moreover, it could enhance effective working liaisons between SEN teachers in schools and SEN tutors in HEIs.

Urgent attention also needs to be paid to the failure of a 'permeated approach' for SEN in ITE courses. This can only be tackled if *all* tutors working in teacher education are acutely aware of SEN issues, the underpinning legislative basis for those who have learning difficulties, and of the kinds of interventions most likely to be effective with SEN children. We would argue that there is a role for a 'Special Educational Needs Coordinator' in HEIs: at the present time the coordinating function for this is highly informal, and results in very uneven quality of experience by students, and an even more disjointed and *ad hoc* arrangement for the professional development of HEI tutors in SEN matters.

There are important matters to be addressed in CPD as a result of the failure of many HEIs to provide a solid grounding in the principles and practice of SEN. Given that ITE has, like schools themselves, largely become subject-orientated, and that the Code of Practice views the classroom or subject-teacher as the person who will initially identify, assess and intervene in cases of SEN, a major initiative is required to equip these teachers with an appropriate level of awareness and skill to act in this capacity. This, as we have implied, requires a coherent and incremental approach which is well resourced. It should not be left to the mercy of financial exigencies or of what may currently be the fashionable topic in SEN. Moreover, CPD in SEN should form an integral part of all staff appraisals, including those of senior management teams.

The potential for using the skills and background of teachers working in special schools has long been acknowledged as important in both ITE and CPD. Regrettably special schools have almost wholly been excluded from partnership arrangements in ITE, with the result that the kinds of stereotypical responses to children educated in these contexts, reported for example by Garner (1994), are likely to prevail. HEIs need to grasp the nettle in this respect by promoting more widespread, formal collaboration with their local special schools. This arrangement can be of mutual benefit, ensuring that staff in special schools are given appropriate status within teacher education as a result of the intrinsic skills which they have traditionally used, whilst reinforcing to all teachers that children in segregated settings should be viewed neither as objects of pity or fear.

The foregoing does not represent a complete or ordered shopping list, nor a prioritisation of the issues involved. Reading the various chapters which comprise this volume, however, we are struck by the frequency with which these themes occur. Moreover, many of the authors in this book demonstrate that a considerable amount of innovative work is being attempted in responding to the demands for effective SEN provision in ITE and in CPD. It could be argued, therefore, that our point of departure from the 'crossroads' is immaterial, so long as the route taken allows us to reach the desired destination: a positive contribution on the part of the teacher in addressing the needs of children.

References

ACSET (Advisory Committee on the Supply and Education of Teachers) (1984) *Teacher Training and Special Educational Needs*. London: HMSO.

Croll, P. and Moses, D. (1985) *One in Five. The assessment and incidence of special educational needs*. London: Routledge and Kegan Paul.

Dean, J. (1991) *Professional Development in School*. Milton Keynes: Open University Press.

Department for Education (1993) *The Initial Training of Primary School Teachers: new criteria for courses* (Circular 14/93). London: DfE.

Department for Education (1994a) *Code of Practice on the Identification and*

Assessment of Special Educational Needs. London: DfE.

Department for Education (1994b) *The Organisation of Special Educational Provision.* London: DfE.

Department of Education and Science (1990) *Special Educational Needs in Initial Teacher Training.* London: DES.

Elliott, J. (1991) 'A model of professionalism and its implications for teacher education', *British Educational Research Journal,* **17** (4), 309–318.

Elliott, J. (ed.) (1993) *Reconstructing Teacher Education.* London: Falmer Press.

European Association of Special Education (1995) Declaration on Education for All. *Information from EASE,* 2.

Furlong, J. (1992) 'Reconstructing professionalism: ideological struggle in initial teacher education', in M. Arnot and L. Barton (eds.) *Voicing Concerns: sociological perspectives on contemporary education reforms.* Wallingford: Triangle Books.

Galloway, D. and Goodwin, C. (1979) *Educating Slow-learning and Maladjusted Children.* London: Longman.

Garner, P. (1994) 'Oh my God, help!: what Newly Qualifying Teachers think of special schools', in S. Sandow (ed.) *Whose Special Need?* London: Paul Chapman, 129–140.

Garner, P. (1996) 'Go forth and coordinate! What special needs coordinators think about the Code of Practice', *School Organisation,* **16** (2).

Gipps, C., Gross, H. and Goldstein, H. (1987) *Warnock's Eighteen Per Cent: children with special needs in primary schools.* Lewes: Falmer Press.

Hartley, D. (1991) 'Democracy, capitalism and the reform of teacher education', *Journal of Education for Teaching,* **17** (1), 81–85.

Hinson, M. (1991) *Teachers and Special Educational Needs.* Harlow: Longman.

Institute for Public Policy Research (1993) *Education: a different version. An alternative White Paper.* London: IPPR.

Jordan, R. and Powell, S. (1995) 'Skills without understanding: a critique of a competency-based model of teacher education in relation to special needs', *British Journal of Special Education,* **22** (3), 120–124.

Lawlor, S. (1990) *Teachers Mistaught: training theories or education in subjects.* London: Centre for Policy Studies.

Lewis, A. (1995) *Special Needs Provision in Mainstream Primary Schools.* Stoke-on-Trent: Trentham.

McClelland, V. and Varma, V. (1996) *The Needs of Teachers.* London: Cassell.

Mittler, P. (1992) 'Preparing all initial teacher training students to teach children with special educational needs: a case study from England', *European Journal of Special Needs Education,* **7**, 1–10.

Mittler, P. (1993) 'Special needs at the crossroads', in J. Visser and G. Upton (eds.) *Special Education in Britain after Warnock.* London: David Fulton.

Mittler, P. (1995) 'Special needs education in England and Wales', in P. Mittler and P. Daunt (eds.) *Teacher Education for Special Needs in Europe.* London: Cassell.

Mittler, P. and Daunt, P. (eds.) (1995) *Teacher Education for Special Needs in Europe.* London: Cassell.

Office for Standards in Education (1993) *The New Teacher in School.* London: HMSO.

Office for Standards in Education (1996a) *Guidance on the Inspection of Primary Schools.* London: HMSO.

Office for Standards in Education (1996b) *The Implementation of the Code of Practice for Pupils with Special Educational Needs.* London: HMSO.

Sayer, J. and Jones, N. (eds.) (1985) *Teacher Training and Special Educational Needs.*

London: Croom Helm.

Smith, C. (1996) 'SEN – forgotten again', *British Journal of Special Education*, **23** (4), 204.

Special Educational Needs Training Consortium (1996) *Professional Development to Meet Special Educational Needs*. Stafford: SENTC.

Tansley, A. and Gulliford, R. (1967) *The Education of Slow Learning Children*. London: Routledge and Kegan Paul.

Teacher Training Agency (1996) 'The future use of TTA INSET funding', 12 December.

Teacher Training Agency (1997) *Training Curriculum and Standards for Teachers*. London: TTA.

Times Higher Educational Supplement (1996) 'Whitehall to Run Teacher Training', June 14.

Thomas, D. (1993) 'Gritty, sensible and utilitarian – the only model? Special educational needs Initial Teacher Training and professional development', in A. Dyson and C. Gains (eds.) *Rethinking Special Needs in Mainstream Schools*. London: David Fulton.

UNESCO (1994) *The Salamanca Statement and Framework for Action on Special Needs Education*. Paris: UNESCO.

Upton, G. (ed.) (1991) *Staff Training and Special Educational Needs*. London: David Fulton.

Wideen, M. and Grimmett, P. (eds.) (1995) *Changing Times in Teacher Education*. London: Falmer Press.

CHAPTER THREE

Modernist Knowledge and Prejudice: Special Educational Needs

David Coulby

This chapter examines the curricula and assessment systems of schools and universities with regard to their function in legitimating and embodying particular views of SEN. It has become commonplace to examine the ways in which the processes and indeed the structures of schooling serve to pick out some children and young adults as being, in whatever way, different. These differences then become the focus for educational intervention in the learning, the life style and indeed the life chances of the individual concerned. What differentiates this individual from others, rather than what s/he may have in common with them, then becomes the focus for intense educational interest and activity. Much remains to be done to rectify these processes and structures. It is the contention of this chapter, however, that these processes and structures themselves are underpinned by *knowledge systems and knowledge protocols* which, in so far as they impact on children and young people perceived to have SEN, have so far remained largely unchallenged. This chapter examines firstly knowledge systems and then knowledge protocols.

Knowledge systems: science and normality

Knowledge systems have been subject to a high level of critique from a position which might be broadly categorised as postmodernist (Lyotard, 1984; Jameson, 1991). Modernist knowledge has been critiqued as being sexist. It is knowledge about men, men's activities, achievements and interests, constructed by men, according to criteria and values which are important to men. The roles of women in knowledge and the criteria they might apply to its construction and organisation have largely been ignored (Coulby and Jones, 1995). Similarly, as far back as Marx, knowledge and culture were seen to be those products and activities most pleasing to the ruling class of any particular epoch and most likely to assist in the extension of their wealth and power (Marx, 1977). More recently, modernist knowledge systems have been understood to be Eurocentric, white and racist (Coulby, 1996a; 1996b). The achievements and even the presence of black people are frequently ignored. The role of Europe, and more now the United States, in relation to the rest of the world, epistemological as well as economic, political and environmental, has been presented as a one-way process. Knowledge and particularly science are seen as being the product of only the Western part of the world. The knowledge systems of other areas of the world have been overlooked or denigrated; their impact upon European knowledge neglected and understated.

As the postmodernist critique gained speed, parallel critiques have been made from a variety of particular positions: to take two more examples, gay rights and environmentalism. Knowledge has been seen to privilege heterosexual forms of human relationships. The achievement of homosexual people in cultural, scientific and other areas has been concealed, disguised, marginalised or sanitised. Homophobic prejudice has been reinforced by school and university knowledge: the way in which the Aids scare has been transposed into health education is an example of this. Whilst perhaps not explicit in the curriculum, health education plays into the media presentation of HIV as a disease of *others* – Africans, drug users, homosexuals. Environmentalists and ecofeminists have found modernist versions of knowledge inadequate to meet the crises of unequal distribution and pollutive production (Beck, 1992). The knowledge of schools and universities is almost exclusively that which will perpetuate modes of production which exacerbate the ecological crises. Modernist knowledge does not offer forms of production and behaviour which might serve to avert or at least diminish these crises.

A similar critique of modernist knowledge with regard to people who are perceived to be disabled is yet to emerge. It is of particular importance to the institutions of education since these are the sites where knowledge is legitimated and reproduced for those perceived to be disabled. Equally, but not so obviously important, they are the sites where knowledge is legitimated and reproduced for those not so perceived. In this respect this chapter focuses on science and in particular medicine. However, it is a mode of analysis which urgently needs to be conducted with regard to a whole range of curricular areas. How much of the literature studied in schools and universities, for instance, has been written by people perceived to be disabled? To what extent does this canon of literature accurately reflect the experiences of such people, distort these experiences or ignore them all together (*Richard III, Jane Eyre, Jude the Obscure, The Idiot*)? Parallel, though less easily formulated, questions can be asked of music and art (*Lucia di Lammermoor, The Scream*). To what extent does history address the circumstances of people perceived to be disabled and their relationships with each other and with people not so perceived? What provisions and institutions were created for them? What philosophies underpinned and legitimated these forms and processes?

In this case, of course, Foucault (1967; 1973) has provided some of the answers. However, the Foucauldian view of *Madness and Civilisation* is not one which has progressed very far in the school and university history curriculum. In all subjects the question of representation remains. To what extent do illustrations in science and technology texts emphasise the activities, achievements and possibilities of those perceived to be disabled? Stephen Hawking has recently become a widely known example of such achievement. To what extent does the discourse of educational subject knowledge stress the arrangements, facilities and technologies necessary to facilitate total inclusion?

It is science which is the central subject with regard to the way in which modernist knowledge excludes and stigmatises those perceived to be disabled. Medical students at London University are privileged to be able to visit a collection of freaks (I am now in an area where inverted commas must proliferate; I am therefore leaving readers to provide their own). The skeleton of the Elephant Man, for instance, has not been respectfully buried or cremated but is there for the critical attention of medical students. A scrutiny which did not end with death. What is here in its most extreme form is a set of confusions which underpin Western medicine. Health is associated inextricably with normality. More tendentiously, health and normality are associated with wellbeing and even with benevolence. It is the opposite formulation of these confusions which affects people perceived to be disabled: difference from the artificially constructed normal is equated with sickness, with misfortune and, again tendentiously, with malevolence. In the reverse process, that which is criminal or wicked is seen as being necessarily unhealthy or unbalanced (Szasz, 1972) consider the use of words such as 'twisted' or 'sick'. It is science here which makes the association which literature and popular culture can all too readily take up and amplify (the psychopath, for instance, in crime fiction or Hollywood movies). The medicine which is taught at universities and the school science which feeds into it is a knowledge system which supports segregation and stigmatisation. It does this because it is committed to a notion of normality which is restricted in terms of physical and behavioural conformity. Its attitude to that which fails to conform to its normality is prurient, excluding, invasive, stigmatising and often punitive.

I am aware that this is rather a large statement but let us consider the three main tools of Western medicine: pharmaceuticals, invasive surgery and counselling (please do not forget those inverted commas). Pharmaceuticals are increasingly being used to control people's behaviour and even emotions. Pills and potions help people to sleep, to behave in a socially acceptable way, to feel good about themselves and to be happy. Increasingly pharmaceuticals such as Prozac and Ritalin are used as a first level intervention to control behaviour in children and young people. Tranquillisers and anti-depressants are considered appropriate treatment for people who have suffered serious physical injury or who are considered to be physically disabled. The sordid history of enforced lobotomies, sterilisations and castrations recalls that medical surgery has also been used to control behaviour. Plastic surgery provides a further example of the relationship between medicine and normality enforcement. Medicine is used to eliminate perceived disfigurement, ugliness and abnormality. In the process it is clear that youth, normality and beauty are medically endorsed as vital elements in human health. Medicine has proliferated a sequence of nonsensical categories for people whose behaviour differs from and upsets the norm: psychotic, schizophrenic, depressive, autistic, dyslexic, etc. These categories are used to cover behavioural, sexual, legal and even political (not only in the former Soviet Union) deviations from the norms of mental health. Surgical and pharmaceutical interventions are justified for such deviations. The people concerned are also subjected to waves of medical or paramedical counselling. If your body or behaviour do not match medical normality, or even if you are in the process of enduring grief or unhappiness, then you are a candidate for counselling. Counselling reminds you subtly what the norm is, sympathises with you for your failure to achieve it, instructs you how to handle your inadequacy so as not to offend the normal and how to conform in as many ways as counselling considers you capable.

Prenatal screening allows an increasing number of deviations from the medical norm to be recognised before birth. The social consequence of abortions in such cases is that some categories of people's whole existence can be seen as a mistake. If a child is fortunate enough to survive a condition where medicine would routinely terminate a pregnancy, how are they and others to regard the condition of their existence? Is human life only to be allowed to those whom medicine regards as normal?

It may be argued that I am selective in the aspects of medicine which I portray; that this is bad medicine but that most of Western modernist medicine is good: antibiotics and miracle surgery. These two examples, of course, are not without their negative aspects. The stress of the argument, however, is rather that if the aspects described and questioned in the above two paragraphs are recognisable components of medicine, and actually rather significant components, then the whole edifice of Western modernist medicine is flawed not only in relation to those perceived to be disabled but also in relation to those not (yet) so perceived. I am not asserting that there is no such thing as health and sickness or even of real disablement: rather I am insisting that in Western medicine these concepts have become so associated with socially derived notions of normality, conformity, beauty and happiness as to render their continued implementation as theory and practice prejudicial to the population at large and in particular to that segment of it perceived to be disabled.

It is in educational institutions that this version of medicine is taught. It is important to emphasise that this does not involve only university medical schools. Aspects of medicine are now taught to a whole range of would be paramedical professionals. Furthermore, medicine is seen to be one of the peaks of modernist science; it constitutes in North America and in Western Europe one of the most desirable and most difficult to attain careers for those pupils and students most successful within the education system. In universities it is usually recognised as an elite subject and medical courses are characteristically longer than most others. One of the important functions of school science is the preparation of young people for medical and paramedical courses. Schools and universities not only teach modernist medicine, they also teach that it is right, good and desirable. Other modes of diagnosis, aetiology and therapy (acupuncture, homeopathy, faith healing, herbalism, etc.) are marginalised or denigrated. The actual construction of the school and university curriculum, then, underpins those processes and institutions which have been so prejudicial to people perceived to be disabled.

A trend in much writing on SEN has been to criticise, rightly, the application of what has been called the medical model in cases where it is inappropriate (Sandow, 1994). With regard to upsetting behaviour or to underachievement in school, for instance, it has been recognised that the use of medical terminology and procedures, far from assisting either understanding or intervention, is likely to be prejudicial to the people to whom they are applied both by offering possibilities for stigmatisation and also by taking the responsibility away from those most closely involved in working with the child or young person, almost always teachers. This chapter is arguing something considerably beyond this: that it is not the inappropriate application of the medical model which is the difficulty, but the whole medical model itself and the Western modernist version of medicine and science which underpins it. Both as a version of scientific knowledge and as an institutionalised professional practice, this modernist medicine has been highly prejudicial to, amongst others, those children and young people perceived to have SEN.

Knowledge protocols: stratification and normality

Knowledge protocols refers to the way in which school knowledge is selected, organised, valued and assessed. Again there is a range of issues concerning the postmodernist critique of modernist knowledge which can be seen to be relevant to the education of children and young people perceived to have SEN. Is underachievement, for instance, determined by the nature of the knowledge which is selected to be taught in schools and universities, or by the way in which it is organised? If a different aspect of knowledge were selected – cooperative and environment-enhancing, say, as against competitive and exploitative – or if it were organised differently – in an integrated, holistic way, for example, rather than in distinctly separated subjects – would those currently perceived as underachieving be seen as successful? and an entirely different cohort of pupils be discovered to be underachievers? If this revolution were to be achieved might there not be predictable but different winners and losers in terms of race (mental inverted commas remain necessary), gender or social class? Certainly there are cross-cultural differences in the status awarded to particular cognitive activities (Labov, 1969). In considering the underpinnings of the prejudicial processes and institutions of SEN, these issues remain to be addressed. The rest of this chapter is concerned with only one of the knowledge protocols, that of assessment.

Assessment is an important protocol for modernist knowledge. It allows institutions to recognise those who are succeeding and those who are failing. It allows for success to be rewarded and failure to be remedied. It allows rational, generalist decisions to be made instead of traditional particularist favouritism.

The opening of the civil service in the United Kingdom to entrance by competitive examinations, in the mid-nineteenth century, rather than by social sponsorship, is an example of the liberal, progressive policy making favoured by the Enlightenment. Assessment, as a modernist protocol, opens careers to talent, provides an apparently rational filtering mechanism for successive levels of education, allows for remedial action for those seen visibly and measurably to be failing.

In England and Wales the implementation of the National Curriculum has recently industrialised the assessment process (Bash and Coulby, 1989; Coulby and Bash, 1991). All school age children are assessed in at least three subjects at at least four points during their school careers on tests which are set and, at least in rhetoric, standardised nationally. The result of this industry is that all school age children can be calibrated, to the satisfaction of politicians and OFSTED, according to their progress in at least three subjects. Data are available to compare them to the norm of their own school, of their local area and of England and Wales as a whole, again in at least three subjects. The results of these assessments are communicated to teachers and to parents or carers but only in terms of their individual children. The results of other children in the class and school are meant to be confidential. Conversations between parents or carers and children as well as playground gossip by both parties, mean that the results even for individuals do have some public currency. In terms of aggregate results for schools and for local authorities, increasingly these data are being tabulated by government and media into league tables.

These assessment arrangements set in motion at least two further educational processes, competition and stratification. These are not unforeseen outcomes of the 1988 legislation, rather they are part of its clear intentions (Jones, 1989; Simon and Chitty, 1993). The assessment sets child against child, teacher against teacher, school against school and local authority against local authority in a competition to get the highest scores. Those who formulated and adopted the Act believed in the positive social consequences of competition and that, in educational terms, these competitions would serve to raise standards of attainment. With regard to stratification, the assessment arrangements highlight the successes and the failures of children as well as the strengths and weakness of each individual. Again this was seen as positive since the perpetrators of the Act were clearly committed to an ideology of individual difference whereby some people are more intelligent (don't forget the missing punctuation) than others and thus they are more successful in schools and universities and thence in the wider society and economy. The assessment arrangements make visible the hierarchy of success of pupils from a very early age and that is how life is. This hierarchy will reasonably enough be reflected in subsequent life chances.

This theory of individual difference with its reliance on a notion of generalisable intelligence or ability (gifted pupils, the less able and so on) is itself a product of high modernity. The science of intelligence and its associated modes of mensuration, not to mention fundamental racist and sexist assumptions, was developed by psychologists working around the turn of the century (Blum, 1978; Evans and Waites, 1981; Scarr, 1984). It is by no means absent from the underpinnings of educational psychology in the United Kingdom today. More generally it informs the day-to-day assumptions and linguistic frameworks (a high flyer) not only of politicians but also of many teachers and lecturers. The literature which exposes intelligence as a political rather than a scientific construct is familiar (Kamin, 1974): more important to this chapter is the insistence that what is seen to be intelligence, that is performance on a range of high status, high visibility tests, is itself dependent upon decisions made within other knowledge protocols. If knowledge had been differently selected or organised then other and different pupils would have been the more successful in performance, that is, would have been more intelligent.

Central to this part of the chapter are the effects of stratification, itself a consequence of the assessment protocol, on pupils' lives. In England and Wales these effects can be summarised under three categories: the facilitation of labelling; the legitimation of the existence of some the categories of SEN; the inhibition of inclusive education policies. The assessment arrangements provide a ready label for each child: level one, not-very-good-at-maths, low ability etc. (A fundamental flaw in the current debate about the (un)desirability of mixed ability teaching in secondary schools is that it utilises the highly questionable concept of ability as if it were a taken for granted truth.) These labels carry the endorsement of government sponsored judgement; they result from the apparently scientific and rational testing industry. It would be difficult for parents or carers to resist the accuracy of the government sponsored label and to insist that the child in question is actually rather good at maths or that the whole notion of ability is politically and educationally fraudulent and retrograde and should therefore never be applied to their child. More likely the parents or carers and then the children themselves accept the label from the early age of seven and start living with ways of adapting to both it and its consequences. A critically important way in which they will adapt to the label is by not risking the failure that would be involved in challenging it. The child will accept the not-very-good-at-maths label and thenceforth will feel exonerated from making too much effort in school mathematics. The result of this relaxation of effort, of course, will be to make the judgement retrospectively correct. An apparent correctness all the more likely to be repeated and further entrenched by each successive round of assessment.

The processes of self-fulfilling labelling have been described before and so have the ways in which pupils internalise labels used about them (Hargreaves et al., 1975). The apparent fulfilment of the label appears to legitimate its use. By internalising the label, the subject of it gives the whole process an authenticity. When a pupil realises that s/he is not-very-good-at maths this has consequences for subsequent educational and probably economic success. But failure at school and in the workplace can be made to seem fair and correct because I *was not-very-good-at-maths*. This then places the burden of responsibility on the individual and removes any blame or indeed possibility of positive action from educational institutions and their processes and personnel. In internalising the label the subject defends her/himself against the hurt of educational, social and economic failure. The assessment system is seen to be just and the subject acknowledges her/his place in a hierarchy with the minimum amount of stress. *I failed at school because I was not-very-good-al-maths but I am happy about what I did.* Instead of labelling being identified as one of the causes of educational underachievement, it is taken on by both agents and victims alike as 'proof' that the system is just and that everybody is happy. It is in terms of children perceived to have SEN, however, that these processes have real power. Those consistently at the lowest end of the performance scale in the national assessment will have labels applied to them even more pernicious than not-very-good-at-maths. In the segregative school system of England and Wales such labels can all too often be transformed into institutional arrangements whereby pupils are subjected to a restricted curriculum and a negatively selected peer group.

More than the consequences for individual pupils, the national assessment arrangements function to legitimate whole categories of perceived SEN through low attainers groups via remedial classes to moderate and severe learning difficulty. The differential performance on the national tests proves that people have different natural abilities. They ensure that there is always a category of children who are at the lowest level of this stratification. They demonstrate that this category of pupils 'needs' (finally I can no longer resist) a different form of educational provision, preferably segregated from the rest of the age cohort and ideally in a separate institution, out of sight and out of mind. *And in legitimating one form of special need the others too are brought into more concrete existence. Once there is a science which taxonomises children according to their perceived ability/need/disability, then other forms of difference, blindness or a tendency to upsetting behaviour, say, can be brought in as other sub-categories of this rational and ameliorative science.*

In fact the wider consequences of the assessment arrangements introduced by the 1988 Education Act have been further to inhibit the development of inclusive schools. The published test results are not part of an abstract competition: there is a real and tangible prize. It is assumed, with only some degree of accuracy, that parents and carers will use the published test results, the league tables, when selecting to what school to send their children. Since funding now numerically accompanies pupil numbers, a parallel provision of the 1988 Act, schools are in the main anxious to recruit as many children and young people as they possibly can. This is not only a test of popularity, it is the way of ensuring continuing employment for teachers and buoyant budgets for the information technology department. Schools are therefore looking increasingly cautiously at pupils who are likely significantly to reduce their aggregate test scores. This applies to those children and young people who are themselves scoring at the bottom end of the tests. It applies even more to those pupils who schools consider are likely to impede the scores of other children due to the extent of their upsetting behaviour. The assessment arrangements actually constitute a disincentive to the creation of inclusive schools. Instead they perpetuate the demand for exclusion and for segregative provision.

It is knowledge systems and their associated protocols, at least as much as the embedded institutional arrangements which they underpin, which are responsible for legitimating and reproducing prejudicial attitudes towards children and young people perceived to have SEN. Prejudices and stereotypes are intrinsic to the modernist knowledge system. This has been recognised and challenged by increasing numbers of groups which this system attempted to reduce to victims, inferiors, patients, perverts, etc. The challenge on behalf of children perceived to have SEN is taking place within and beyond schools and universities. As well as developing the critique of modernist knowledge, this will take account of non-prejudicial ways of constituting, organising, legitimating, sharing and evaluating knowledge and knowledge systems.

The implications for the education of teachers both in terms of their initial preparation and their CPD are stark. Teachers have themselves come through a system, indeed often been among the successes within it, which perpetrates modernist notions of normality. It is the task of unpicking and contextualising these notions which will be critical to developing within the profession a more inclusive understanding of what it is to be a human being. Some of this work goes on within SEN courses as well as in some humanities and social sciences subject work. It needs to be consolidated and made much more central to the professionalism of all teachers.

References

Bash, L. and Coulby, D. (1989) *The Education Reform Act: competition and control.* London: Cassell.

Beck, U. (1992) *Risk Society: towards a new modernity.* London: Sage.

Blum, J. M. (1978) *Pseudoscience and Mental Ability: the origins and fallacies of the IQ controversy.* London: Monthly Review Press.

Coulby, D. (1996a) 'Ethnocentricity, post modernity and European curricular systems', *European Journal of Teacher Education,* **18** (2/3), 143–154.

Coulby, D. (1996b, forthcoming) 'European curricula, xenophobia and warfare', *Comparative Education.*

Coulby, D. and Bash, L. (1991) *Contradiction and Conflict: the 1988 Education Act in action.* London: Cassell.

Coulby, D. and Jones, C. (1995) *Postmodernity and European Education Systems: centralist knowledge and cultural diversity.* Stoke-on-Trent: Trentham.

Evans, B. and Waites B. (1981) *IQ and Mental Testing.* London: Macmillan.

Foucault, M. (1967) *Madness and Civilisation: a history of insanity in the age of reason.* London: Tavistock.

Foucault, M. (1973) *The Birth of the Clinic: an archaeology of medical perception.* London: Tavistock.

Hargreaves, D., Hester, S. and Mellor, F. (1975) *Deviance in Classrooms.* London: Routledge and Kegan Paul.

Jameson, F. (1991) *Postmodernism or the Cultural Logic of Late Capitalism.* London: Verso.

Jones, K. (1989) *Right Turn: the conservative revolution in education.* London: Hutchinson Radius.

Kamin, L. J. (1974) *The Science and Politics of IQ.* New York: John Wiley.

Labov, W. (1969) 'The logic of non-standard English', *Georgetown Monographs on Language and Linguistics*, **22**, 1–31.

Lyotard, J-F. (1984) *The Postmodern Condition: a report on knowledge.* Manchester: Manchester University Press.

Marx, K. (1977) 'The German ideology' in D. McLellan (ed.) *Karl Marx: selected writings.* London: Oxford University Press.

Sandow, S. (ed.) (1994) *Whose Special Need? Some perceptions of special educational needs.* London: Paul Chapman.

Scarr, S. (1984) *Race, Social Class and Individual Differences in IQ.* London: Lawrence Erlbaum.

Simon, B. and Chitty, C. (1993) *SOS – Save Our Schools.* London: Lawrence and Wishart.

Szasz, T. S. (1972) *The Myth of Mental Illness.* St Albans: Paladin.

Note: I am grateful to Val Richards and Ron Ritchie for comments on an earlier draft of this chapter.

CHAPTER FOUR

Values, Initial Teacher Education and Special Educational Needs

Linda Thomas

Introduction

People responsible for leading those HEIs which provide both ITE and CPD courses in education frequently use words like 'permeation' and 'partnership' to indicate commitment to ideals such as inclusion and cooperation. They also feature in the recent literature on SEN. But what if the intention suggested by these expressions is never realised because of lack of control over the circumstances in which such activities occur? Could the use of this vocabulary become a way of legitimising ideologically suspect dogma and/or economic expediency? In such contexts as ITE, which is highly politicised, and SEN, which is chronically under-resourced, these questions deserve serious attention. This is what I intend to give them in this chapter by establishing a set of values-based standards for our work. Drawing on my own experience of teacher education, I shall consider the implications of such standards for the way we tackle two issues affecting ITE and SEN – student teachers' perceptions of their role and the introduction of a competence based teaching, learning and assessment model. In conclusion I will emphasise that there are no quick and easy solutions to the problems raised. If the profession wants to use such words as permeation and competence in the context of SEN within ITE not as rhetorical devices but with a degree of authority and concern for ideals it must be prepared to make them work in practice.

What do we value?

It is my belief that, at the heart of the ITE enterprise, there must be a vision, something in which it is possible to have faith, that gives meaning to activity, that inspires and unites. In this respect, ITE is no different from any other kind of education, including that aiming to develop an understanding of mathematics or management, or to provide learning experiences for individuals with SEN.

Brunel University's School of Education uses the following statement of aims to represent its vision. In my view they are unexceptional and unlikely to be controversial.

A new age of learning

All educational institutions, including Brunel's School of Education, are having to respond to the implications of a knowledge revolution which is transforming the ways in which we work, live and learn. We believe education must lead rather than follow in the context of these changes. Through our research and teaching we are committed to certain courses of action which we feel will provide a necessary foundation for the age of learning. We are therefore seeking to generate and to contribute to the fundamental change with which society as a whole will eventually have to engage.

- We recognise the importance of meeting the learning needs of the individual in the new post-industrial age. We are therefore emphasising, within research and teaching, that area traditionally known as special educational needs. In our teaching, in programmes uniquely incorporating the results of research, we are seeking to promote skills such as those developed in the area of supportive education and to prepare teachers to help *all* pupils of *all* abilities to develop their full potential in *all* areas of work;

- In common with the National Commission on Education, we believe that communities through learning will promote a sense of common identity and active participation in shaping their future. We therefore value the opportunities provided by our position within the vibrant multi-cultural community of West London to explore, within research and teaching, the parameters of this challenge and to develop new routes to learning;

- In our view the age of learning will require full integration between action and thought, theory and practice. Our research and teaching is already being enriched by the partnerships established between ourselves and schools, both locally and nationally.

Are these aims good enough? Do they represent a vision which is capable of commanding respect and allegiance, giving a worthwhile focus and a sense of purpose to everyday endeavours? One way of establishing whether this is so is to test them against the standards set by people who are sceptical of education. Postman (1996), for example, attacks the tendency, within education, to replace those inspirational narratives which traditionally defined its purpose with stories that are 'thin, crass, and certainly without transcendent meaning' (p.15). He argues that, in the past, the purpose of education was informed by a nobler set of values than at present: by democratic ideals (schools were for teaching about citizenship and the protection of liberty); by humanitarian ideals (schools were for teaching about safety and freedom); by the Protestant ethic (schools were for instilling the virtues of hard work and deferred gratification). In contrast, schools are now about preparing young people for entry into economic life (in response to an ethic which affirms that we are what we do for a living), about maximising consumer satisfaction (we are what we own), or about tooling up for technological advance (we are what technology requires us to be). Whilst we may not be wholly persuaded by such a bleak and devastating critique, it certainly reminds us of the need to offer students something noble to serve and fight for. *This* is why proclaiming our adherence to enlightened ideals such as inclusivity, community and partnership is so vital in giving purpose to our educational enterprise and to SEN within it.

It is also important to do more than that. The educational system is highly complex and dynamic and new practices and structures are constantly developing in response to changing circumstances. We should, therefore, consider the implications of our principles for new ideas and practices as they emerge. In the context of SEN within ITE, I would like to pin-point two issues as deserving particular attention – (i) student teachers' perceptions of their role in relation to the education of *all* pupils and (ii) the notion of competence.

Implications: student teachers' perceptions

I believe that the focus of ITE, like every other educational activity, must be the individual student and the understanding that s/he develops of the meaning of education. If one of my aims is to prepare student teachers to help *all* pupils to develop their full potential in *all* areas of work I must at least wonder about what it takes for student teachers to experience a programme of university and school-based work in that way. What does it take on my part? What does it take on theirs? The real problem is that I have no easy answers to either question. The next section of this chapter will address the former question. With regard to the latter, all we know is what we can glean from recent small-scale research. Garner's (1996) study, for example, examines the views of 52 randomly selected NQTs (primary and secondary). The conclusion of the study is clear:

> Although the status of SEN as a topic for teachers in training is further confirmed in Circular 9/92, this official view is not supported by the training experiences of the NQTs. (p.163)

What is less clear is how the respondents perceived the task of learning to teach all pupils, including those with SEN. There are hints here and there. One student is quoted as saying that school-based work was:

> by far the most informative and useful part of my SEN work . . . [giving] me some good, basic and no-nonsense insights into the kind of things I would be facing when I began teaching. (p.160)

Another shared an anxiety:

> I still worry a lot about my inability to fit into the role of a support teacher; I get a bit fazed [also] when a more experienced teacher acts as support to an SEN pupil in my own class . . . I wasn't prepared for any of this sort of thing. (p.160)

Others claim that:

I was not involved with SEN pupils on placements so had no experience. Now, as an NQT, everything I do relating to SEN pupils has been 'learnt' from my school's SEN Coordinator. (p.160)

Or that, because they did not have formal contact with SEN staff in school, they were prevented from:

any meaningful application, in a practical sense, of some of the ideas discussed in college. (p.161)

It is tempting to conclude that one of the main problems may be student teachers' perceptions of what learning to teach is all about but that temptation must be resisted. What is not available, here or elsewhere, is a systematic account of students' perceptions of learning to teach in relation to SEN. Without it, it is impossible to explore the effect of those perceptions on students' approaches to and experience of their ITE.

Why is this so important? It has been established in empirical and theoretical studies (for example, Marton and Booth, 1997) that, in a broad range of learning contexts the outcome of learning is logically related to the learner's approach to learning. It has also been shown (Wood, 1996) that this is true of learning to teach – student teachers who adopt a surface approach to learning to teach achieve restricted outcomes whilst those who adopt a deep approach achieve an understanding of what is required for meaningful pupil learning.

Research (Wood, *op. cit.*) on student teachers' experience of teacher education produced a set of qualitatively different conceptions of teaching which suggested that there were three significantly different ways of understanding teaching:

- In the first case, the focus is on *the agent of teaching*. The emphasis is on the teacher not the learner as the agent of learning. Teaching matter is seen as imparting knowledge to pupils. The outcome, described as learning, is an increase in pupils' knowledge but the meaning of knowledge is not attended to. Rather attention is drawn to the communication process by which knowledge is understood to be imparted. Successful teaching is associated with personal qualities of the teacher – such as firmness, charisma, being respected and having power.
- In the second case, the focus is on the *act of teaching*. Teaching is understood as preparing pupils to use knowledge. The focus is on the communication process but in this case, in contrast to the first, it is understood as a two-way process between teacher and pupils, and not simply from teacher to pupils. Teachers' questions are emphasised. Through some kind of Socratic dialogue with the teacher, the learner is encouraged to respond to an issue or problem and, through interaction with the teacher, modify that response in the course of teaching. The dialogue demonstrates the weaknesses in pupils' thinking and skills when applied to problems or issues or an explanation of a phenomenon.
- In the third case, the focus is on the *object of teaching*. The object of

teaching is understood as changing the way pupils understand phenomena. The effect of teaching on pupils' 'thinking' is the focus of the teacher's attention. Teaching is understood as preparing pupils to think and to be aware of their own thinking and learning. Teaching understood in this way involves a willingness on the part of the teacher to discover what and how others think about any particular content in order to give it meaning, and to work pedagogically with that thinking. According to this understanding, the teacher is also a learner.

The variation in student teachers' experience of learning to teach was directly related both to qualitative differences in approaches to learning to teach (deep or surface) and to the outcomes of the ITE programme – the student teachers' conceptions of teaching. In other words, what student teachers experienced was what they learnt. Furthermore, what they experienced was related to how they approached learning to teach (deep or surface).

This research study did not directly address the area of SEN. Nevertheless it throws doubt on attempts during ITE to cover this area without reference to the various ways in which students are likely to approach, experience and learn from such attempts. If the SEN agenda is about anything, it must surely be about the individual learner; learning to teach in this area may therefore be conditional on the achievement of the third way of experiencing learning to teach and of understanding teaching. One of the implications of this conclusion is that, if we are really interested in making provision for SEN within teacher education, we should foster a deep approach to learning to teach and engage with student teachers' differing levels of awareness and understanding of the variation in their pupils' thinking and learning. This is an urgent learning/research task for those in HEIs and their partners in schools.

Implications: defining professional competence

If student teachers are to experience a teacher education programme in such a way that they are fully prepared for the task of helping *all* pupils to develop their full potential in *all* areas of work, what does it take on the part of teacher educators? Is it possible within a competence based model of teacher education?

The introduction of the competence based teaching, learning and assessment model was achieved through DfE circulars 9/92 and 14/93 which list the competencies expected of newly qualified secondary and primary school teachers respectively. HEIs, schools and students are to focus on these statements of competence throughout the whole period of initial training.

Newly qualified secondary teachers are required to demonstrate competence within subject knowledge (e.g. demonstrate knowledge and understanding of the National Curriculum and attainment targets, and the programmes of study in the subjects they are preparing to teach, together with an understanding of the framework of the statutory requirements); subject application (e.g. produce coherent lesson plans which take account of National Curriculum and attainment targets and of the school's curriculum policies); class management (e.g. devise and use appropriate rewards and sanctions to maintain an effective learning environment); assessment and recording of pupils' progress (e.g. identify the current level of attainment of individual pupils using National Curriculum attainment targets, statements of attainment and end of Key Stage statements where applicable) and further professional development (e.g. a working knowledge of their pastoral, contractual, legal and administrative responsibilities as teachers). The requirements for newly qualified primary teachers are similar.

Why is this introduction of competence statements a potential problem? Barnett (1994) uses the term 'operational competence' to signal an area of concern and suggests that the introduction of a competence based system:

> may lead to a narrowing of human consciousness. Understanding is replaced by competence; insight is replaced by effectiveness; and rigour of interactive argument is replaced by communication skills. (p.37)

Barnett (*op. cit.*) argues that a competence based system is capable of permeating ideas, institutions and language and, as a result, almost without our noticing, can affect the way we think – the medium becomes the message. Ideas such as vocationalism, mastery, transferable skill development, audit, capability and enterprise, although seemingly distanced from education, become embedded in its fabric through managerial and quality assurance practice. Words and phrases which are relatively neutral such as the learning society, learning how to learn and critical thinking skills are incorporated within education when, in fact, they are elements of larger, less benign constellations of social practices and ideologies.

> Competence, skill, knowing-how, getting things done, technique, effectiveness, operation: all these are coming to form a constellation of concepts marking out a discourse and a set of interests. (p.170)

Barnett (1994) argues that this form of discourse must be constantly examined and challenged even when it sounds persuasive because it represents a denial of the independence of mind which should characterise human *being*.

> What is sought is a response to a given situation: an input-output notion lies not far under the surface of operational competence. What is prized is not a genuine personal interpretation of a situation (for that could lead to an unduly challenging world-view) but a reprocessing of presented sense data. Real independence of mind cannot be tolerated. Real minds would be liable to challenge the given definitions of competence and outcomes. 'Mind', therefore, falls outside the constellation of concepts containing competence and outcomes. (p.173)

This is an important warning which suggests that the whole educational community, including those in teacher education should be constantly vigilant.

But independence of mind cannot become reality if the educational community resists it. The challenge for teacher educators (in universities and schools) is to withstand a wholly competence-driver approach, to unpick the conceptual web, repatriate the concept of competence and redefine it within a professional framework of teacher education. Marton's (1988) analysis is a useful starting point. He suggests that there is:

> a kind of competency which seems to be different from, and more fundamental than, two other kinds of competencies, ordinarily called skills and knowledge. This is because the words 'skills' and 'knowledge' refer respectively to how we handle, and what we know about, phenomena that are already discerned and already apprehended in one way or another. 'Understanding', on the other hand ... refers to the way in which the phenomena are discerned and apprehended ... both the skills and the knowledge related to a phenomenon rest on – or, rather, should rest on – a particular way of understanding that phenomenon. It is in this sense that I want to argue that there is a competency, simply labelled 'understanding', which is different from and more fundamental than the two other kinds of competences, commonly referred to as skills and knowledge. (pp.3–4)

Marton (*op. cit.*) uses work on the development of children's early number concepts to illustrate his definition of competence as a particular way of understanding or experiencing. He also shows how a teaching programme, designed to foster mathematical competence, achieved success in meeting the needs of one group of Swedish pre-school children diagnosed as running the highest risk of developing mathematical difficulties. Because the programme brought about changes in the children's experience and understanding of basic 'number facts', their mental arithmetic skills and knowledge were also significantly improved.

Is it possible to teach student teachers so that they develop Marton's kind of competence? In one ITE programme (Wood and Thomas, 1996), this was achieved by using variation as a tool simultaneously to change two things: the content of learning to teach as it was experienced by student teachers and the way in which the act of learning to teach was experienced. The programme aimed to:

- create, as a deliberate intention, the *relevance structure* that is required if student teachers are to experience teaching in an advanced and complex way;
- focus student teachers' attention on the *variation* in their pupils' learning and understanding of subject matter, that is, variation in pupils' understanding of the content of learning and variation in pupils as experiences of that content (e.g. how they approach the task of learning);
- focus student teachers' awareness *metacognitively* on themselves as experiences of a learning to teach programme and on the dimensions of variation in that experience.

The programme's success was recorded in terms of teaching skills (as measured by the award of QTS) and knowledge (as measured by successful completion of PGCE assignments). More important, the programme was successful in encouraging student teachers to adopt a deep approach to learning to teach, to experience it through the variation in their own and their pupils' thinking and learning, and to achieve professional competence in Marton's (*op. cit.*) terms, in the majority of cases (as measured by student teachers' focus on the object rather than the act or agent of teaching). This success is sufficiently convincing to merit further exploration by those who aim to assist student teachers to experience a teacher education programme in such a way that they are fully prepared for the task of helping *all* pupils to develop their full potential in *all* areas of work.

An action plan for special educational needs within initial teacher education

It is my contention, on the basis of the above arguments that it is possible to promote the highest educational ideals in situations and contexts which often appear unhelpful. But it is also my contention that it will require further exploration and research to identify the basis of student teachers' perceptions of learning to teach in inclusive education settings, to generate programmes of work, and to evaluate the effects of various interventions. Furthermore, this whole enterprise will need to be conducted, in a spirit of collaborative learning, by teacher educators within university and school partnerships.

In my view the profession is capable of undertaking this task so that preparing student teachers for inclusive education becomes an inclusive element of learning to teach. Whether or not it is willing to devote the necessary effort and goodwill remains to be seen.

References

Barnett, R. (1994) *The Limits of Competence*. Buckingham: The Society for Research into Higher Education and the Open University Press.

DfE (1992) *Initial Teacher Training (Secondary Phase)*, Circular No 9/92. London: DfE.

DfE (1993) *Initial Teacher Training (Primary Phase)*, Circular No 14/93. London: DfE.

Garner, P. (1996) 'A special education? The experiences of newly qualifying teachers during initial training', *British Educational Research Journal*, 22 (2), 155–165.

Marton, F. (1988) *Phenomenography and 'The Art of Teaching All Things to All Men'*, invited address presented at the annual meeting of the American Educational Research Association, April, 1988, New Orleans, USA.

Marton, F. and Booth, S. (1997, in press) *Learning and Awareness*. Hove: Lawrence Erlbaum.

Postman, N. (1996) 'School's our, forever', *Guardian*, 21.12.96.

Wood, K. (1996) *Learning to Teach: a phenomenographic perspective*, unpublished

PhD thesis, University of London.

Wood, K. and Thomas, L. (1996) *Assessing Meaningful Teacher Learning*, paper presented at the International Symposium, Exploring Futures in ITE, University of London Institute of Education, September.

CHAPTER FIVE

The Views of Newly Qualified Teachers Concerning SEN Provision in ITE Courses

John Dwyfor Davies and Philip Garner

At various points in this book individual contributors express a concern that the SEN experiences of students on ITE courses are often unsatisfactory, in terms of both their volume and their content. The reader could be excused for suspecting a degree of self-interest in such claims: after all, most of our contributors have a stake in what some see as a 'special needs industry'. Nevertheless, the current ITE scenario for SEN is worrying, as is outlined in the opening chapter of this book. What we have summarised is a prevailing shortfall of the SEN component in ITE courses, which, according to Cains and Brown (1996) results in students' concern 'about their level of preparedness to deal with pupils with SEN'. The first part of this chapter uses the views of students who have recently completed ITE courses in order to investigate such claims in more detail. The evidence presented suggests that the diminution of SEN input to ITE courses is very real, with the implication that, without considerable reformulation, an even bleaker future for SEN within ITE may exist. In the overall spirit of this volume, which seeks as much to celebrate existing good practice as it does to critique current difficulties, we then go on to offer three recent examples of effective practice taken from ITE courses. We realise there are many similar approaches in HEIs and their partner schools, which, given the constraints facing course leaders, SEN tutors and schools, is a tribute to the creativity of all involved. Such examples offer pointers for the reinstatement of SEN as an essential feature of effective ITE provision, a position which can be justified not only in terms of equity and natural justice but also in respect of current guidelines for the 'training' of teachers, with their emphasis on developing teacher-skills which ensure access for all.

Sorry tales: what NQTs say about special educational needs in the 1990s

A questionnaire was sent to 100 randomly selected BA or BSc/QTS (Primary) and PGCE (Primary) students who had just completed their teacher-education courses at four higher education institutions in the south-east of England. All were in their first term of teaching. A 40% response-rate was achieved, with 30% of the replies from those who had followed BA/BSc courses and the remainder from PGCE students. The questionnaire concerned four aspects of the students' ITE course: (a) the structure, staffing and mode of delivery of SEN elements (b) the range of SEN topics covered (c) the nature of school-based SEN content and (d) the teachers' views concerning the effectiveness of their SEN preparation in the light of their early experiences of working full-time in schools. Subsequently, two students from each institution were interviewed in order to elicit more detailed comments. Although the sample used in this study has the limitation of being both small and opportunistic, the data obtained is nevertheless indicative of the difficulties involved in sustaining SEN matters as a central focus in current ITE programmes.

i. Structure, staffing and mode of delivery

The evidence gathered from this group of students shows that less than 20% recall receiving two or fewer SEN-specific lectures during their course, whilst only 15% recalled more than six sessions of input. The responses indicated that free-standing SEN input was the favoured option in PGCE courses, BA/BSc (QTS) courses adopted the 'permeation' approach, where SEN issues were subsumed within general education or subject-specific elements of an ITE course. Encouragingly, the respondents noted that most of their SEN-specific sessions were delivered by a specialist SEN lecturer.

The lack of time devoted to SEN left many students in the survey feeling that they had received inadequate preparation in their college-based courses. One student observed that 'the mainstream teaching course does not offer enough input on specific special needs of children that one might encounter in future work placements', whilst another, commenting on the permeated nature of SEN in her course, recognised that 'SEN needs to be a special course on its own due to its complexity'. One respondent claimed that she was 'totally frustrated by the way in which the lecturer jumped from one aspect of special needs to another', but added that 'I suppose this was bound to happen because he only had one session with us.' Each of the students interviewed regarded SEN provision within their college to be something of a lottery, with a SEN-dedicated written assignment being required in each of the PGCE courses but in only two of the BA or BSC (QTS) courses. As one respondent put it, 'I didn't get the chance to do an essay about special needs, which I was really interested in, but Louisa [PGCE student] did. I think it should be compulsory for everyone.'

ii. The range of SEN topics covered

The data reveals the somewhat *ad hoc* nature of the coverage of SEN issues in college-based courses, whether dedicated SEN lectures, subject-based studies or in general education lectures. On one level, for example, it may be understandable that little emphasis was given to the education of children with SLD; on the other hand, it could be argued that such an omission will do little to develop in young teachers an understanding of the concept of inclusivity, applied to cover the whole school population (Garner, 1994). According to the students, classroom management, identification and differentiation were the three topics on which they received most direct input. This is reassuring, given that most practising teachers might say that these are the most critical elements in effective SEN provision. Sessions dealing with each of these issues were generally well received by the students, one observing that 'without that [behaviour management] input I think I might have failed my final teaching practice.'

Twenty per cent of the students felt that subject-based studies dealt with SEN matters very poorly, whilst only 27% believed that SEN had been dealt with 'quite well'. No-one considered the quality of subject-based coverage to have been 'good' or better, and on talking to individual students it became apparent that there was a wide variation in quality: one student argued that 'All subjects should offer the level of input that Maths, English and Science offer for subject-specific SEN support' and that she 'could offer no help to a physically handicapped child in Music, Art or PE, for example'. Amplifying these comments, another student felt that 'different subjects dealt with SEN with variable success. English, Maths and Drama were good, and Science was OK, but the rest were poor. PE was useless.' Given the key role being assumed by the classroom teacher under the Code of Practice for the initial assessment of, and provision for, SEN these observations are cause for concern.

General education lectures fared somewhat better, with 45% of respondents rating coverage here as being at least 'good'. A worryingly high proportion of students (42%) felt that the SEN focus in general education lectures was insufficient, especially as such sessions were seen as opportunities for the students to examine the broad context of SEN in schools; this view is typified by the comment that 'when you are starting out in teaching you need to know something about where these [SEN] kids have come from, and what schools usually do with them, in a general sense. It's about a personal philosophy really.'

iii. The nature of school-based SEN

Almost 60% of the students said that they were not given an opportunity to be involved in generic SEN work whilst on school placement, although this overall percentage masks the fact that the one-year PGCE course, because of its shorter duration, is less able to fit a specific SEN element into school experience. Eighty five per cent of the students said that they did not receive a visit from a college tutor who was a SEN specialist whilst on school placement, whilst a similar percentage was given no opportunities to visit special schools during their course.

When interviewed about this aspect of their SEN experience all of the students commented on the variation in quality between schools. This was neatly summarised by Helen, a PGCE student, who said that 'SEN experience all depended on what school and age-range you were with on teaching practice.' Nevertheless, the students all regarded the school-based element of their course as an important way in which they could gather practical advice and experience about meeting SENs. One, for instance, advised that 'I think it would be very helpful for a NQT to watch a specialist SEN teacher in action and have the chance to discuss with them different types of strategy to motivate SEN children and improve their self esteem.' Clearly, though, the pressures currently being faced by many SENCos as a result of increased responsibilities, may severely militate against such initiatives.

The failure of HEI-based courses to provide students with access to special schools as a mandatory part of the student experience was seen as a major drawback. Angela, for example, could see no reason why, on a four-year ITE course, she was not given the opportunity to 'visit a special school, any special school really, because the bit I've read and heard about them makes me think they'd have a different way of working with the children. I think we all should see that, even if it's just for a week or so.' Not surprisingly, such a view, which stresses the importance of teachers and schools working in collaboration in order to enhance their expertise in SEN, has been the focus of considerable attention in recent years (Norwich *et al.* 1994).

iv. SEN training in retrospect

About a quarter of the respondents felt that their preparation in SEN matters whilst undertaking their ITE course was inadequate to meet the learning difficulties of children in schools. Only 6% felt that their college-based course as 'highly effective' in this respect. As a result, one student advised that 'Early provision of extra training during the first year (of teaching) would be helpful as classroom experience always adds a dimension which cannot be reached by theory alone.' Perhaps the most encouraging response was that over 55% of the students indicated that they intended to maintain a professional involvement in SEN when they begin teaching on a full-time basis. This provides an indication of the degree of interest in, and commitment to, SEN amongst students in training, and is a basis of optimism for the future of SEN provision in schools.

The above accounts, by students following ITE programmes, are not unusual in their illustration of the level of student concern about their state of preparedness to work with children with SEN. Cains and Brown (*op. cit.*) report that many new teachers feel unable to assist 'slow learners', as they have not accumulated the necessary skills and strategies to intervene. Aubrey (1996) reinforces this concern, noting that, in her sample of 98 students, almost 20% reported that they felt 'unqualified in the detection of learning difficulties. . . specifically, the difficulty in distinguishing between normal and atypical developmental variation among young children' (p.16).

Making a difference: the role of generic, free-standing SEN courses in ITE

In the previous section of this chapter we have noted two types of SEN input to ITE courses – 'permeated' and 'free-standing' courses. Few of the NQTs in the study experienced anything other than the occasional SEN-specific lecture: this is now part of an approach which argues that, as SEN is such an important issue for NQTs, it should percolate into every aspect of the student's experience, not least into the inputs provided by 'subject studies' staff in HEIs. Few of the respondents expressed any great satisfaction with this type of arrangement, the students feeling that free-standing SEN courses, comprising a series of associated lectures and workshops over a given period of time, were of more value. Although the NQTs questioned demonstrated that this approach to SEN provision was being increasingly curtailed, the value they placed upon such 'free-standing' inputs was evident in their comments. Three examples of work in this area are now illustrated to further emphasise its potential. In the first two, the accent is upon HEI-based courses, whilst our third example, recognising the need for ITE providers to offer ongoing support to teachers newly entering the profession, illustrates a school-based programme in SEN.

HEI A

In this example, an SEN programme operated within a PGCE course and involved collaboration between a partner school and an HEI. The partner school was located in an outer London borough and was a mixed comprehensive community school (11–18) with over 1,300 pupils on roll. An area survey in 1989 had revealed that 12.6% of the existing roll in that year had some involvement with outside agencies, and the catchment included a number of areas of social and economic disadvantage. At the time of the project, statements of SEN had been prepared for 3% of the school's population. SEN provision within the school was organised from a department, which had five teachers and whose facilities included a resource room, a special unit, a support-teacher network providing in-class intervention, and a 'sanctuary' for pupils who were regarded as having behavioural difficulties.

A programme was jointly prepared by HEI and school staff. Fifteen PGCE (Secondary) students were placed in the school for one term (13 × 3 hour afternoon sessions). Each session had a specific focus, although at the outset of the programme individual students were allocated a 'target' pupil, who was in receipt of a statement. The structure of each day comprised (i) an initial briefing by school/HEI staff, outlining the day's focus (ii) participation by the students in teaching activities, according to the school's timetable (iii) reporting/ debriefing session. Importantly, the students had received three three-hour preparatory sessions at the HEI on general SEN issues, supported by course readings and handouts. They also received written information concerning the school's expectations of them during their SEN placement. Emphasis was placed upon regular and punctual attendance: both issues were seen as essential to the development of an effective relationship between the SEN pupil and the student-teacher. There was, according to the school, a danger that SEN pupils could be trivialised by one-off or irregular input. Finally, the placement provided the students with a focus for their assessed work in SEN, which comprised the development of a learning package for a pupil or group of SEN pupils. This was supported by a notebook or diary, which each student maintained for the duration of the placement.

The course explored a wide range of SEN issues which were arranged in such a way as to demonstrate the incremental process of SEN work. Thus, the first session dealt with individual student perceptions of what constituted a 'special need'; this was followed by a session on identification and assessment and subsequent activities on setting learning-objectives, task analysis and differentiation. Considerable focus was placed throughout on the key areas of literacy and numeracy. A further important aspect of the programme was a consideration of 'problem behaviour' by pupils, and its association with underachievement. An overarching theme was the organisation and resourcing of SEN provision within the school.

How was it for you? PGCE students' opinions of school-based SEN courses

A short questionnaire was distributed to the students at the end of their school-placement. This sought their opinion on (a) course organisation (b) content and (c) perceived relevance to their first year in teaching.

Thirteen out of fifteen respondents felt that the course was well-structured. Ron, for example, stated that 'It was pretty good that we got the lectures in the first term as they prepared us for what was to happen later on. I think I'd have been a bit lost if I was just plonked next to a kid with SEN'. Several students welcome the opportunity to focus on the learning needs of a particular student: 'I felt I really got to know Karen [Year 9 pupil] during my time in the school. We talked about lots of things other than her work, and I think at the end of it we were both sorry to say goodbye' (Marsha, PGCE student). Maintaining a notebook/diary was seen as particularly beneficial, with eleven students indicating that this was an important part of their learning process. Pete, for instance, felt that it 'gave me reflection time on my own work and my own feelings. As the [PGCE] course is pretty full, you need to have some kind of formal way of making sure that you think about what you do, rather than just doing it like a robot. The diary helped me very much on this.'

There were a few logistical problems. A number of students viewed the course as problematic in terms of its timing. Several had to leave HEI-based sessions early in order to arrive at the school on time. The school was situated about four miles from the HEI, and transport was also identified as a problem. Several students were also unable to attend sessions because of job interviews. Nevertheless, all fifteen of the students indicated that the course was important to them, as there was 'no ivory tower stuff . . . [and] I don't think a college-based lecture each week would have given me enough to cope with the real world' (Hillary).

Most of the respondents felt that the content of the course was about right. 'The course has covered most things, and I'm glad that, as I will soon be in school myself as a qualified teacher, I at least know the basics about teaching reading' (Bill), and 'I was fascinated, and very encouraged, to see the sort of things that could be done to help kids who cause behaviour problems. Knowing something about why these pupils behaved in that way is, I think, very important to all new teachers' (Ron) were two typical responses.

The students were especially complimentary about the manner in which the school-based location of the course enabled various aspects of theory to be seen in practice. Thirteen of the students referred to this in their responses. This not only applied to their work with their allocated SEN pupil, but also to their contact with SEN staff and other teachers, an opinion summarised by Wendy, who stated that 'I have appreciated the "hands on" experience with both the pupils and staff from [the] school'.

The students made frequent reference to the potential value of the course when they begin teaching. Such comments were apparent in all three parts of the questionnaire, and all students, without exception, saw the course as a prerequisite to their first year of teaching. 'It has given me confidence, whilst realising more than ever that SEN is a huge area and that I won't be able to do everything when I start teaching. The best thing is that I have seen teachers making a difference, and this has made me very enthusiastic about starting full-time teaching' (Felicity) is a summary of the positive nature of the feedback.

Such a free-standing course was not without its problems, however. It was labour-intensive, and therefore relied on the commitment of the senior management and SEN staff in the partner school. Some teachers were concerned about the impact that fifteen students would have on the ethos of the school, whilst at least two saw the initiative as counter-productive, arguing that it was at once voyeuristic and unreal. As one staff-member noted: 'These students will never get the luxury of working one-to-one with difficult [sic] pupils, and it is also unrealistic to assume that they will get the kind of support that they have received here.'

The initiative also depended upon both the support of a partner school which had a well-established SEN provision and that of a head of department (this was prior to the CoP) who was enthusiastic about the school's role in teacher education. Within the HEI, SEN had long been recognised as a key element within ITE courses, a principle which had the continued commitment of the head of department, the course leaders and the teaching team. It may perhaps be difficult to provide such SEN-specific input in establishments which lack such resolve.

In spite of these difficulties, identified by teaching staff, HEI tutors or the students themselves, the overall impression given was that the free-standing input did its job efficiently and in a highly practical manner. The sharp differences between the responses of these students and those outlined earlier by the group of primary ITE students is of particular note.

HEI B

The second example is taken from an ITE programme that operates within a modular structure and where a module was designed and validated specifically to provide a group of students with the opportunity to spend regular periods of time over one term working closely with pupils with SEN, within a mainstream setting. This module was offered alongside several others focusing on SEN issues. Students undertaking this particular module had selected it specifically because they wished to develop further their skills, understanding and knowledge of working with pupils with MLD. These students were consequently generally highly motivated.

The programme had been designed and negotiated between the HEI tutor and the host school, which had volunteered to participate in the exercise. That voluntary element was also significant since it too added an element of commitment to the exercise. Comparisons may immediately be drawn between this situation and the current statutory requirement that HEIs and schools enter into partnership arrangements.

The term's programme was presented in two discrete parts. The first half consisted of six two-hour taught sessions at the HEI during which time the students attended lectures and workshops on SEN issues. These were designed to build on earlier work undertaken by students on SEN, and focused on three discrete, but interrelated areas of study seen as pertinent to the practice based element of the module, to be undertaken during the second part of the term. These were (a) barriers to learning (b) learning/teaching styles and (c) match and differentiation.

The underlying theme for the practical exercise was that of 'problem solving'. Students were required to work as a group – in collaboration with a teacher from the host school – designing a programme of activities that would support pupils with MLD in resolving challenging problems.

Students, class teacher and an HEI tutor met during the early part of the term to consider the needs of the children in the group and to agree on the nature of the activities that would be designed for the practical element of the task. Depending on these negotiations, participating groups elected to undertake a wide variety of approaches with pupils, ranging from problem solving through drama, to practical activities in the playground or main hall, and to exploring imaginative approaches to tackling the reading difficulties which some pupils were experiencing. Consideration was also given at this time to the nature of support resources that would be required and how these could best be created.

Following an initial period of familiarisation, the students spent an afternoon each week over the rest of the term working with pupils on the jointly prepared exercises. Students agreed to share responsibility for different aspects of the school-based work and rotated the tasks of leadership, support, observation and analysis so as to ensure that each gained experience in addressing each of these by the end of the term. Where appropriate, the lessons were recorded on video and closely analysed by the group at a later time. The students also worked together in compiling a document for assessment. This required them to present not only an analytical account of the work undertaken, but also an analysis of its effectiveness in meeting the initial aims of the exercise and to suggest modifications that might be made on future occasions.

The value of this approach for student teachers was generally well received. They appreciated the greater insight gained in working closely with pupils with SEN in mainstream settings – which would support their practice as teachers in future. They frequently commented positively on the support received from collaboration with peers in analysing, reflecting and documenting the process and its outcomes for pupils and for the teachers themselves. The sharing of *real* workplace situations, and the management issues that invariably arose, also attracted considerable attention.

The module culminated with a meeting of students and teachers, during which the observations gleaned from the above process could be shared publicly. In addition to providing an opportunity to disseminate skills and approaches to working with pupils with SEN, this offered students a further opportunity to rehearse skills of presenting oral accounts of their learning and to respond to questioning and challenges from peers.

HEI C

Teachers entering the profession have traditionally found difficulty in accessing CPD opportunities provided by HEIs in the area of SEN, as a result of stringent entry requirements to programmes of study leading to higher diplomas or degrees. This has meant that for many, the very support they require as NQTs has been unavailable to them. More recently, this has been more widely recognised, as reflected in the recommendations of the SENTC report (1996) and by the TTA (1997).

A large independent school in the south-west of England has long recognised this difficulty and attempted to provide additional professional support for its

NQTs. This, however, presented some difficulty, since the number of NQTs entering the school varied from one year to the next. There would be occasions when the viability of such a group could not be guaranteed. The fact that it was offered exclusively to those employed within the school, also limited the value of such a programme, restricting the range of ideas and opinions that NQTs were exposed to. Whilst NQTs invariably welcomed this additional support – and despite the constraints identified here – its value was diminished by the fact that their enhanced learning could not be recognised formally within HEI-validated programmes. Through discussion with a local HEI, the school was able to negotiate a programme of study that was to address all the limitations recognised above.

In order to widen access to such a programme and to make it more likely that a viable cohort could be recruited on a regular basis, it was agreed that this should be advertised to NQTs working in LEA schools across the region.

The school provided a venue in which NQTs could meet on a regular basis. A room was specifically allocated for CPD activities and furnished appropriately. In recognition of the fact that these teachers were attending this programme of CPD on a voluntary basis, care was taken to ensure that they would be made to feel comfortable and welcomed.

A senior member of the school's staff had been designated as its CPD coordinator and as well as the responsibility for ensuring appropriate support for colleagues generally, that person had the responsibility for liaising with the HEI in devising support modules for NQTs. It was found necessary to identify those areas of their work that NQTs felt most in need of support and further guidance. Accessing that information was relatively easy. However, providing high quality programmes was somewhat more challenging.

A survey of NQTs within the region suggested that SEN was one of the main areas where they felt most in need of further support. Their views closely reflect those of NQTs reported elsewhere (Cains and Brown, 1996; Garner, 1996) with the majority of respondents stating that, whilst their ITE courses had familiarised them relatively well with recent legislation on SEN, they felt less secure in the practical application of a range of strategies designed to meet the learning and behaviour difficulties experienced by their pupils.

Through negotiation between the HEI tutors and senior managers at the school, the expressed needs of the NQTs were considered and a programme of study defined. This was validated within the HEI's programme for CPD and formed the content of two modules, which could be delivered jointly by HEI staff and senior managers at the school over a period of one year. The group met regularly throughout that time and drew upon the content of the course in support of school-based enquiries, exploration and analysis of their own work with pupils with SEN. The outcome of that exercise was presented to the HEI for assessment and subsequent accreditation, which could be used towards a further qualification by those who so desired.

Participants in this programme expressed their satisfaction with this approach to NQT support, which has attempted to build upon the skills and competencies that they had begun to refine whilst on ITE courses. This timely intervention has not only provided new teachers with opportunities to access the kind of support that they have themselves identified as a priority, but it has also allowed them to engage in a coordinated programme of CPD at a crucial point in their careers. By so doing, they have embarked on recognised course of progressional study which captures their early enthusiasm for teaching and which forms a much needed bridge for teachers during their induction phase. As a result of the success of the initiative it is now intended that further programmes will be devised to offer these teachers a coherent progression to CPD as their skills and knowledge develops.

Conclusion

In this chapter we have argued that the level of content of SEN input to ITE courses is inadequate, both in real terms and in relation to the likely numbers of SEN children that NQTs will be involved with in their teaching career. We have, in addition, outlined some ways of organising SEN input to ITE courses, as a means of providing more emphasis on this aspect of the ITE 'curriculum'.

The focus of most post-1988 guidance and legislation in ITE has been towards the establishment of competent teachers. Whether or not we agree with the moves towards a skills-based approach, at the expense of what Fish (1989) has called 'professional artistry', a solid argument can be made that free-standing inputs are more likely to result in new teachers who are able to meet the various learning difficulties of the children who they will encounter in their future careers. Ultimately, however, the principle underlying such provision is likely to be more important than its organisation and content. That principle should recognise the right of all children to participate in educational practices that are inclusive. All ITE providers, whether generically associated with SEN or not, need to have a forthright commitment to this.

References

Aubrey, C. (1996) 'From the beginning', *Special Children,* June/July, 15–19.
Cains, R. and Brown, C. (1996) 'Newly qualified primary teachers: a comparative analysis of perceptions held by B.Ed. and PGCE trained teachers of their training routes', *Educational Psychology,* 16 (3), 257–270.
Fish, D. (1989) *Learning through Practice in Initial Teacher Training.* London: Kogan Page.
Garner, P. (1994) 'Oh my God, help! What newly qualifying teachers think of special schools', in S. Sandow (ed.) *Whose Special Need?* London: Paul Chapman Publishing.
Garner, P. (1996) 'A special education? The experience of newly qualified teachers during initial training', *British Educational Research Journal,* 22 (2), 155–163.
Norwich, B., Evans, J., Lunt, I., Steedman, J. and Wedell, K. (1994) 'Clusters: inter-

school collaboration in meeting special educational needs in ordinary schools', *British Educational Research Journal*, **20** (3), 279–292.

SENTC (1996) *Professional Development to Meet Special Educational Needs: Report to the Department for Education and Employment*. Stafford: SENTC.

TTA (1997) *Special Educational Needs: next steps in training*, post-conference report. London: TTA.

CHAPTER SIX

Partnership in Initial Teacher Education: Three Case Studies of Special Educational Needs

Pat Dodds, Alexis Taylor and Lynne Thorogood

As a result of DfEE Circulars 9/92 and 14/93 the training of teachers for the Secondary and Primary phases has undergone considerable change. These circulars specify national criteria for the assessment of teaching competence, increased school-based experience and a requirement for ITE to be based on partnership between schools and HEIs. The partnership model formally sets out the greater responsibilities that schools are expected to undertake in the preparation of NQTs.

The partnership model of the School of Education at Brunel University is based on the belief that, as partners, the learning community (in this case, school and university) will develop a sense of identity. This belief underpins our commitment to partnership in ITE as a first stage in career-long academic, professional development and learning. Our aim is to achieve sustainable school-focused ITE through a process of negotiation, continual review and refinement which recognises the strengths which schools and the University bring to the partnership.

Three principles guide our expectations of partnership. *Mutual Benefit*, which implies that working in partnership will contribute to enhanced teacher learning (in schools and in the university), enhanced student learning (school and university students) and enhanced knowledge of teaching, learning and teacher education. *Mutual Esteem* is a recognition by the university of the value of its school-partners' contribution to its aims by giving them special access to its expertise, resources, course programmes and accreditation systems. At the same time the partner schools demonstrate the value they place on the university's contribution to their aims by the use they make of the university as a source of expertise for their teachers and students. *Shared Responsibility* means that both partners recognise their joint responsibility for the professional education of students and their continuing academic and professional development through induction and beyond.

Brunel University was one of the few institutions which trained primary ITE students to teach in SLD schools until this was curtailed by the DES in 1984.

Moreover, SEN has always formed discrete elements within primary and secondary mainstream ITE courses (Garner, 1992) and it has remained a popular area of study within the university's Academic and Professional Development programme. This background has provided the necessary expertise to enable training for SEN within ITE to develop within the new model for partnership established since 1992.

The Code of Practice for SEN requires all teachers to play an integral part in the identification of, and provision for, SEN in their class. Not only do we acknowledge the importance of this role, but we further believe that all students must recognise that teaching and learning is based on the principle that pupils, irrespective of their abilities, aptitudes or behaviour, are entitled to a curriculum that is understandable and accessible. The following three case studies illustrate some of these principles in operation.

Case study one: secondary undergraduate course

The secondary undergraduate course is a four-year course leading to a BA or BSc Honours Degree with QTS. Students study, within a modular programme, a main subject of physical education or geography, with a subsidiary subject of English, information technology, geography or religious education. Partnership work in schools is a major feature of two modules in the last two years of the course. In Year 1 students take a foundation professional module, which introduces them to the world of secondary education in general. Visits to partner schools provide opportunities to work collaboratively with pupils and school staff. During Year 2 students develop their professional competence through a module related to teaching and learning in their main subject. Work in partner schools focuses on planning programmes of study and individual lessons, the students being encouraged to reflect critically on these activities. Provision for pupils with SEN is a significant feature of this module, both in university and school-based work. It is worthwhile noting that both modules, with their heavy emphasis on school-based experience, were established prior to the publication of Circular 9/92. This, we believe, represented the good practice to be found in many other HEIs, well before government intervention.

The last two years of the course are the main professional years, with Year 3 being heavily weighted towards school-based work. Circular 9/92 requires students to be based in partner schools for 160 days over the whole course. This emphasises an increased focus on partnership, and a more sophisticated management of the process. In the light of this it was decided to establish a pilot partnership project, reflecting this increasing level of cooperation, prior to its implementation in Year 3 of the course.

The partnership pilot project

We began the partnership pilot project with a planning conference. Senior staff from six partner schools, who had previously worked closely with the university through the more traditional 'teaching practice' arrangement, were invited to attend. The conference established a Partnership Planning Group (comprising university tutors and senior school staff), which took responsibility for partnership policy and implementation through regular planning meetings. A time-schedule for the project was determined, and there was agreement that groups of students (approximately six/seven) of mixed gender and subject, would spend one day per week in a partner school for six weeks during the latter part of the spring term.

It was decided that the focus of the pilot project was to be SEN, with the intention that students would be introduced to this area of provision by their active contribution to the SEN work of the partner school. A mixture of pragmatism and principle governed this choice. An SEN focus would allow students to build on their earlier work in partner schools, whilst providing a relevant practical element to the university-based module which focuses on 'schools as organisations': SEN forms a vital element of this, with individual sessions on assessment, differentiation, recording and reporting, home/family links and pastoral care. Moreover, previous evaluations have indicated that students had requested 'more work on special needs' and we were acutely aware that we were educating future teachers who would be responsible for implementing the Code of Practice, one of the central features of which was the role of subject- and classroom-teachers in the identification of SEN and their involvement in subsequent 'Stage 1' provision. Prior to this, Circular 9/92 had indicated a requirement that NQTs should have the necessary foundations to develop an awareness of individual differences. Finally, we were aware that SEN provision in ITE courses was deemed unsatisfactory by many students (Garner, 1996).

What did the students do in school?

The schools themselves wanted to take the lead in planning a SEN programme that was appropriate to their own institutional context and needs. In each school the SENCo, supported by the university link tutor, prepared a programme of activities for the students. These included:

- placement in their main and subsidiary subject departments, preparing materials, undertaking whole class support and collecting departmental documentation;
- support for statemented pupils in a variety of curriculum areas;
- involvement in whole school initiatives, such as numeracy and literacy projects through, for example, paired reading;
- shadowing the SENCo and working in the Learning Support Department;

- collecting information concerning the whole-school policy on SEN, and exploring how it was implemented within the school;
- preparation of differentiated materials, and work with pupils using the material. The materials become both a personal and school resource;
- review of existing worksheets, previously aimed at the middle ability range;
- observation of intervention methods and techniques used by class teachers;
- interviews with pupils, with a focus on their learning;
- examination of IEPs (amended to maintain confidentiality), including investigation of their use by the school; preparation of a draft IEP.

Evaluating the project

The pilot project was evaluated at the conclusion of the students' placement. SENCos, senior staff responsible for students, and subject teachers all participated in this exercise, together with the university link tutors and students. Each school group was asked to make a brief presentation describing their programme, their initiatives and some indication of what they, as a group, had learnt. Students were also asked to complete an individual written response. Student comment included:

- 'a very well organised and planned project; a worthwhile experience';
- 'it linked theory and practice';
- 'it gave me valuable information about differentiation';
- 'helping SEN pupils to read and supporting them in other lessons than my main subject was valuable';
- 'learning what an IEP was and how to complete relevant documentation for SEN pupils was useful';
- 'I realised the extent of SEN in schools and how teachers help and how I could help';
- 'it helped me to be aware of difficulties encountered by SEN pupils in the classroom';
- 'the SEN project and school visits gave me an insight into how to plan for PE and physically disabled pupils';
- 'the maths lesson gave me a real perspective – I worked in the bottom set';
- 'I worked with children in the Learning Support Department. This helped me to analyse specific learning needs, which I hadn't encountered before';
- 'I came away with personal resources, such as differentiated worksheets we could use. It gave me a buzz to know that I had written them.'

A number of benefits accrued for the participating schools. According to the teachers these included:

- having the flexibility to plan their own SEN programme, suited to their own needs;
- meeting with other SENCos in project planning meetings. This provided

opportunities for discussion and shared good practice;
- additional students in school meant that more pupils received one-to-one support;
- an understanding of current university-based arrangements in ITE, and an opportunity to explore links between research and practice;
- a greater whole-school awareness to SEN issues.

As far as the university was concerned the project was viewed as a success because it:
- contributed to the professional developmental link tutors;
- developed genuine 'partnership in action';
- made stronger links with SENCos in a variety of schools;
- developed further the concept of ITE as part of a teacher development continuum, in which SEN was an important element.

Summary

The project, with its SEN focus, was generally considered to be a success and greatly informed the planning of Year 3, the main professional year of the course. The Partnership Planning Group agreed that SEN should remain as a central theme for the whole of the spring term. During this time students would spend two days a week working on a further school-based programme in SEN. Other pastoral activities, such as attachment to a tutor group, initiating an extra curricular activity and teaching Personal and Social Education were also included, and seen as a valuable extension of SEN activities. At the time of writing our students are following this programme, and we await their evaluations with optimism.

Case study two: PGCE primary course

PGCE primary courses at Brunel University have traditionally provided a high-profile SEN component, included within a 'Teaching Studies' programme. This comprised a block of four core lectures, supported by a learning pack. One of the three major pieces of mandatory assessed work was a project based on provision for SEN support, at individual (pupil), school and LEA levels. The course attracted, and continues to attract, large numbers of well qualified graduate applicants, many of whom cited the SEN component as their main reason for selecting this course as their first choice. Regrettably, however, the impact of Circular 14/93 has meant that the discrete SEN component has survived only by reducing the number of core lectures to a single session. The SEN learning pack, together with subject-based work, have become the most significant elements of SEN provision within the university-based part of the course.

An area of particular interest to many students is that of supporting those children whose SEN is related to reading difficulties. The emphasis on reading within the English component may be one of the reasons for this, and the high profile and publicity which 'reading standards' have always been given in the media may be a further contributing factor. Whatever its origins, however, the course team (university- and school-based) regard it as an important aspect of SEN intervention. One example of this focus on reading difficulties is the partnership scheme with one of our local primary schools which was one of the first centres in the UK to offer 'Reading Recovery', an early intervention programme for struggling readers. This is a highly intensive scheme, in which children learn to combine attention to detail in both reading and writing, with a focus on meaning. It also helps children to develop more effective 'self help' strategies, so important to those who have learning difficulties.

Student participation in a Reading Recovery programme

Reading Recovery is now well established in many Surrey schools, and the partner school is recognised as one of one of the most experienced and successful in the area. The training of teachers, tutors and trainers/ coordinators described in this case study is highly structured, and carefully monitored. Reading Recovery is not a generalised method or approach to reading, but a very highly specific and tightly controlled programme, to be delivered only by those who have undertaken an accredited course. Research evidence (Wasik and Slavin, 1993) has established that one of the challenges for any educational programme is to ensure its implementation remains faithful to the original model. For this reason, 'dabbling' in Reading Recovery is not encouraged, and consequently students working at the school are not able to participate fully in teaching sessions in the centre. They are, however, welcome to observe teaching, monitor individual children's progress over a number of weeks and discuss issues arising with members of staff. As students work in schools for a period of eighteen weeks, including intermittent and block placement, it is often possible to 'track' an individual child through the programme from beginning to end and monitor his or her development.

Student observations

Students are invariably interested in, and usually impressed by, both the methods used and results obtained by Reading Recovery. Whilst it is necessary to protect the integrity of the programme, and avoid any 'drift' away from its intention as a means of working with a very specific targeted group, there are a number of features from which students find they can generalise, and subsequently use in their teaching of reading. They also gain insights into individual children's learning needs which inform their later work with these pupils. Observations taken from students' SEN files, maintained throughout their participation in the Reading Recovery Programme, include the following:

- 'It shows how important it is to begin with extensive diagnostic assessment . . . [to] find out what they do know and build on that.'
- 'A programme of work is tailor-made for each child.'
- 'Aaron began his session by retreading two familiar books to develop fluency and get into his reading; he knew these books from memory – no matter, as it meant he felt he was achieving in reading, and could do it.'
- 'When Sara was reading a new book, Mrs. Francis [Reading Recovery teacher] drew her attention to the strategies she was using to de-code, as she may not have been aware of what she was doing. At least if children know what they are doing, they may remember to use that strategy next time, for example: "I like the way you stopped there and went back . . . well done for reading on to find the meaning of that word . . . that was good the way you used letter sounds to work that word out . . . you recognised that letter pattern, didn't you, 'ing', here and here, well done".'
- 'The teacher gave heaps of positive praise.'
- 'Children who often misbehave in the classroom relish the one-to-one attention they receive, and can improve dramatically. I wonder how much of Aaron's awkwardness and naughtiness in the classroom is rooted in the fact that he can't read.'
- 'It is important not to intervene too quickly when a child is "stuck".'
- 'There is no chatting, socialising or time filling. The intensity of each lesson is tremendous, but the children seem to love it.'
- 'Carefully structured lessons and use of time. Plenty of variety for the children, but highly focused.'
- 'A combination of reading, phonic work, handwriting practice, writing for a purpose, and letter, word and sentence construction meant that Rena was engaged in a 'whole literacy' programme, not just reading support.'
- 'It seems far better to intervene with this programme at the end of year one than to wait until they reach KS2 and are really behind and frustrated.'
- 'Mrs. Francis [Reading Recovery Teacher] told the child directly about what strategies he should use, for example: "Now what could you do here to find out what this word is . . . let's think . . . you could read on . . . go back again . . . you could use the picture . . . look at the first letter . . . look at the end . . . the middle sound . . . don't just rely on one clue".'

These student comments, made after seeing Reading Recovery in action, are typical of the kind of reflections which help students to develop and refine their own teaching, particularly their work in SEN. The importance of an individual programme, devised after careful analysis of the child's abilities, achievements and needs is demonstrated. The significance of security, success and praise are shown, and the willingness of children to work intensively if motivated by interest and personal achievement is illustrated. Early intervention is recognised as vital and the effect of learning difficulties on behaviour and conduct is also acknowledged. For the teacher of reading, a good many insights into the reading process are offered, and without compromising the Reading Recovery programme itself, lessons learned from the programme can be generalised by the students into mainstream classroom work with the majority of children.

Case study three: primary undergraduate course

The primary undergraduate course at Brunel University has a SEN component within its 'Professional Education' programme. This is supported by phased inputs on assessment, child development, planning and teaching a differentiated curriculum and subject-specific issues in SEN. 'School Experience', an extended attachment to one school over the duration of the course, has now become central to ITE provision. During this time a range of activities have been developed to allow the students to observe, participate and demonstrate a developing competence in meeting the SEN of pupils. These activities are seen as mutually beneficial: student competence (and confidence) grows whilst children develop and benefit from the support of additional 'educators'.

In Year 2 of their school experience, all students participate in a reading development project which forms part of the Primary English modules (at least 50 hours of which must focus on the teaching of reading). The project is based on our understanding of the central importance of students' ability to be effective teachers of reading, not least to meet the SEN associated with this type of learning difficulty.

The project builds upon the students' work in Year 1 of their course by extending their understanding of planning, and then teaching, an effective reading programme. It provides additional regular, individual and structured teaching for children, especially those with SEN, and aims to help them develop an enjoyment of reading for a variety of purposes. Finally, the project offers students a real problem solving situation in SEN, which frequently leads to high-quality reflection and direct experience with children with learning difficulties over an extended period of time.

Project outline

Each student visits their partner-school for an induction week in late September. This is followed by twelve day visits. During the induction week a profile group (six children) is identified and the students, with support from the classroom teacher, begin to undertake diagnostic assessments. From the profile group one child with SEN is identified for the reading project. The project itself comprises four distinct steps.

Step 1: develop a detailed, formative reading assessment of the child
- Have a reading conference to explore the child's knowledge and attitude to reading. In the university-based session students devise a series of open-

ended questions, having been given such guidance as 'Listening to Children Read – some questions to ask', based on Arnold (1983).

• Share the child's current reading text and talk to them about the story/text with a focus on understanding. Students are guided in ways of setting questions and in a range of comprehension questions that go beyond literal understanding.

• Undertake a miscue analysis, using a text that is at instructional level for the child. The class teacher is asked to guide the student with the selection of a text (students are advised to use a tape recorder as part of the assessment process so that they have full data to analyse).

• Present the 'results' of the formative assessment on a record sheet (provided) and discuss this with the class teacher.

Step 2: devising and teaching a structured reading programme

Having assessed the child's strengths and areas of development the student prepares an individual teaching plan for reading to cover ten sessions of 40–45 minutes each. The plan will include activities related to the NC PoS for Reading (developing the range of reading and key skills).

An outline structure for the 45 minute session is provided, on the understanding that it must be adaptable to meet individual pupil-needs.

• reading the 'class reader' intervening as planned and discussing the text (10 minutes);

• reading activity based on assessed needs (20 minutes). Examples of this include:
   – a game to develop phonemic awareness;
   – reading a chosen short text to focus on an aspect of 'reading for meaning';
   – crossword puzzle devised to reinforce particular vocabulary;
   – listening to a taped story or poem and then a focused discussion or activity;
   – an activity based on a non-fiction text to develop research skills;

• reading class reader or review new text (10 minutes).

Following each session the student completes an A4 record sheet with sections describing the activities, analysing and critically reflecting on them, and presenting some possible future strategies.

Step 3: reviewing progress

After the completion of the ten sessions each student devises strategies for evaluating the child's progress.

This will include:

• a miscue analysis using a text chosen to include aspects that the reading programme has focused upon;

• child's self-evaluation task;

• evidence from the ten sessions to show progression.

Step 4: reporting on progress
The student completes a record sheet to give to the class teacher and provides verbal feedback on the work. Giving both an oral and written report introduces students to the competence 'prepare and present reports on pupils' progress' at an early stage of their training.

Reflections

In their evaluation of the first year of the project the participants (classroom-teachers, students, children and headteachers) indicated widespread satisfaction.

Teachers:
- 'the greatest benefit to Josie was a change in attitude towards reading';
- 'David really gained from the individual teaching that I am unable to give';
- 'it was interesting to observe the student's growing confidence as the weeks went by';
- 'I learnt a lot from the professional discussion about Ian with the student';
- 'Some of the phonic and book activities that the student planned were so creative – I'll keep them for myself'.

Students:
- 'it was great to see Marie able to read a book with enjoyment';
- 'it was hard work planning such an intensive and structured 45 minutes';
- 'I really noticed that Alex was more willing to "have a go" at reading';
- 'I'm beginning to understand how self esteem and lack of achievement are linked';
- 'the child really looked forward to our reading time';
- 'I felt that I was offering something worthwhile to my school';
- 'teaching reading is a very complex issue – there are no simple solutions';
- 'the project gives us time to focus on the teaching of reading. The university sessions have more relevance as we are in school every week as well'.

Children:
- 'I like Miss Davies [student], she gives me fun things to do';
- 'We share reading. If I get stuck Mr Norris [student] helps me';
- 'We play "funny" games with words – I like it';
- 'Mr Raynor [student] took me to the library – I enjoyed it";
- 'Reading is boring but Miss Fairchild [student] brought in some ace books and she lent me one';
- 'Reading helps you learn – I can do it better now';
- 'Mrs Morris [student] will still hear me read, I like reading to her';
- 'If I get stuck I can try and sort it out'.

Headteachers:

- 'it is a real "payback" to the school for involvement with ITE';
- 'the SENCo has been fully involved and used the profile sheets in reviews'.

The positive comments from the students indicate the real benefit gained in relation to their understanding of the development of the reading process in action, and of related SEN issues in particular. The demands of being involved in actual teaching compelled the students to prepare in a very focused way, resulting in a very positive contribution to pupil learning. Most students commented that they would have liked the project to have continued throughout the remainder of the year. This is not to say, however, that the project was without its difficulties. Sometimes a targeted child (or a student) could be absent, whilst there was a need to monitor very carefully the input of weaker students and provide them with appropriate support. Nevertheless, the positive aspects of the course far outweighed its drawbacks.

Conclusion

These case studies, from ITE courses provided by one HEI, illustrate many of the current changes in teacher education that have taken place in recent years. There is a tendency to problematise issues surrounding ITE, particularly in respect of the time available to attend to each aspect of what will eventually become a 'national curriculum' for ITE. Our view is that, to use a much-abused managerial saying, 'problems are opportunities'. In each of the case studies illustrated in this chapter there are indications that effective SEN inputs can be made, providing that the notion of partnership is actively adopted. Similar initiatives probably exist in many HEI-school partnerships throughout the country. It is to these, rather than to the doom-mongers, that we should turn to refine and enhance the SEN experience of our students.

References

Arnold, H. (1983) *Listening to Children Reading*. London: Hodder and Stoughton.

Garner, P. (1992) 'Special educational needs and initial teacher education: a recent PGCE development', *Support for Learning*, **7** (3), 125–129.

Garner, P. (1996) 'A Special Education? The experiences of newly qualifying teachers during initial training', *British Education Research Journal*, **22** (2), 155–164.

Wasik, B. and Slavin, R. (1993) 'Preventing early reading failure with one-to-one tutoring: a review of five programmes', *Reading Research Quarterly*, **28** (2), 179–200.

CHAPTER SEVEN

From Survival to Reflection: Locating Child Protection in Teacher Education

Anne Sinclair Taylor

Introduction

'there is ample evidence to show that what happens in the early years, and in particular in the family and in schools, is most influential in determining attitudes to violence' (The Gulbenkian Foundation, 1995). Concern about violence and abuse relating to children has increasingly become a media focus (Connett and Henley, 1996). The ways in which schools can contribute to the prevention of violence and abuse through behaviour, bullying and child protection policies has been well documented at international, national and local levels (Cooper *et al.*, 1995; David, 1993; DfEE, 1995).

This chapter concentrates on how students and teachers can be prepared to meet the needs of pupils who have suffered from, or are experiencing abuse. Research increasingly demonstrates that such children are likely to experience difficulties in learning, under-perform academically and suffer long-term behavioural and emotional difficulties. They are likely to require special help to support their learning; in other words, they are likely to have SEN of some kind.

There is a consensus that children have a right to protection from harm in and outside school. Accordingly many LEAs and schools have policies on bullying and child protection as part of their overall pastoral/PSE strategies. However questions remain about whether the resources and expertise exist in schools in the United Kingdom to translate policies into practice. Educational reforms of the 1980s and 1990s have resulted in a continuous restructuring of the education system – from pre-school to higher education – in England and Wales. Major policy initiatives such as the ERA, 1988 and the introduction of a National Curriculum have altered the platform on which equal opportunities issues such as child protection work in schools can be discussed (Hatcher *et al.*, 1996). Child protection can be construed as an equal opportunities issue, because children who are maltreated suffer unique and pervasive disadvantage due to the harm inflicted upon them. The responses of their teachers and schools can help to ameliorate or, conversely, exacerbate their problems. Teachers, therefore, need to be open to the idea that the abuse of children is a feature of our society and that they have an important role in minimising the profound negative effects on children's educational development and emotional well-being.

Special support for meeting the unique needs of abused children is clearly stated in an important piece of international law, the UN Convention on the Rights of the Child, ratified in 1991 by the UK. Governments are required to scrutinise their legislation and policies to ensure that the principles contained in the Convention are developed and implemented to the maximum extent possible. Article (6,2). states that 'state parties shall ensure to the maximum extent possible the survival and development of the child; not only physical health but mental, emotional, cognitive, social and cultural development' (Franklin, 1995, p.x).

Now that a prescribed National Curriculum has been in schools for eight years, there has been a shift in focus from interactive views of school effectiveness as evidenced, for example, by Mortimore *et al.* (1988) to assertions about effectiveness being linked to teachers' subject expertise (TTA, 1997) and the time allocated to whole class teaching (Woodhead, 1996). Quality in education is being measured by such factors as a school's ability to deliver the National Curriculum, the degree of curriculum match and, of course, the all-pervading ability to do well in league tables of SATs (now SSAs).

The way in which children are now judged is through their ability to learn, and be tested on, prescribed bodies of knowledge. Children, and their schools, have their performances ranked in local, national and international league tables. The dominant Government education agenda has consequently become progressively more systemic and reductionist (OFSTED, 1996).

This is reflected in teacher education. There has been a commensurate push to focus on 'the basics', defined as numeracy and literacy, and there is the prospect of an even more instrumental approach to teacher education, which would concentrate on the acquisition and transmission of subject matter. The essential core for the new National Curriculum for ITE will focus on trainee teachers' own knowledge of subject matter, what their pupils should be taught; effective teaching methods and how and when to use them, and the standards of achievement they should expect of their pupils (DfEE, 1996a).

While these Government initiatives have been gaining momentum, researchers and practitioners have continued to assert that the relationship between teaching and learning is complex and interactive. The range of models and theories to capture these complexities have been, and continue to be, debated (see, for example, Novak and Gowin, 1984; Sotto, 1994). Scrutiny of the validity and reliability of National Curriculum content and SATs is, however, less in evidence. Even so, there have been challenges to more recent assertions about the efficacy of whole class teaching. Alexander (1996) argues that cultural borrowing of, for example, whole class teaching, as evidenced in Taiwan and transposed to the UK, is inappropriate, as it fails to reflect the wider socio-political contexts which impact upon classrooms and learning. It can be argued that single factor explanations for human activities are seldom satisfactory and the introduction of one technique to solve all learning needs – in this instance whole class teaching, must be flawed.

Teaching and learning comprise a symbiosis between what the child brings to the classroom and what the teacher provides. This is influenced by a variety of other factors including teacher actions, resources available and community/ familial influences. Additionally, the child at the heart of this process is a complex being with a social, emotional and intellectual life. Viewing the school population as homogeneous, required to meet national targets of attainment, underestimates the diversity of ability and need which exists. Certainly such a view marginalises children with learning difficulties. This can be illustrated when scrutinising the literature about children who are abused. Evidence shows that children who live in fear of abuse and neglect are likely to under-perform academically (Kurtz *et al.*, 1993; Kendall-Tackett and Eckenrode, 1996). In their study of 139 school aged children, Kurtz *et al.* concluded that 'school problems, both academic and behavioural, have emerged as the single most dramatic and consistent risk factor for school aged abused and neglected children' (p.588). In a more recent study of 324 neglected children and adolescents, it was found that neglected children consistently achieved lower grades and had more suspensions, more disciplinary referrals, and more grade repetitions . . . neglect in combination with physical or sexual abuse was related to lower grades and more suspensions (Kendall-Tackett and Eckenrode, 1996, p.161).

As a conservative estimate, 10% of children live in homes where there is cause for concern about how they are being treated (see Reder *et al.*, 1993). Research shows a link between children's emotional and cognitive patterns (Athey, 1990). It is therefore argued that a more sophisticated level of analysis to assessment and intervention in their learning is necessary for children who are abused than simply focusing on subject-knowledge acquisition and behaviour control. In fact, the case can be made that teachers need to take the social and emotional dimension of all children's lives into account when planning for effective learning. This multi-layered, inter-active approach, however, is not indicated in current or draft advice for ITE.

Achievement and the affective domain

In this chapter I want to draw attention to the important role which the affective domain plays in pupil achievement and emotional welfare, specifically in relation to children who are abused. Over-emphasising the cognitive and more narrow conceptions of pedagogy tends to draw attention away from the social and emotional aspects of their development. It is timely to reassert notions of the 'whole child', paying as much attention to the social and emotional dimensions of the child's condition as to the intellectual/cognitive (Nutbrown, 1996). There is now a considerable body of research evidence on school effectiveness which clearly signals the importance of such an approach

(Brighouse and Tomlinson, 1991). Regrettably, however, there is a trend in some of the more recent official literature and guidance (OFSTED, *op. cit.*) to stress the importance of the teacher's subject mastery, rather than expertise in developmental and interactive pedagogy.

For schools to be effective in promoting learning, teachers not only need to be competent and well prepared, but also humane and responsive to the social and emotional aspects of children's lives. According to Mortimore *et al.* (1988), Rutter *et al.* (1979) and Kyriacou (1995) effective schools (in terms of academic achievement and good behaviour) show evidence of the following features:

- positive interactions between staff and pupils by the use of rewards and reinforcement more than punishments and negative feedback.
- an ethos which recognises, rewards and values individuals of all abilities within the community of the school.
- staff who demonstrate concern for pupils' wellbeing both within the school and as members of their community (this includes children's wellbeing at home).
- a questioning and reflective culture where aims, practice and outcomes in relation to pupils' learning and wellbeing are constantly questioned.

Research shows that, to be effective, teachers must be competent not only in their mastery of subject matter, but also in their concerns and understandings about individual pupils.

Children and home: pupils who are 'at risk'

According to the NSPCC, at least 10% of children are living in circumstances where there is 'cause for concern'. This figure is, however, contestable as much depends on how abuse is defined and responded to (Lawlor, 1993). Some commentators, such as Maher (1987), have argued that the figure is possibly nearer 20%. Children who are living in homes where they are deemed to be 'at risk' are living in conditions which have a profound impact on how or whether they learn at school. While some children may retreat into academic study as a coping strategy, evidence shows that children who live in fear of abuse and neglect are likely to under perform academically and suffer long-term behavioural and emotional difficulties (Silverman *et al.*, 1996).

The teacher's role in child protection also becomes relevant when assessing the academic achievements of under-performing and non-conforming pupils. There is a crucial role for teachers in assessing the ability of children to learn given their home circumstances. In other words, are the children in their classes safe enough to learn? Or, are the pressure of their lives such that they are unable to concentrate and consequently achieve?

Teachers and child protection

Advice to the education service in England and Wales on child protection has recently been issued by the Government (DfEE, 1995), which explicitly acknowledges its importance:

> As well as this statutory duty (sections 27 and 47 of the Children Act, 1989), schools and colleges have a pastoral responsibility towards their pupils and should recognise that pupils have a fundamental right to be protected from harm. Children *cannot learn effectively unless they feel secure* [my emphasis]. Every school and college should, therefore, develop a child protection policy which reflects its statutory duties and pastoral responsibilities. (DfEE, 1995, 4, p.3)

The guidelines go on to emphasise the role of teachers in protecting children, and state that 'Because of their day to day contact with individual children, teachers ... are particularly well placed to observe outward signs of abuse, changes of behaviour or failure to develop' (DfEE, 1995, 8, p.5). They advise that 'the appointment of a designated teacher with specific responsibility for child protection should not be seen as diminishing the role of all members of staff in being alert to signs of abuse and being aware of the procedures to be followed' (DfEE, 1995, 8, p.5).

According to a report by HMI, NQTs felt less than adequately prepared for their role in relation to pupils with SEN and for their pastoral duties. Of the 172 teachers surveyed 50% felt unprepared for the SEN element and 33% for their pastoral responsibilities (OFSTED, 1993). If it is acknowledged that child protection work is likely to straddle both dimensions, there is clearly a need to consider most carefully the likely content of the new ITE curriculum, in respect of both these areas.

Student teachers and child protection

According to the DfEE's own advice *(op. cit.)* NQTs need preparation for their role in child protection. Prior to any school experience, students also need some understanding of how to deal with children who disclose abuse to them, as well as how to recognise the signs of abuse and how to support children who have a child protection plan. Child protection plans are drawn up by a core group under the leadership of the social worker (key worker) designated to children who are 'at risk'. These plans define the roles and responsibilities of all agencies concerned with children, including teachers (see, for example, Whitney, 1996, p.47). There are pragmatic, legal and moral reasons for including child protection awareness training in ITE. The pragmatic reasons are linked to minimising behavioural and learning difficulties whilst the legal relate to the requirements of the UN Convention (1989), as well as DfEE (1995) advice. The moral issue concerns the social/ethical responsibilities teachers have to their pupils.

However, there is a crucial difference in the context in which child protection work takes place in England and Wales, as opposed to other countries. A recent conference at the University of Warwick, involving participants from Australia, Canada and the USA , reported that child protection training and accreditation is mandatory for teachers (Sinclair Taylor, 1996). For example, in the United States, '51 jurisdictions mandate the reporting of child abuse and neglect by school teachers and administrators to child protective services' (Crenshaw *et al.*, 1995). As it is mandatory for teachers to report their suspicions, it is also mandatory for student teachers to be provided with appropriate training. This is not the case in England and Wales, where there is no specific requirement or guidance relating to ITE. However, it is *possible* to interpret the framework of competencies in such a way that child protection can be located under the categories of subject expertise and the management of pupil behaviour. Thus:

2.5   newly qualified teachers should be able to:

2.5.1   identify and respond appropriately to relevant *individual differences* between pupils

2.5.2   show awareness of how pupils learn and of the *various factors which affect the process*

2.6.2   create and maintain a purposeful, orderly and *supportive* environment for their pupils' learning

2.7   Newly qualified teachers should have acquired in initial training the necessary foundation to develop:

2.7.1   a working knowledge of their contractual, *legal, administrative and pastoral responsibilities* as teachers

2.7.4   the ability to identify and provide for *special educational needs* and specific learning difficulties (my emphases)

2.7.6   a readiness to promote the *spiritual, moral, social* and cultural development of pupils.

A developmental model for teaching student teachers about child protection

A model for teaching at undergraduate and postgraduate ITE and post-experience levels has been developed out of teaching on BA (QTS), PGCE and Masters courses at the University of Warwick. It was designed so that students' understandings and professional skills could be developed incrementally, starting at *survival* level and moving to *reflexivity*. This represents a broadening wedge of issues which relate to the educational perspectives of child protection work. At the basic *survival* level students need to know what to do if a child discloses abuse to them or what their role and responsibilities are, in terms of recording or reporting information for a child already known to be at risk or who has a child protection plan. At the *reflexivity* level students examine

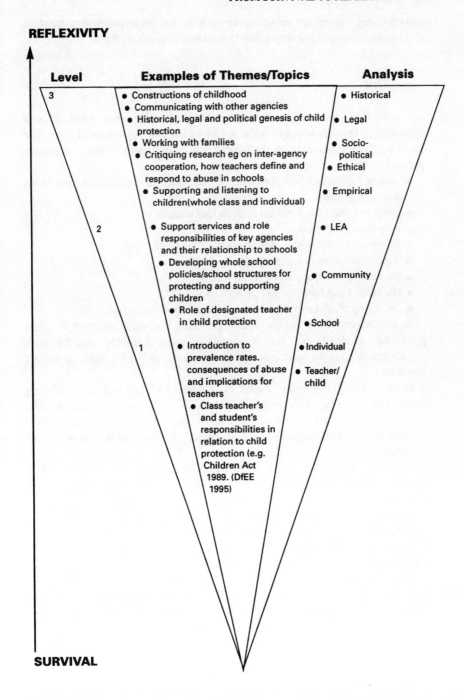

REFLEXIVITY

Level	Examples of Themes/Topics	Analysis
3	• Constructions of childhood • Communicating with other agencies • Historical, legal and political genesis of child protection • Working with families • Critiquing research eg on inter-agency cooperation, how teachers define and respond to abuse in schools • Supporting and listening to children(whole class and individual)	• Historical • Legal • Socio-political • Ethical • Empirical
2	• Support services and role responsibilities of key agencies and their relationship to schools • Developing whole school policies/school structures for protecting and supporting children • Role of designated teacher in child protection	• LEA • Community • School
1	• Introduction to prevalence rates. consequences of abuse and implications for teachers • Class teacher's and student's responsibilities in relation to child protection (e.g. Children Act 1989. (DfEE 1995)	• Individual • Teacher/child

SURVIVAL

Figure 7.1   Child protection – a development model for teacher education: from survival to reflexivity

underpinning theoretical perspectives such as the socio-political context of child protection and how they relate to constructions of childhood.

Level One

At Level One students are introduced to the Children Act, 1989. This is presented by lawyers who specialise in Child Law, and a guardian *ad litem*. The focus of these sessions is on the educational implications of the Act and, in particular:

- parental responsibility as it concerns schools, and in particular, who holds that role in law;
- Section 1 Welfare checklist with its inclusion of:
  a. educational needs,
  b. ascertainable wishes and feelings of the child;
- supervision orders and non school attendance;
- the role of the education welfare officer;
- the role of teachers in child protection;
- 'enabling children to expose abuse, discrimination or injustice'.

This is followed by a lecture which provides a contextualisation of child protection in schools, in terms of prevalence rates, definitions and the cross class, cultural, gender and age aspects of abuse and their implications for teachers.

Specific seminar activities based on a number of key sources (including DfEE, 1995) together with samples of a number of LEA guidelines for schools to follow. Activities focus on defining abuse, teachers' specific roles in child protection work and analysis of LEA and school policies and their implications for practice.

Students are shown a video which charts the experience of a teacher who suspects a child in her class is being abused. The video was originally shown on national television and although it contains no visual representation of the child concerned, it nevertheless illustrates the range of emotions which such work can arouse, as well as the complex nature of defining and responding to abuse. A selection of journal articles which examine the issues critically and empirically is also made available to students.

There is always the possibility that child protection work will stir up powerful emotions. For students (and staff) who have been victims of abuse or who are close to those who are suffering or have suffered abuse, special provision needs to be made. They are all, therefore, given local and national help-line numbers, including the University counselling service and told that they can talk to their tutors about any difficulties and if necessary, disengage from this strand of their work, to follow alternative activities.

Having discussed this issue with both course members and tutors, some of whom may have been victims of abuse themselves, there remains a strong feeling – given the safeguard outlined above – that child protection needs to be addressed in the initial education of all new teachers. Teachers in their everyday work in schools will come into contact with children who are being abused. They therefore need to be prepared to face this possibility and have a working knowledge of what to do in this situation.

Level Two

At Level Two the focus broadens from the micro-level, the individual child, teacher and classroom, to closer scrutiny of whole-school, LEA and inter-agency work. Thus students are introduced to:

- whole-school policies, which look at the hierarchy of responsibilities and the role of the designated teacher with responsibility for child protection.
- school mechanisms for record keeping (including 'need to know' decisions). These include storage and retrieval and data protection, as well as listening to children who disclose, and recording information. The fact that records may be used as evidence in court is also discussed.
- the role of the support services and their responsibilities are covered and inter agency co operation emphasised as being key to good practice (for example where possible representatives from police, social services and NSPCC offer contributions).
- the importance of relationships in creating a climate of trust between staff, and staff and pupils, is discussed, together with aspects of listening to children and strategies such as Circle Time and developing thinking skills, as part of a preventative approach (Elliot, 1986; Mosley, 1993).

Level Three

At this Level the agenda is both deepened and broadened. Whilst, throughout Levels One and Two reference is made to empirical evidence, at Level Three, critiquing and evaluating research becomes more important. This includes:

- the historical and political origins of child protection work;
- constructions of childhood and the power relations between adults and children, including the gendered, racialised and disability/ability dimensions of childhood, as well as economic/class parameters. Comparative international perspectives are also referred to at this Level;
- the issue of confronting and dealing with teachers' own feelings ;
- listening to children, children's rights and choices in decision making;
- the legal context;
- the implications for teachers of working with abused children and their families.

Student feedback

Problems exist in trying to assess and analyse the value of the kind of intervention described in this chapter. The ultimate test of child protection work, however, resides in the classrooms of NQTs. Feedback was gathered from students who had completed courses based on the three Levels of the model previously described as part of their BA, PGCE or CPD courses. Evaluative comments have been gathered over three years from 257 students. The overwhelming message is that students consider this dimension of their course to be both important and useful, even though the child protection component covers a small percentage of respective programmes.

Comments from Year Two undergraduate (BA QTS) students, on part of their professional development course based on Level One of the model include the observations that:

> 'Child abuse work was the most thought provoking and *useful* part of the course.'
> 'Child abuse issues need to thrashed out, we need to know how to handle these situations.'
> 'Child abuse work is interesting and very helpful to me for classroom practice. I feel I now have some understanding of what I should do.'

These students were a quarter of the way through their ITE courses and some had already experienced children disclosing to them matters relating to abuse, or had been involved in on-going cases whilst on school experience. The profound impact on students directly involved with such cases, was clear. One student became distressed because her partner was undergoing therapy for the abuse he had suffered as a child. For another student it brought her own experiences of abuse to the surface. For others there was a general sense of horror which raised the need for support for them in dealing with their feelings of anger and distress. In the light of these considerations it may be that there is a need for introductory training in child protection prior to a student's first school placement. This would benefit not only the students, but also the children who are involved.

In Year Four of the BA (QTS) programme an optional SEN module is provided. This option includes child protection, because of a recognition that abused children are likely to manifest behavioural and learning difficulties. The course reviews Level One but focuses mainly on Level Two. Students may choose this topic as the basis for an assignment and thereby move into Level Three of the model. Student comments on this Level of the course include:

> 'The aspect of the course which has been of most value to me is child abuse and ways of helping abused children. We all need this as a matter of course.'
> 'Child protection issues have been one of the most valuable to me as someone about to enter the classroom full-time.'
> 'I found the child protection work and the effect of the home life on a child's

education has been of great value. As someone hoping to teach pupils with special needs, I see this as essential.'

Many of the students would take first teaching posts in mainstream primary schools and some would immediately move into posts dealing with pupils with SEN. Here their ability to identify and respond to abuse might be conflated with responsibilities to pupils with SEN in general. With the complex demands of the Code of Practice (DfEE, 1994), as well as National Curriculum requirements, how likely would it be that they would receive training in child protection once in post? Much would obviously depend on the priority and resource availability, which individual schools attached to this area. It appears, however, that a substantial element of GEST funding is focused on subject based training. Circular 13/96, which offers guidance on GEST training for 1997/1998, does not highlight child protection training as a specific priority area. The training which is available is for senior teachers with designated responsibility in those schools and Pupil Referral Units where children are deemed to be most in need (DfEE, 1996b).

Students on the PGCE programme were equally convinced of the value of this work:

'I have found child abuse sessions interesting. How to deal with these situations is useful as this is the sort of thing you could panic about if you didn't know what to do.'
'Child protection is essential to think and know about.'
'Child protection issues and information was vital. We definitely need to be made aware of these.'
'Many areas covered, particularly on child abuse, have helped enormously to quell some of my main anxieties.'
'It is necessary for me as a professional to know how to recognise abused children and what to do about abuse.'
'The most interesting session has been on child protection – if interesting is the correct word!'
'Child protection made me aware of issues and how, if they arose, I would deal with them.'

The students whose course evaluations are discussed above received an intensive course of taught and practical experience at the level of survival and awareness. The fact that students spend half of their time in schools means that there is a necessity for mentors in schools, and tutors in universities, to ensure this element of training is developed.

Concluding remarks

It seems that hardly a day passes without reference to some scandal involving child abuse. The horrors of the Fred and Rosemary West case and of the recent events in Belgium punctuate the steady trickle of reports about child abuse in individual families, such as the tragic case of Rikki Neave whose mother physically abused him over a long period until his death at the age of six (Elliott and Mullin, 1996). According to Reder *et al.* (1993), 197 children die at the hands of their parents or carers each year in England and Wales and the *real* prevalence of abuse remains unknown, although it is thought to be around the 10% figure. For a discussion of the problems of assessing the extent of abuse, see Wiehe (1996).

Child abuse has become increasingly visible in society whilst paradoxically, it is in danger of becoming less important as an ITE focus. A national curriculum for ITE should, as in other countries, such as the USA, include a compulsory element on child protection (Crenshaw *et al., op. cit.*). It would be a kind of cultural borrowing that could be readily justified. Currently, training in child protection in this country is subsumed under competencies specified in circulars 9/92 and 14/93 (Sinclair Taylor, 1996). This means that institutions can choose to give greater or lesser emphasis to child protection as they see fit, or as pressures on time allow. The prospect of a new ITE curriculum provides an opportunity to reconceptualise and assert the importance of this area of professional development.

The model discussed in this chapter provides a basis for discussion about the place of child protection work in ITE – with particular reference to pupils with SEN. The next phase of development in ITE needs to acknowledge that children who are abused or who live in fear, carry the emotional, behavioural and learning consequences of this treatment into school. The DfEE recognises that teachers are in a unique position to monitor the wellbeing of children, because of their daily contact with pupils. And, with discussion proceeding on the formulation of a 'national curriculum' for teacher education, the TTA now has an opportunity to reflect DfEE thinking in order to ensure that child protection training takes place on all future ITE courses.

References

Alexander, R. (1996) *Other Primary Schools and ours: hazards of international comparison.* CREPE Occasional Paper. University of Warwick.

Athey, C. (1990) *Extending Thought in Young Children – a parent–teacher partnership.* London: Paul Chapman.

Brighouse, T. and Tomlinson, J. (1991) 'Successful schools', *Education and Training Paper*, No.4. London: Institute for Public Policy Research.

Bright, M. (1996) 'Truth behind the classroom war for moral high ground', *Observer*, 9 June.

Connett, D. and Henley, J. (1996) 'The pedlars of child abuse: we know who they are. Yet no one is stopping them', *Observer*, 25 August.

Cooper, A., Hetherington, R., Baistow, K., Pitts, J. and Spriggs, A. (1995) *Positive Child Protection: a view from abroad.* Lyme Regis: Russell House Publishing.

Crenshaw, W., Crenshaw, L. and Lichtenberg, J. (1995) 'When educators confront child abuse: an analysis of the decision to report', *Child Abuse and Neglect*, **19** (9), 1095–1113.

David, T. (1993) *Child Protection and Early Years Teachers.* Milton Keynes: Open University Press.

DfEE (1994) *The Code of Practice on the Identification and Assessment of Special Educational Needs.* London: DfEE Publications Centre.

DfEE (1995) *Protecting Children from Abuse: the role of the Education Service* (Circular 10/95) London: DfEE Publications Centre.

DfEE (1996a) 'Shake up of teacher training and new focus on leadership skills for headteachers, Shephard', *DfEE News* 302/96.

DfEE (1996b) *Grants for Education Support and Training 1997–1998* (Circular 13/96). London: DfEE Publications Centre.

Elliott, C. and Mullin, J. (1996) 'A short and brutal life. Rikki Neave: a boy abandoned', *Guardian,* 31 October.

Elliot, M. (1986) *Keeping Safe: a practical guide to talking to children.* London: NCVO.

Franklin, B. (ed.) (1995) *The Handbook of Children's Rights: comparative policy and practice.* London: Routledge.

Hatcher, R., Troyna, B. and Gerwitz, S. (1996) *Racial Equality and the Local Management of Schools.* Stoke-on-Trent: Trentham Books.

Kendall-Tackett, K. and Eckenrode, J. (1996) 'The effects of neglect on academic achievement and disciplinary problems: a developmental perspective', *Child Abuse and Neglect*, **20** (3), 161–169.

Kurtz, P., Gaudin, J., Wodarski, J. and Howing, P. (1993) 'Maltreatment and the school aged child: school performance consequences', *Child Abuse and Neglect*, **17** (5), 581–589.

Kyriacou, C. (1995) *Essential Teaching Skills.* Cheltenham: Stanley Thornes.

Lawlor, M. (1993) 'Assessment of the likelihood of primary school teachers believing children's disclosures of sexual abuse', *Child Abuse Review*, **2**, 174–184.

Maher, P. (ed.) (1987) *Child Abuse: the educational perspective.* Oxford: Basil Blackwell.

Mortimore, P., Sammons, P., Stoll, L., Lewis, D. and Ecob, R. (1988) *School Matters: the junior years.* Wells: Open Books.

Mosley, J. (1993) *Turn Your School Round: a Circle Time approach to the development of self-esteem and positive behaviour in the primary staffroom, classroom and playground.* Wisbech: Learning Development Aids.

Novak, J. and Gowin, D. (1984) *Learning How to Learn.* Cambridge: Cambridge University Press.

Nutbrown, C. (1996) *Respectful Educators – Capable Learners: children's rights and early education.* London: Paul Chapman Publishing.

OFSTED (1993) *The New Teacher in School: a survey by H M Inspectors in England and Wales 1992.* London: OFSTED.

OFSTED (1996) *The Teaching of Reading in 45 Inner London Primary Schools: a report by Her Majesty's Inspectors, in collaboration with the LEAs of Islington, Southwark and Tower Hamlets.* London: OFSTED.

Reder, P., Duncan, S. and Gray, M. (1993) *Beyond Blame: child abuse tragedies revisited.* London: Routledge.

Rutter, M., Maughan, B., Mortimer, P. and Ouston, J. (1979) *Fifteen Thousand Hours.* London: Open Books.

Silverman, A., Reinherz, H. and Giaconia, R. (1996) 'The long-term sequelae of child and adolescent abuse: a longitudinal community study', *Child Abuse and Neglect*, **20** (8), 709–723.

Sinclair Taylor, A. (1996) 'Child protection; relative values', *International Journal of Early Years Education*. **4** (2), 70–75.

Sotto, E. (1994) *When Teaching Becomes Learning*. London: Cassell.

Teacher Training Agency (1997) *Training Curriculum and Standards for New Teachers*. London: TTA.

The Gulbenkian Foundation (1995) *Children and Violence, Summary of the Report of the Commission on Children and Violence*. London: Calouste Gulbenkian Foundation.

Whitney, B. (1996) *Child Protection for Teachers and Schools. A guide to good practice*. London: Kogan Page.

Wiehe, V. (1996) *Working With Child Abuse and Neglect: a primer.* London: Sage Publications.

Woodhead, C. (1996) Interview, BBC *Panorama*, 'Hard Lessons', 3 June.

CHAPTER EIGHT

A Different Tale of the Sorcerer's Apprentice: Towards a New Model of Teacher Development in Special Education

Christopher Blake

Introduction

Special education largely reflects conventional practices in teacher development at both preservice and inservice levels. This means that Special educators are trained using apprenticeship models, especially at the preservice level, that provide a double dosage of andragogy (Knowles, 1980) in a rigid format: specialised content for study; and experiential internships designed to assess practical competencies. This approach reflects a dual, interdependent notion of teaching as a management activity and teaching as an exercise in scholarship (Applebee, 1989). Such a training model is, furthermore, rooted in a rationalistic view of learning (Knowles, 1980) and a technicist view of performance (Smith, 1994). The end result is a system of teacher development that can be understood figuratively in terms of the career ladder: novice at the bottom, barely equipped for the ascent and expert at the top, with an elevated and informed perspective, in which various levels of skill conformity are discernible at each intervening rung of the ladder (Berliner, 1994).

This chapter describes an ethnographic account of one preservice teacher's experience in that hierarchical system, which occurred as part of an exchange programme between teacher education universities in the USA and Britain. Jerry was sent in the Spring of 1996 from Baltimore to a west London comprehensive to complete his dual certification programme in secondary mathematics and special education, through a final teaching practice. His certification by the State of Maryland depended on success in this seven-week internship, which followed earlier school internships.

Whilst at Lovegrove School, Jerry began to keep a weekly journal that progressively revealed his professional development and insight into his relationship with the supervising mathematics and SEN teachers, and illuminated key weaknesses of the teacher education discourse. What was most striking was that the heart of his professional growth centred on knowledge and skills outside of the formal structures that were used to evaluate him and that underpin the precepts of teacher education. Jerry became an effective, valuable teacher not because of the structural models, but despite them. Critically, he also came to view pedagogy not only in terms of student learning, but also in its potential challenge to the relationships between beginning and veteran teachers.

In the famous tale of the sorcerer's apprentice the power-knowledge axis is clear: the untrained and unsupervised apprentice recklessly creates mayhem until the sorcerer redeems the situation and chastens him for arrogantly acting beyond his means. The same power-knowledge axis typifies our assumptions of the relationships between teachers in the training discourse. Jerry's story tells a different tale, one of professional disquiet, reflection and vision that belongs to the apprentice and that causes upset not in the working arena but in the views and attitudes of veteran teachers. This apprentice's account, rooted in human dynamics and variables, helps us to reconsider and reframe the debate about teacher education and the cultural politics of the SEN classroom (Kincheloe, 1993).

Special education certification in the State of Maryland

Jerry's journey from the States to Britain presented him with little culture shock in terms of the teacher training experience. A similar model of content specialism and apprentice internship is required for special education certification on both sides of the Atlantic. For Jerry, who held a maths degree, his dual certification by the State of Maryland in mathematics and special education was built around a core of taught courses in subject content and a teaching practice internship.

This typifies the process of obtaining special education certification and some illustration of the nature of special education training in Maryland would be helpful here. The majority of special educators in the state, such as Jerry, gain a 'generic' certificate, which licenses them to work in one educational phase: Primary (Kindergarten through Grade 3); Elementary (Grades 3 through 6); or Secondary (Grades 6 through 12). Since the Individuals With Disabilities Education Act (1990), these generic special educators have worked in environments where 'mild' cases of learning disability, emotional and/or behavioural disorder, and physical or mental disorder are formally identified. This diagnostic process is undertaken by a Screening Committee, made up of a school senior administrator (e.g. principal), school psychologist, school counsellor and a senior special educator, upon receipt of a classroom teacher's reports and recommendations on an individual student. The Screening Committee's deliberations often result in an IEP – individual educational plan – which ascribes to the student a 'category of exceptionality'. The range of categories this covers includes learning disabilities, mental retardation, ED/BD, autism, physical impairment, health impairment, visual impairment, hearing impairment, traumatic brain injury, and other impairments (such as ADHD). The IEP then entitles the student, through a code known as 'Public Law 101.476', to guaranteed special education services and eligibility for 'related services' (e.g. specialised transportation). The IEP will also decide whether the student receives the officially preferred 'inclusive' provision within mainstream classes, or separate education.

This clinical and bureaucratic process is matched by a training regime which is similarly uniform. The beginning special educator studies for the state's Professional Eligibility Certificate (PEC), initially valid for five years, through an approved thirty-nine semester-hour programme (either undergraduate or baccalaureate) at an accredited university, with a testing requirement upon completion. The programme is broken down into specified content matter: three semester hours in historical and legal foundations of special education; six semester hours in human growth and development; nine semester hours in assessment, diagnosis and prescriptive techniques, including three semester hours at the appropriate age/grade level; twelve semester hours in curriculum and instructional methodology, of which six must be specific to special education; three semester hours in communications skills, emphasising parent counselling; and lastly six semester hours in an internship or 'practicum' at the appropriate age/grade level.

Several points can be made about this system. Firstly it reinforces the role of specialist knowledge that is natural to a clinical view of special education: the SEN teacher herself is thus rendered separate from the corporate body of teachers and special education is an activity alienated from the 'ordinary' teacher. Secondly, the concept of professional development is linked explicitly to the process of certification, whereby a teacher is required to upgrade her qualifications as a prerequisite to continued practice. Not surprisingly, this lends itself to an hierarchical and formalised view of professional expertise in special education, since the veteran has 'jumped the hoops' demanded by the training procedure. Consequently, the model of professionalism this endorses is essentially a selective and bureaucratic one, rather than one rooted in the organic and interactive experiences of professionals working in a teaching capacity. And importantly, in contrast to Jerry's account below, the bureaucratic model fails to embody the means of qualitative, intersubjective professional growth, whereby the forging of complex relationships is the primary basis of teacher development.

The new apprentice and the tricks of the trade

Jerry was another beginning teacher in mathematics and special education, noteworthy because of his success in gaining the opportunity to take his final 'practicum' in Britain, an option permitted under state regulations for teacher certification. He came to London through an exchange scheme between

Towson University in Baltimore and Brunel University in London, after a very successful internship in a Baltimore middle school. His supervisor reported (Martin, 1996) on that internship that:

> his easy going personality almost disguises his superior ability ... He casually includes extra information in his classes so the students are learning more than they realise. He is very flexible in handling the content ...

Upon arrival at Lovegrove School, in west London, Jerry was assigned a university supervisor from Brunel and given a teaching assignment that included two low-achieving Year 9 maths sets, in a department where mathematics was taught across four achievement sets. This rigid differentiation was new to Jerry, contrasting with more heterogeneous class groups in the States. At the time of his introduction to the school Jerry began to keep a weekly journal, initially for his own purposes but increasingly used as a focus point for discussion with Michael, his university supervisor.

The journal for his first week reveals an ambivalence in Jerry: respect for the school's pluralist ethos, but uncertainty about the curriculum organisation he was to take part in (Carlton, 1996):

> Throughout the school's wide range of abilities and cultures, there is a positive atmosphere and the students and staff respect and adjust to the differences. In the mathematics department, the students are grouped by ability, based on the skills of a student and their level of performance. . . The ability group that a student is in also determines the maximum grade attainable. This means that someone in my level four group, the lowest, could only earn a D as their highest mark. I am strongly opposed to this system. Overall the week has been positive, though, and I feel students and myself will benefit from this exchange of knowledge and experience.

This latter theme of teacher-student reciprocity was an important element within Jerry's developing reflections on pedagogy and its relationship to the organisational framework for his internship. By the second week his caution about achievement setting in mathematics had turned into opposition, matched by a growing awareness of the critical role of teacher behaviours and values within the curriculum organisation: in short, his journal shows an awareness that teacher agency cannot be discounted from organisational structure. He records his frustration at being kept away from classroom teaching on account of extracurricular events at the school and through a mistake by the head of mathematics, Fred Hodges, in scheduling his timetable. But he used this time to observe key figures in the mathematics and special needs departments, and the first reflections on teacher typology and its significance can be found in his journal at this point (Carlton, *op. cit.*):

> I have found the role of the teachers I have observed at Lovegrove to be very limited. Traditional methods of teaching can be very useful and effective, but in this case the converse is true. It is not the method used but rather the way

that it is being implemented . . . these approaches have produced students that blindly follow guidelines to obtain meaningless solutions. They are not taught to predict or to find solutions in a variety of ways. They are not taught to respond to 'what if' or 'why' questions. In effect, the students are not learning mathematics. I plan to teach these students mathematics whether or not they are called 'bottom set'. I plan to build their self-esteem so they become more aware of their own potential. These have always been my most basic goals as an educator.

This criticism of the department's pedagogical approach did not appear to hinder his relationship with the mentor teachers nor Jerry's valuing of the internship. The sombre comments of the journal's second week are starkly contrasting to the up-beat mood of week three, when he records his enjoyment of participating in various field trips, especially since they 'enabled me to establish a good rapport with more students'. He also received very positive observation comments from both Michael and Fred on separate occasions, with Michael remarking on Jerry's professional skill in reconciling his own values with departmental expectations and attitudes (Hunter, 1996):

he is building an excellent relationship with staff and students alike, and not always in the easiest of circumstances. His colleagues I'm sure regard him as a gifted teacher, and for some that may pose a challenge. It is my view Jerry has already proved himself to be a valuable member of the teaching profession.

Jerry's enthusiasm and confidence about his own values and pedagogy received an additional boost that third week when a call from the States brought him a job offer at a diversified, urban Baltimore 'magnet' school for mathematics. This combination of feedback from his university supervisor and employment success back home appeared to consolidate his reflections on the shortcomings of the pedagogy he perceived in the department at Lovegrove. A long and incisive entry for the fourth week details an overarching critique of the differentiation used in mathematics, starting with its motivational weaknesses across the achievement range (Carlton, *op. cit.*):

Once students become part of a bottom set class, they feel unsuccessful and unable to advance . . . while students in the top sets are expected to excel academically with minimal impetus. Teachers seem to find this satisfying. They plan less and life is that much easier.

Critically the first record appears of a negative reaction to Jerry's approach to teaching from veteran teachers, contrasting with the highly positive endorsements given by Michael and by Sally, the deputy headteacher (Jensen, 1996). Jerry records an intriguing exchange between himself and the maths teacher responsible for 'low' achievement sets, which captures the basic variance of values and pedagogy that set Jerry apart from his veteran mentors:

> Most [of the department] feel that the traditional approach is the only 'real' way to teach mathematics. When discussing alternative methods, Bill stated that they did not have time for the 'the fun stuff'. Another teacher went so far to say, 'if they [the students] like you, then you must not be any good'. I thought that he was joking, but he was not.

This leads Jerry to consider the problem in terms of the power-knowledge axis that dominates teaching and organisational hierarchy in the training process. He sees it in blunt terms, in a reflection on the above interaction:

> many teachers are consumed with power and control. It is in these ideas that they lose sight of their obligation to students: to teach students in the way that the students learn best. This is the challenge.

From this a critical point is deduced and recorded in Jerry's journal shortly after, turning training theory effectively on its head. For Jerry, perhaps somewhat naively, the training 'deficit' belongs not to himself as the new apprentice but to the veteran teachers who have failed to develop a repertoire of knowledge, skills and attitudes to meet contemporary student needs (Carlton, *op. cit.*):

> In fairness to these teachers, they are equipped with neither the strategies nor resources to deal effectively with the range of students in their school.

It is evident from his final entry in the journal that this issue came to a head in the final days of his teaching practice. The journal record continues until the fifth week and ends on a high note, both in terms of his assessment of student learning and his impact on colleagues. The consensus amongst his assessors (Michael, Fred and Sally) is that the students in low achieving mathematics sets have shown marked improvement in interest and performance. As Jerry puts it (Carlton, *op. cit.*):

> students have demonstrated a gain in interest in math which I attribute to a combination of recent success, variety of lesson presentation, and genuine respect . . . Success breeds confidence. Being confident in their own abilities, students begin to trust their own judgement.

Jerry's reflections end not with the students, however, but with an awareness of his relationship with his mentor teachers and how his internship has effected both his and their views of teaching. This is the crux of his school experience. The journal itself concludes with an optimistic account of how he challenged the assumptions of the department without causing resentment or hostility. He notes that only when several maths teachers observed his teaching did they begin to inquire into his pedagogical views. As a result, one teacher engaged in a lengthy discussion with Jerry about sharing techniques for teaching mathematics to students with learning disabilities. Here the first signs of reciprocity were evident, with at least one experienced professional considering the possibility of learning from the 'apprentice' and setting aside the mantle of expert for the sake of professional development. Jerry details their shared plans for trying out several techniques in presenting data and managing a specific group, and ends with a hopeful estimation of what his presence might mean for the department in the long run:

> Actions speak louder than words! When they saw my actions in the classroom some of the teachers have begun to listen to my ideas. Of course the department will not change overnight, but the seed has been planted.

This might sound arrogant and short on self-evaluation, but the evidence from Sally, the deputy headteacher, suggests otherwise. Her report (Jensen, *op. cit.*) described Jerry as 'an extremely reflective practitioner' who 'readily accepted advice throughout the course of the practice'. Elsewhere (Jensen, *op. cit.*) she noted his 'charisma' and indicated, tellingly, that he 'behaves professionally at all times and is a good role model for pupils and colleagues'.

In the case of Jerry at Lovegrove School, therefore, it would be fair to say that central to his professional training was a capacity to reflect on and critique those traditions, both pedagogical *and* andragogical, surrounding him. In so doing, he became a means for professional reflection and change amongst more senior and experienced colleagues. This, of course, can bring difficulties of human relations, but it would seem that these were avoided through sensitivity and communication. As a result, Jerry's presence signified opportunities for teacher education beyond the formal intentions of the training process.

Towards a new view of teacher development in special education

At its heart special education confronts us with the challenge of equity and justice in education, in the face of a differentiated society. This is why special education has rightly paid as much attention in recent years to socio-economic and cultural parameters facing educators as to the range of pedagogical knowledge and techniques that teachers may employ in reaching students (Ornstein and Levine, 1997). This values base to special education is made especially vulnerable by the hegemonic, but ill-suited models of teacher education on which the profession relies, and which confronted Jerry so starkly. These models embody an hierarchical and linear notion of expertise that inhibits the process of professional development on both sides of the Atlantic and that Jerry's case so refreshingly challenges. The importance of this is acute for special education, since such models pose a direct threat to the value system that special education naturally embraces. As Mussington (1996) puts it:

> teachers tend to be educated and socialized in ways that reinforce culturally insular beliefs and attitudes. At the center of the educational enterprise is a teacher force whose formative years have often not prepared them to foster or promote egalitarian or multicultural beliefs. (p.9)

The case of Jerry reminds us of the radical possibilities of teacher encounter and that special education should be a curricular activity where teacher education hegemony can cogently be critiqued. By implication it is time to reconsider the role of adult learning, or *andragogy*, in teacher education in general and Special Education in particular: this has tended to be overshadowed by the historical priority given to *pedagogy*. Such a role for andragogy would necessarily require the deconstruction of the current discourses in teacher education. But in so doing it need not replace them with a myopic view of individualism. One of the shortcomings common to a range of post-structural learning paradigms, such as andragogy, perspective transformation, or self-directed learning is an over-reliance on psychological foundations and a tendency toward individualism. Instead, what is needed as a replacement to the existing framework is the recognition, as Flannery (1995) remarks, that:

> learning and knowledge must be acknowledged as a cultural phenomenon, intricately interwoven in the setting in which they occur. In reality, all cognition is dialectically structured by activity and setting. (p.153)

This awareness of the social and cultural context of learning empowers us to critique the existing weaknesses of bureau-management and/or educo-psychological models of teacher education, and to look to an alternative vision of human learning for our training needs. Particularly valuable in this respect should be special education, given its values-base in democratic and egalitarian ideals. Such a new vision is not unrealistic for schools. Teachers are highly familiar and skilled in translating such values into processes and actions on a daily basis in their actions. Any experienced teacher knows fully the significance of social and cultural factors in, say, leading a department through a process of reflection and development. This search for a new, risk-taking 'collegiality' is an overdue essential in teacher education, and it is not achieved simply by designating certain individuals as mentors or supervisors. Instead we need flexible frameworks that connect people and, in McKenna's (1997) words, enable us to 'celebrate the fact that complex, paper-generating components in teacher induction are not necessarily better' (p.54).

Jerry's apprenticeship story is ultimately about this celebration of successful communal connection and growth, embedded in a view of shared culture, and resistant to the hierarchies of stratified professionalism in a capitalist workplace. In such communities we are all learners and teachers, and expertise lies not in climbing figurative ladders but in creating a shared culture of interaction and growth. If teachers, and especially special educators, hold to these principles in their dealings with students, then it is time to question why they are insufficiently present in their arcane dealings with fellow beginning teachers.

References

Applebee, A. (1989) 'The enterprise we are part of: learning to teach', in P. Murphy and B. Moon (eds.) *Developments in Learning and Assessment*. London: Hodder and Stoughton, 215–223.

Berliner, D. (1994) 'Teacher Expertise', in B. Moon and A. Shelton Mayes (eds.) *Teaching and Learning in the Secondary School*. London: Routledge and the Open University.

Bishop, A. (1989) 'Mathematics education in its cultural context', in P. Murphy and B. Moon (eds.) *Developments in Learning and Assessment*. London: Hodder and Stoughton, 85–97.

Carlton, J. (1996) Unpublished personal journal of school internship experience in West London. Twickenham: Brunel University.

Flannery, D. (1995) 'Adult education and the politics of the theoretical text', in B. Kanpol and P. McLaren (eds.) *Critical Multiculturalism: Uncommon Voices in a Common Struggle*. New York: Bergin and Garvey, 149–163.

Hunter, M. (1996) Unpublished supervisor's interim report on Jerry Carlton's internship at Lovegrove School. Twickenham: Brunel University.

Jensen, S. (1996) Unpublished deputy headteacher's final report on Jerry Carlton's internship at Lovegrove School. Hounslow: Lovegrove School.

Kanpol, B. and McLaren, P. (eds.) (1995) *Critical Multiculturalism: uncommon voices in a common struggle*. New York: Bergin and Garvey.

Kincheloe, J. (1993) *Toward a Critical Thinking of Teacher Thinking: mapping the postmodern*. Westport, Connecticut: Bergin and Garvey.

Knowles, M. (1980) *The Modern Practice of Adult Education: andragogy versus pedagogy*. New York: Association Press.

Martin, J. (1996) Unpublished supervisor's final report on Jerry Carlton's middle school internship. Towson, MD: Towson University.

McKenna, G. (1997) 'Collaborative components for teacher induction', *Kappa Delta Pi Record*, **33** (2), 52–54.

Moon, B. and Shelton Mayes, A. (eds.) (1994) *Teaching and Learning in the Secondary School*. London: Routledge and the Open University.

Mussington, C. (1996) 'What do preservice teachers believe about equity and social justice?', *Renaissance Group: research that makes a difference*, **3** (3), 9–10.

Ornstein, A. and Levine, D. (1997) *Foundations of Education*. Boston: Houghton Mifflin Co.

Smith, R. (1994) 'What makes a good teacher?', in B. Moon and A. Shelton Mayes (eds.), *Teaching and Learning in the Secondary School*. London: Routledge and the Open University.

CHAPTER NINE

Modular Programmes: A Market Response in Troubled Times

Sarah Sandow

Teachers and teacher-educators concerned with the education of children with SEN are becoming increasingly anxious about the dwindling supply of professionals with an understanding of and commitment to the twenty per cent of children who experience difficulties in school. The 1990s have seen the end of ITE for children with SLD. It has also witnessed the dramatic reduction of the special education element in subject- or phase-based ITE courses, which had been promoted following the 1981 Education Act, mainly as a result of the changes in teacher training required by DES circulars 9/92 and 14/93. Even in 1987, HMI expressed concern about the adequacy of special needs training in ITE (DES, 1987) and a detailed, and anxious, analysis of the current situation is provided by SENTC (1996). The present situation for children in mainstream and in special schools is that their teachers are unlikely to have received significant input on special needs during their initial training, and may have limited opportunities for INSET (SENTC, 1996).

In-service programmes for teachers in special education, as for other teachers, are currently provided in one of three ways: very short school-based sessions, GEST courses, and diploma or Masters courses offered in HEIs, usually within a modular framework. GEST courses are sometimes incorporated within these latter modes of study. The 1990s have seen a dramatic increase in the number of modular courses offered in HEIs, to the point where this is now the universally approved method of course delivery. This chapter will attempt to trace the development of such modular courses, and to identify particular implications for special education of the service they offer to teachers.

Looking back: what happened before modularisation

From the standpoint of CPD provision in 1996, it is instructive to look back at practice fifteen years ago. Traditional diploma courses were then the main, often the only, means by which teachers could extend their knowledge and their professionalism. These one-year full-time or or two-year part-time courses were usually oversubscribed. Teachers were still awarded secondments through the pooling system by LEAs. Mostly these were arranged in a positive spirit, sometimes as opportunities for retraining or a change of career direction, occasionally clearly because LEA employers sought to find a niche for essentially redundant staff. Staff in HEIs were accustomed to the luxury of interviewing and selecting their students from a range of applicants.

In special education courses (which were often still referred to as the 'education of handicapped children') teachers studied a range of provision on an awareness basis; the content was heavily discipline-focused, including sociology and psychology as well as identification, assessment and curriculum. Courses were thus a mixture of 'liberal education' with a curricular element which most nearly approximated to what Bines and Watson (1992) have described as a 'technocratic' model. The emphasis was on learning difficulties and the emphasis on the child inevitably led to a defect approach; even the range of visits to different establishments, to ESN(S) (SLD), ESN (MLD), PH, partial hearing unit, school for the blind etc., tended to support this. During the 1980s, while still largely retaining this 'within-child' model, the courses gradually pulled away from prescription, but teaching placements and visits still focused on special schools and units. Teachers in ordinary schools looked for new knowledge and experience in special schools, and little attention was given to the problems facing children in mainstream schools.

Notwithstanding the limitations, which at a distance of fifteen or more years we can now recognise, courses organised in this way had some advantages. Teacher-students, on full-time courses, had time and facilities in which to rethink their own practice and observe that of others. Teachers who had never seen the inside of a special school discovered what went on behind their doors. Conversely, special school teachers were able to remind themselves about practice in the mainstream. Full-time courses ensured generous staffing in HEIs, so that staff had time and opportunity to update and reinforce their knowledge of provision and curriculum development (it was even common for the course tutor to go *with* the students on school visits!). During the 1980s, the establishment of the CNAA Special Needs Panel involved a number of PCFC SEN staff in the development and validation of courses. This raised the quality of the debate and presented many valuable opportunities for networking. Such inter-institutional contacts are today mainly confined to the artificial atmosphere of the examination board and the occasional conference.

DES Circular 5/83, which radically changed the arrangements and funding for in-service education for teachers, led to the gradual decline of secondments throughout the 1980s (Gaunt, 1992). Groups on full-time courses began to shrink, with no guarantee of viability from year to year. Part-time courses in the early 1980s were seen very much as the poor relation; teachers attended in larger groups although the course content was very similar to that of the full-time courses, often being merely 'sliced up' without being adapted to the specific needs of part-timer students. Thus it did not draw upon teachers' own daily experience to any great extent. In an effort to retain the breadth of experience beyond the teacher's own school, visits to other establishments were a requirement on one course, but not supervised or reported, and rarely analysed effectively. Eventually, because of financial constraints on LEAs and schools, release for even these visits was discontinued and they ceased altogether.

Changes

So, by the late 1980s, full-time courses had all but disappeared, even though as late as 1990 HMI were expressing concern about their demise (HMI, 1990). LMS, delegated budgeting and the GEST system of designated priorities for training meant that LEAs were no longer in a position to fund a serial programme of planned secondments. More and more teachers were expected to finance their own CPD. This is an expensive business. Thomas expresses the concern that

> . . . at the advanced studies level and higher degree levels these (university) departments see their potential clients as self funded teachers. *In other words, access to the upper levels of professional development will be available to those who can afford it. There will be National Health level care for the many and BUPA for those who can go 'private'.* (original italics, Thomas, 1991, p.82)

A system which enabled some sort of interim payment for course units was therefore necessary if teachers were not to beggar themselves or abandon award-bearing courses altogether. At this time, two major enabling changes took place: semesterisation and modularisation. Semesterisation, or dividing the academic year into two parts with a break halfway through the spring term, provided a capsule of time within which an aspect of education could be studied; the 14–15 week model meant that each semester contained a short holiday period at Christmas or Easter, as well as half-term breaks, which could be utilised for the preparation of assignments. The traditional one-year three-term model did not provide the same flexibility, and a one-term, ten-week course was too short to deal with issues in sufficient depth. Course units, or modules, were designed to fit the new timescale, and teachers were able to finance the courses they studied on a module by module basis. In the old 'polytechnic' sector, PCFC was only partially supportive of this new approach; it recognised for funding, as late as 1989, only one-year full-time or two-year part-time courses. The eligibility of modular courses for funding was only achieved by requiring students to formally register for an award at the start of their studies, whether or not they actually intended to obtain the qualification. That so many did stay the course and go on to accumulate enough credits for an award was and remains a tribute to the commitment of both teacher-students and their tutors.

The new system meant that an element of choice could be included within whole courses. Essentially teachers could construct their own learning package according to their need. In several Institutions, such as Manchester Polytechnic (now Manchester Metropolitan University), Oxford Polytechnic (now Oxford Brookes University), Bristol Polytechnic (now the University of the West of England, Bristol) and The West London Institute (now part of Brunel University), new courses were designed to fit the semester pattern; incorporating several subject areas within one system. This range, coupled with an element of choice for students, enabled economies of scale and ensured larger and more viable teaching groups. To begin with, this was often seen as problematic. How could students justify a course containing elements of very different units? What could religious education have to add to computing, or special needs to modern foreign languages? Teachers working in differing establishments and with different age-ranges were often wary of one another, and sometimes questioned the virtues of working together. Many had a respect for their own specialism which contrasted with the distrust they offered to others.

Thus, courses in SEN became part of larger series of in-service courses, which meant that, for the first time, teachers pursuing different outcomes worked together on the same modules. This meant that teachers who saw themselves as primary, secondary or subject specialists were exposed to SEN as a specialism in its own right. Conversely, teachers with experience and interest in special education began to encounter mainstream subject teachers and to recognise some of their problems and concerns. This drawing-in of teachers from a wide range of schools and specialisms was an unlooked-for bonus of modularisation. Enrolling through curiosity, mainstream teachers were soon 'hooked'; the differentiated curriculum in particular attracted many who found themselves teaching a wider range of ability than before. Behaviour management was another area of concern which was included under the general umbrella of SEN, but which was perceived as increasingly relevant by 'ordinary' teachers, particularly after the publication of the Elton Report (1989).

Most of these course were validated by the now defunct CNAA. Validating committees were concerned to ensure two things: 'coherence' and 'progression'. Clearly both these qualities are easy to specify and to identify within a conventional course, but more difficult to create within the new systems being constructed. CNAA recognised two ways in which this coherence and progression, which characterised effective professional development, could be achieved: either by specifying pathways to named awards and a number of prerequisite courses wihin it, or by allowing the teacher-student to identify their own route through the available modules. The

predetermined pathway . . . locates progression and coherence in the sequenced learning constructed by the scheme design. In other schemes . . . the reflective and reflexive practitioner is believed to require more individualised routes because autonomy can be fostered by reflecting self critically on perceived professional development. In this approach, coherence and progression must reside in the individual teacher, and therefore the scheme must facilitate negotiated routes to a range of appropriate award level skills, knowledge and understanding. Such schemes establish mechanisms which negotiate, formalise, approve and maintain this reflective negotiated professional development. (CNAA, 1990, p.8)

Modularisation was not, at first, welcomed by all HEI tutors or by all universities. For SEN tutors in particular, the emphasis on curriculum and management meant that the old discipline-based approach would disappear; and many felt that the loss of psychology, sociology and history from ITE syllabi had left a gap which the discipline-based SEN diplomas were able to fill. This was certainly partly true. Ways had now to be found whereby reflective teaching, newly popularised through Schön's (1983) seminal work, could be embedded in a sound understanding of children's development and experience. Structuring modular courses to include the characteristics of the learner as well as elements of common educational principles and reflection was a popular option.

Courses had already changed to accommodate the principles of the 1981 Education Act, but more important was a new emphasis on changing practice in schools rather than on the examination of individual differences within a deficit model. In fact, even if course providers had wished, it would have been impossible to maintain the old ways of thinking. The 1988 Education Reform Act, including the National Curriculum, LMS and Key Stage assessment, all demanded attention within special and ordinary schools. They provided an imperative, therefore, for a new pragmatic element in CPD for teachers. Modular systems which could be expanded and changed in response to these initiatives were in fact best placed to accommodate them. More recently, the 1993 Education Act and the associated Code of Practice have added new dimensions to the range of SEN courses.

The effect of modularisation on the teacher-student population

One of the unexpected effects of the move to part-time modular courses was the increased heterogeneity of the teacher-student population. No longer seconded by LEAs after a number of years service, they now ranged from experienced senior teachers, heads and deputy heads to NQTs and returners, often studying together on the same module. It was interesting to compare this situation in the early 1990s, with the much more homogeneous groups on the still extant full-time courses in Scotland, where LEAs continued to support courses on the old basis for much longer, as in the case of Jordanhill College, Glasgow (now part of Strathclyde University). At that institution, teachers seconded to courses were mainly experienced but unpromoted women teachers, and there were none supporting themselves financially.

With a wide range of experience came a wide range of levels of ability. Universities, old and new, have had to find ways of responding to the needs of this broad-based clientele. Recognising and allowing for personal and professional development meant that progression included increased depth of understanding as well as breadth of knowledge and skill. Differentiation by outcome, and an increased range of awards (Certificate, Diploma, BEd (in-service) and MEd or MA) has developed as a response to this heterogeneity, underpinned by the argument that it is good educational practice for students to build up their abilities over the period of registration for a higher degree, adapting and extending their expectations in the light of tutorial advice. To support students, tutors have had to provide more detailed feedback and to adopt mentoring roles on an individual basis. Teacher-students have also had adjustments to make; as participants in an ever changing scene, they have less identity as cohorts, and therefore fewer opportunities for sustained peer support. Every new module group is an assembly of comparative strangers, in which only a few may have met before. Constructing a community of learners is a difficult task in this situation.

Assessment

One of the most interesting changes which have accompanied the introduction of modular courses has been the development of new ways of assessing students' work. Looking back again to the beginning of the 1980s, assignments then mostly comprised a number of essays, sometimes chosen from an indicative list, and a 'child study' which inevitably focused the teacher's attention on the deficits exhibited by a particular child, rather than on the problems associated with teaching. Such forms of assessment were relatively leisurely affairs and did not relate directly to the teacher's working life. In shorter modular units, there is no time to become gradually socialised into the course; there must be immediate impact and the teacher must focus right from the outset on the relationship between what they are learning during the evening and the work they are doing during the day. So, assignments have changed from traditional essays, which were largely theoretical in character, to studies which enable the teacher to focus on aspects of practice within the workplace and to examine and reflect on issues as they arise. Such assignments can be progressive, as in a notebook or an account of a teaching or management experience, or interactive, as in a seminar presentation.

It may be thought that assignments accumulated over time may represent a disjointed experience. This has been a matter of concern for Golby (1994) who writes that 'Coherence and depth are at risk in modular courses which too often seem to be like beads on a string – but without the string'. To counteract this, institutions have identified different ways of helping students to create their own coherence. At the University of the West of England, Bristol, students negotiate with tutors the criteria by which their work will be assessed from an explicit list provided to them. At Brunel University, teacher-students are required to construct a 'cumulative record' which is submitted at the end of the course with the final assessment. In either case, the intention is to enable teachers to engage with what Rudduck (1988) calls 'the ownership of change'. She writes:

> Professional learning is, I think, more likely to be powerful in its engagement with fundamental issues in education if teachers have constructed their own narrative of the need for change. (Rudduck, 1988, p.213)

Of course, this is a counsel of perfection. Not all teacher-students will be able or willing to engage with fundamental issues; some will seek simply to extend expertise, or gather in-service credits. But this was also true of the preceding system. Thomas (1991) cites O'Hanlon's (1988) distinction between teachers who are 'intuitionist', concerned with relationships, processes and the challenging of institutional norms, and those who are 'teacher technicians' primarily concerned with professional techniques, results, products and outcomes and who are characterised by 'a ready acceptance of institutional norms'. The latter are less likely to be able to 'construct their own narrative' in a way characteristic of a good higher degree student. However, it would be foolish to pretend that such teachers do not work for, and obtain, masters degrees, or that they are ineffective with children. 'Differentiation by outcome' cannot always cope with such subtleties.

The reflective teacher or the competent teacher?

Schön's (1983) formulation of the reflective practitioner has been highly influential in HEIs concerned with ITE and CPD (Carr and Kemmis, 1986; Fish, 1991). Since the advent of the National Curriculum and increased pressure on providers to include increased school experience in ITE courses, the reflective practitioner, squeezed from ITE, has become even more of a goal in CPD programmes. Modular courses have struggled to adhere to a reflective philosophy within relatively short units. Some have argued that this is a doubtful proposition. Thomas (1991) saw a 'danger ... in the production of *reactive* teachers rather than *reflective* ones.' He did acknowledge, however, that modular courses 'have made their contribution by keeping a lifeline open to a good match between the technicist and intuitionistic needs of the reflective practitioner'. Golby (1994) is more severe, arguing for

> ... at the very least, a reasonable period of time over which courses ought to run. In my experience two or three terms of part time work with a group begins to see penetrating work being done. Courses of a few days, or tens of hours spread very thinly achieve very little of academic worth in regard to practice. (Golby, p.72)

It is however possible, in the writer's experience, for reflection-in-action to take place and become part of a modular course, provided that the focus of particular units is made sharp and clear. A progressive approach to assessment, with tutorial support, can produce remarkable insights. Some of these can be found in the extracts from teachers' work utilised by Garner *et al.* (1995). What must be avoided is the kind of undifferentiated and undigested grumbling characterised by one examiner as 'What people in my staffroom are *fed up* about'.

Others see no problem in promoting reflection on practice in any courses which are provided away from the teacher's workplace:

> Any professional development activity away from the employer's premises means that there is the likelihood that participants will begin to question some aspects of the institutional arrangements or policy, as they have the opportunity to engage in active discussion with others from similar and different types of organisation (Burchill and Woolhouse, 1995, p.145)

Hodkinson (1992) is equally positive, noting that

> For effective critical reflection some learning is best done away from the job where pressures of the present and constraints of a specific situation can make such general thinking almost impossible. (p.37)

The new emphasis on the establishment and assessment of teacher competencies identified by OFSTED in Circulars 9/92 and 14/93 brought to a head the conflict between the 'intuitionists' and the 'technicians'. It is clear that the direction favoured by DfE and the TTA (now responsible for monitoring and funding most in-service education for teachers) is towards an increasingly technocratic approach. For special education there are problems with this on two levels: first, because the methodological superiority asserted for some methods of teaching (as in a preoccupation with an exclusively 'phonic' approach to reading) runs contrary to the eclecticism which SEN teachers have adopted in response to the needs of their pupils, and to their experience of prescriptive methods in the past. This eclecticism is characterised by the search for strategies rather than the imposition of tactics. Secondly, in attempting to identify specific competencies for SEN, there is a danger that inclusive education will be threatened. After all, if children with particular difficulties are indentified as requiring highly specialised teacher competencies, it will be too easy for mainstream teachers to recommend their withdrawal from the 'normal' classroom.

The SENTC (1996) report to DfEE, in attempting to accommodate to the officially favoured language of competencies, appears to have fallen into a pit of its own making by listing competencies for ten different groups roughly corresponding to the categories previously abandoned by the 1981 Education Act. If modular CPD schemes were to adopt organisational structures which mirrored these segregated competencies, the ability of the courses to respond to issues and problems raised by teachers from disparate backgrounds working together would be severely curtailed. Of course, if courses comprising a collection of focused modules can be designed to support an appropriate range of competencies without neglecting the reflection needed by the intuitive teacher, this would satisfy both elements. This is, in fact, what most course leaders attempt to achieve today. However, if the DfEE and the TTA adopt such an extreme view, modules could be 'hijacked' for short term ends, such as the introduction of a newly fashionable teaching method or behavioural management style.

Thomas wrote that the method as well as the content of teaching is not value free.

> Teaching styles or methods are loaded with social political and philosophical meanings. In some societies and in particular therapeutic institutions, the 'manner' of instruction or relationships is understood to be more significant than content. (Thomas, 1991, p.78)

So, if staff in HEIs allow themselves to be persuaded that short instructional modules, conceived and 'delivered' without context or philosophy, are an appropriate response to the teacher's need for CPD, competencies may be achieved, but at the expense of reflective practice. There is more to teaching than skill. As Pring wrote:

> We ought to provide not only the knowledge base but also the politically free and critical framework within which potential teachers might acquire the values central to being a professional. Programming teachers for independence? (Pring, 1989, p.1)

Moreover, as Rudduck (1988) insists, the ownership of change depends on the need for reform to be generated from the chalkface and not to be imposed from the top. Good CPD is about constructing teacher researchers through enabling individuals to look with a fresh eye at their teaching, at their management skills and at the preconceptions which underpin what they do on a daily basis. In this way, as Smyth (1987) describes, they learn to challenge their current perception of themselves as teachers, and recognise their career as an 'open ended search for identity'.

Is this compatible with the inculcation of competencies? Certainly, it is very hard to measure these more nebulous professional attributes. Hartley (1995) describing current changes in higher education, borrows Ritzer's (1993) concept of the 'McDonaldisation' of society, characterised by an excessive emphasis on quantification, calculability, predictability and control. It is a powerful metaphor. Hartley continues by identifying the 'double coding' in higher education as a whole, in which institutions try to combine bureaucratic rationality with 'post-modernist notions of choice, ownership, flexibility and diversity'. This is certainly true of CPD in general, and, as expressed in the SENTC report (1996), it is true of SEN in-service education in particular. Perhaps an accommodation between the two codes is possible. HEIs need to adopt, within CPD programmes, a holistic approach to competence, in which, as suggested by Reynolds and Salters (1995), knowledge, understanding and the affective dimension are recognised as essential to competent *performance*, even though they may not be identifiable within competence-based *training*.

Teacher stress and burnout

Both the stressful and satisfying aspects of being a teacher are particularly associated with special education. Such stresses range from the sheer physical exhaustion, and sometimes danger, experienced by those working with SLD or with EBD, to the more mundane stresses of working with low-achievers in ordinary schools pressured by performance league tables. Modular systems, with inbuilt flexibility, enable teachers to participate in courses as they are able, and to interrupt studies when necessary. This is particularly important in an era of OFSTED inspections, which involve teachers in many weeks of preparation and are followed by a necessary 'recovery period', even though the actual visitation is of short duration. The advent of directed time, where teachers are expected to spend a number of hours on school premises after the 'normal' school day, also inhibits participation in off-site courses. The ability of HEI managements to recognise this and to offer popular modules more frequently, on different days and times, and in a range of formats including distance learning modes, helps to circumvent these difficulties. It may also help that the end of any module is never very far away, and the teacher can view with satisfaction the accumulation of credits within a manageable framework.

Conclusion

One of the more irritating examples of management-speak is the oft-repeated statement that 'there are no problems, only opportunities'. It would be quite wrong to say there are no problems here. CPD, particularly in SEN, began to be effective in the mid-1980s as never before. When ITE incorporated elements of SEN practice, new teachers were open to the issues facing them of managing curricula to promote and ensure inclusive education. LEAs employed special education advisers, advisory teachers and support teams. Teachers' Centres provided short courses and facilities which alerted mainstream and special school teachers to new strategies and materials which could be used to help struggling pupils. Exclusion was a comparatively rare occurrence. Had this framework for support survived into the 1990s, how much easier would have been the introduction of the 1993 Education Act and the CoP! How much more ably would teachers cope with the special educational implications of the National Curriculum, key-stage assessment and OFSTED! The death of CNAA has also inhibited the interchange of ideas and the development of good practice. Universities provide their own validation and examination systems, which do not always facilitate effective management of ITE and CPD courses, especially in matters such as admission regulations, assessment and Credit Accumulation and Transfer.

HEIs have responded to these problems by re-designing and repackaging courses for teachers in formats which attempt to offer some solutions. In doing so, they have found opportunities to continue their participation in the development of SEN practice. The present system isn't perfect, and critical voices, such as those quoted in this chapter, will continue to be raised. HEIs must respond to them, and must retain their integrity as well as their ablity to respond to the changing needs of teachers.

References

Bines, H. and Watson, D. (1992) *Developing Professional Education.* Buckingham: Society for Research in Higher Education/Open University Press.

Burchill, H. and Woolhouse, M. (1995) 'The role of learner autonomy in competence based post-compulsory teacher education', *British Journal of In-service Education,* **21** (2), 137–148.

Carr, W. and Kemmis, S. (1986) *Education, Knowledge and Action Research.* Lewes: Falmer Press.

Council for National Academic Awards (CNAA) (1990) *Complex Modular Inservice Education Schemes: a review of CNAA provision.* London: CNAA.

Department of Education and Science (1989) *Discipline in Schools* (Report of the Committee of Enquiry Chaired by Lord Elton) London: HMSO.

Department for Education (1992) *Initial Teacher Training (Secondary Phase)* (Circular 9/92). London: DfE.

Department for Education (1993) *Initial Teacher Training (Primary Phase)* (Circular14/93). London: DfE.

DES (1987) *The New Teacher in School.* London: HMSO.

Fish, D. (1991) *Promoting Reflection.* Twickenham: West London Press.

Garner, P., Hinchcliffe,V. and Sandow, S. (1995) *What Teachers do.* London: Paul Chapman Publishing.

Gaunt, D. (1992) 'Coordinating inservice education for teachers', in H. Bines and D. Watson (eds.) *Developing Professional Education.* Buckingham: Society for Research in Higher Education/Open University Press.

Golby, M. (1994) 'Doing a proper course: the present crisis in advanced courses', *Journal of Teacher Development,* **3** (2), 69–73.

Hartley, D. (1995) 'The "McDonaldization" of higher education: food for thought?' *Oxford Review of Education,* **21** (4), 409–423.

Her Majesty's Inspectorate (1990) *Special Needs Issues: a survey by HMI,* Education Observed series. London: HMSO.

Hodkinson, P. (1992) 'Alternative models of competence in vocational education and training', *Journal of Further and Higher Education,* **16** (2), 30–39.

Jenkins, A. and Walker, L (eds.) (1994) *Developing Student Capability Through Modular Courses.* London: Kogan Page.

O'Hanlon, C. (1988) 'Alienation within the profession: special needs or watered down teachers?', in D. Johnstone and C. O'Hanlon (eds.) *Critical Reflections on Special Education.* Ormskirk: Edge Hill College.

Pring, R. (1989) Editorial, *British Journal of Educational Studies,* **39** (3), 1.

Reynolds, M. and Salters, M. (1995) 'Models of competence and teacher training', *Cambridge Journal of Education,* **25** (3), 349–359.

Ritzer, G. (1993) *The McDonaldization of Society.* London: Pine Forge Press.

Rudduck, J. (1988) 'The ownership of change as a basis for teachers' professional learning' in J. Calderhead (ed.) *Teachers' Professional Learning*. Lewes: Falmer Press.

Schön, D. (1983) *The Reflective Practitioner*. New York: Basic Books.

Smyth, W. (1987) *A Rationale for Teachers' Critical Pedagogy: a Handbook*. Geelong: Deakin University Press.

Special Educational Needs Training Consortium (SENTC) (1996) *Professional Development to meet Special Educational Needs: Report to the Department for Education and Employment*. Stafford: SENTC.

Thomas, D. (1991) 'Reflective or reactive? Role dilemmas for teachers and education tutors', *Support for Learning*, **6** (2), 77–83.

CHAPTER TEN

A Whole School Modular Programme for Continuous Professional Development

Diane Fidler

Brislington is a large comprehensive school in South Bristol with a teaching staff of over a hundred. Until recently its arrangements for professional development reflected the traditional model to be found in the majority of schools across the country, which relied heavily on the provision of external courses and an assortment of school-based activities. External courses and conferences, whilst they were often well attended, did not necessarily meet the direct needs of the school. By their very nature they had to be generalist and were not designed to address issues specific to the school or region. Their ability to recruit course members resided more with the fact that few alternatives existed and teachers, eager to take advantage of an opportunity for professional refreshment and extension, accepted what was offered, although the comment 'It was fine as far as it went, but I can't see us being able to do that in this school' was far too frequently heard.

Nor was it possible to plan a coherent programme of staff development. Support for individuals and school initiatives depended upon what was being offered by the LEA or by various HEIs. Information concerning these courses was often not available to allow for appropriate planning and allocation of funds; details of courses would arrive at various times throughout the year, requiring the school to adopt a 'wait and see' attitude as to whether or not certain CPD needs would be met. Inevitably this situation resulted in funds being held back in order to meet the cost of such courses and conferences and, where they failed to materialise, the rapid and inevitably less prudent spending of residual funds at the close of the financial year. Even when it has been possible to locate relevant professional development activities a number of factors have made it less than easy for the school and individual teachers to participate.

For many teachers, concerned about their professional obligation to their classes, there has always been a tension created when they are asked to disadvantage their pupils through their absence to attend a course which is ostensibly for their own benefit. Nor has it been made easier when the absent teacher has to prepare detailed plans for 'cover' lessons taken by colleagues or supply teacher(s). They also have the responsibility of conveying, on their return, as much of the course content as possible in order to justify their absence.

Each of these points carries whole school implications. Firstly, the issue of covering classes for teachers absent because of attendance on courses raises the question about the teachers' main function – the task of *teaching*. Arguably they are not employed to be released from their teaching to participate in professional development activities, despite the fact that these will ultimately benefit the pupils. It could be argued that if a school is concerned with quality teaching and learning it must also be concerned with the quality of its teaching staff. However, to adopt a CPD programme which disrupts pupils' learning is clearly untenable.

At the same time, when a teacher is absent, supply-cover costs have to be met. Given the limited budget with which schools have to operate, it seems an act of gross mismanagement of funds to unnecessarily double the cost of a teacher. The dissemination of skills and knowledge by the teacher commissioned to attend the course is also thwarted by a number of factors. Whilst there is merit in instigating a 'report-back' procedure by the teacher to other colleagues, there is little to be gained and much naivety in expecting that same teacher to recreate the course and impart more than a second-hand version of what they have experienced. Whatever the usefulness of the 'cascade' model for disseminating purely factual information, its employment is seriously inadequate for more complex areas of CPD.

School-based professional development has gained a stronger foothold due to some of the difficulties associated with external course provision. Yet where school-based courses take place during the day they are likely to mirror many of the problems already outlined. Moreover, the 'self-help' quality of these activities, in which a staff member leads a professional development session, whilst useful for direct exchange of information, is not likely to allow for high quality professional development. By their nature, such arrangements are parochial and more akin to a 'quick-fix' answer to professional development needs than to a structured programme which goes beyond the school's immediate requirements to fundamentally influence classroom practice and the management of learning. Yet despite the disadvantages of this traditional model of staff development, it is the one familiar to most schools. That it is no longer the predominant model at Brislington is due to both the reservations about traditional CPD formats already voiced and the fortuitous coming together of several initiatives.

Teacher Appraisal, introduced in the school in September, 1992, provided the means to define more acutely both individual and whole-school training requirements. The school' s commitment to Investors in People (IIP)[1] in the following year also brought about a reassessment of how teaching and non-

---

[1] IIP is concerned with the way in which an organisation sets and communicates its goals and develops people to meet these goals, so that what people can do and are motivated to do, match what the organisation needs of them. At the heart of IIP is the National Standard for Effective Investment in People. This represents a standard towards which an organisation can work, and a benchmark against which progress can be measured.

teaching staff were being developed to support the declared aims of the school. It was evident that a comprehensive programme for staff development needed to be put in place, which addressed the specific needs of the school in a cost effective way.

The logical solution was for the school to organise its own range of after-school courses for teaching and non-teaching staff. However, it could not be assumed that staff would automatically wish to extend their school day for the purposes of professional development. Yet the concept was a sound one. Courses run on-site, after school, removed disruption to lessons and drastically reduced costs. The issue regarding attendance needed to be addressed in several ways. If staff were to commit to twilight staff development then the courses offered needed not only to be relevant but also of an assured quality. Where possible there also needed to be recognition of attendance through some form of certification or accreditation of each course. A timely partnership provided some of the answers. ITE had already increased the links between the school and its university partners. One of these institutions, to further cement the existing partnership arrangements with the school, provided several places on its modular Masters of Education (MEd) course for the school's staff. In the spring of 1994 negotiations started between Brislington and the University of the West of England, Bristol (UWE) regarding a programme of twilight courses, which linked into their modular course structure. Not all of these courses were to be delivered by university personnel, some in-house expertise would also be employed and, where neither the university nor the school had the necessary provider, outside agencies would be called upon. The main intention was to design a programme of individual courses that met the defined requirements of the staff. What the courses had in common was that they were accredited by the university and as such could be used as part of the modular route towards a Postgraduate Diploma and/or Masters of Education degree.

The resulting programme promised to deliver a great deal. The focus for each course was a direct response to the school's known professional development needs. On an individual level, these needs had already been established through the outcomes of the Appraisal process and in the Professional Development Meetings held with the deputy headteacher responsible for CPD. Other, more whole-school issues had been identified in relation to School Development Plan targets. The programme was, therefore, broad yet pertinent and included courses on:

- preparing for Senior Management;
- preparing for Middle Management;
- improving Behaviour for Learning;
- developing Effective Teaching and Learning Styles;
- Counselling Skills.

Staff were informed that each course had been carefully planned in response to their perceived and stated needs.

Through astute selection of and negotiation with course tutors, issues concerning quality, delivery and outcomes were practically assured.

Furthermore, status had been assigned to the courses by virtue of the accreditation arrangement with the university. There was to be only one cost to staff: their time. All fees and registration costs for further professional qualifications were met by the school. The courses were therefore an attractive proposition for staff. In exchange for their time and commitment, staff gained the means of increasing their professional skills and knowledge, and the possibility of acquiring further qualifications.

The response to this initiative was remarkable. Large numbers of staff elected to extend their day to take advantage of this professional development opportunity. The immediate impact of this response has been the wholesale development of staff in key areas related to their day to day work.

One of the most successful courses to date has been 'Improving Behaviour for Learning'. It was designed to address those difficulties some teachers were experiencing with certain pupils. Clearly, to be effective it needed to provide opportunities for teachers to examine not only their pupils' behaviour but also their own. From this starting point of self-awareness it was then possible to determine appropriate strategies to reduce difficult behaviour and increase opportunities for learning. The course, in common with many others on offer, required teachers not to simply luxuriate in anecdotal accounts but to conduct a focused assessment of what was happening in their classrooms through the application of observation and survey techniques. This section of the course was followed by sessions which examined theoretical models for improving behaviour. Course participants were thus equipped with extended knowledge about their existing practise, an understanding of behavioural theory, giving them a background against which they could confidently develop appropriate strategies to improve pupil performance in the classroom.

The analysis of a teacher's personal practice, which was a major thrust of the course, required sympathetic but firm handling. It also required a close knowledge of the teachers on the course and the context of their work. These points determined that the trainer needed to be 'in-house', with the necessary skills and experience to support and influence staff as they reassessed their own mode of operation and moved towards being more perceptive classroom practitioners. Fortunately, such a person existed amongst the staff of the school: a colleague who had for some years held responsibility for the school's EBD provision. It was therefore with some confidence that staff enrolled for this particular course. It is also significant that course participants included not only the 'rank and file' subject teachers but also a range of middle managers. Dealing with difficult pupils and improving the context for learning was reassuringly being identified as an issue about which all staff, regardless of experience and position, wished to increase their professional competence.

One of the most satisfying outcomes of this initiative has been the level of professional debate generated by the courses. Issues raised during the sessions spill over into discussions in the staffroom or in work-bases around the school. Such discussions are no longer restricted to a handful of 'INSET' days but now form part of an on-going discussion amongst teachers seeking to improve their practice.

The student-like camaraderie amongst the course members – joking about whether or not they have completed their 'course homework' or whether they will manage to meet an assignment deadline – has all been instrumental in drawing the staff together towards a common goal. The fact that over 25% of the teaching staff are now working towards a higher qualification has a direct benefit for the school. Teachers have a further incentive to glean as much from the courses as possible, equipping themselves for the task of assignment writing. In so doing they are required to not only absorb a body of theoretical knowledge but to carefully reflect on their day-to-day practice. The assignments are based on action research and are not simply a passport to a higher degree, they provide a means of clarifying, confirming and making real the skills promoted by each course.

The courses have been successful in introducing a new range of professional experiences to staff. They have also been instrumental in generating an ethos of professional enquiry. These significant outcomes of the programme have been supported by another dimension of the school's professional development work. In conjunction with the UWE, workshop sessions have been provided for teachers, detailing the opportunities available through APEL. Teachers attending the workshops are initially helped to assess those aspects of their work which they might usefully document so as to provide evidence of their professional reflection and progression. At the same time they are given advice about whether or not their attendance on past courses can be recognised for accreditation purposes. For some teachers this is the first step towards embarking on the road to a Masters degree. As a starting point, it gives status to and builds upon an individual's past and present achievement. It is the means by which teachers can translate their day-to-day professional competencies into academic credentials. For many teachers the APEL workshops and an appreciation of how a modular programme for CPD can work for them is the point at which they realise that a Masters qualification is within their grasp.

Furthermore, the flexible negotiated nature of the initial stages of the modular Masters programme allows individuals to manage the pace of their academic progress. This has proved an important feature when encouraging colleagues to consider the benefits of increasing their professional qualifications. It has thus been possible for teachers to plan the acquisition of module credits towards a Masters degree according to their professional and personal circumstances. Some will take the maximum amount of time permissible before completing all stages of the Masters programme; others will complete within three years. Hence the inducement to individuals to promote their own career development is supported by ownership and control. The majority of teachers at Brislington School who are working towards a higher degree have chosen to do so by gaining accreditation through a combination of APEL and course attendance and assignment. Whatever the balance of choice, both options have direct relevance to the quality of professional development taking place within the school, promoting reflective and well-trained practitioners.

The guided nature of the modular approach ensures that tutor support is available on request to steer teachers through their decision making about the options to take and to monitor progress with assignments. Appropriate guidance enables teachers to select a focus which recognises both their own interests and the needs of the school and it is rare that these interests do not match. For example, the school's main target is 'to raise pupil achievement'. It is central to all of the courses organised for the twilight programme and crucial to the work of all teachers whatever their subject specialism. Agreeing a focus for an APEL or course assignment, therefore, is unlikely to find the teacher wishing to stray far from this central theme. Furthermore, for those teachers wishing to enhance their career prospects, gaining a Masters degree is not simply an end in itself; it is essentially an educational process which facilitates a more astute grasp of issues central to the concerns of any school. As such, teachers are highly likely to select an assignment focus which is pertinent to the school's concerns.

Further negotiations with the University of the West of England, Bristol, have resulted in the introduction of a 'Professional Portfolio' for teachers. Teachers not wishing to study towards a higher degree are nonetheless able to record details about their INSET attendance and its impact on the management of pupils' learning. This portfolio can be submitted at a later date for accreditation should the teacher decide to pursue the Postgraduate Diploma/Master of Education route. The programme has recently been further refined to provide a direct entry for NQTs. There is a year's Induction Course for NQTs which can be included in the portfolio or converted into an accredited module. At present the school and university are exploring the possibility of providing a similar portfolio/qualifications option for non-teaching staff.

In a relatively brief period there has been a significant culture change within the school. Whereas the emphasis had primarily been on pupils' learning, with the occasional awkward inclusion of staff 'training' to facilitate this key function, the focus is now clearly on the *continual learner*. The school is fast becoming a learning institution in the fullest sense, providing improved educational opportunities for its pupils and its staff. The link with the university has had other benefits. Several student teachers, based at the school for their ITE, have gained posts at the school on completion of their PGCE. They are inducted into a school culture which supports and even demands their continued development as 'experts' in their field. The personnel providing the courses for this sustained professional growth are both their new colleagues and tutors from their student days. For some teachers, therefore, the transition from student to qualified status (QTS) is almost seamless.

One of the key concerns in the Brislington School initiative has been to ensure both quality provision and outcome. A determined commitment to pursuing the type of activities detailed above and the associated support for CPD has had undeniable financial implications for the school. Most schools operate a relatively small staff development budget. Brislington, as a large school of over 100 teaching and 50 non-teaching staff, has access to an unusually large budget. Whilst this allows for a more creative use of funds, costs, nonetheless, have to be justified and evidence provided that the investment made is benefiting the school. Evaluating the impact of training on staff is therefore a means to both refining the progressional development and justifying its continuation. Evaluation, in this context however, is not a straightforward task, especially when what we are attempting to measure must ultimately be the impact of the professional development on pupil learning. In order to obtain an informed position the school has pursued three methods of evaluating its activities, each investigating the various levels of impact of the programme on the work of the school.

Firstly, at the same time that the CPD initiative was launched, the school committed to Investors in People (IIP) as a means of working towards a Quality Standard. Operating within IIP criteria has both brought a more critical note to the planning, implementation and evaluation procedures for the CPD programme, as well as promoting a wider application of what had hitherto been understood to be 'equality of opportunity'. The most useful aspect of the process for the school's evaluation purposes however, arose during the final assessment for the Quality Standard. At this stage twenty eight staff were interviewed by an assessor to determine how the school's professional development needs were being met and whether or not the provision was effective. The assessment was followed by a detailed report and the award of the Standard early in 1996.

As a means of gauging staff opinion (both teaching and non-teaching) the feedback both confirmed the school's developing strength in this area and highlighted areas for further improvement. In the final analysis, however, what has been obtained is only evidence of increased staff participation on courses and of the commitment of individual teachers to their own professional growth. Whilst this is intrinsically good, it offers no hard evidence to confirm that these activities were benefiting pupils. Further exploration of this point was required and again took the form of an outside evaluation.

The school therefore, made a submission for a National Training Award which entailed an assessment not dissimilar to that required for the IIP award. However, in this instance there was a greater emphasis on how the school evaluated its professional development outcomes. The assessment resulted in Brislington receiving a Regional Training Award for 'Excellence in Training' with the attendant advice that the school's evaluation procedures needed to be extended even further, beyond the course participants' assessment to the more fundamental issue of how such professional development was impacting on pupil achievement. It was no longer enough to be acknowledged as a 'high quality training provider'. If the school was to move forward with its declared aims, it had to have a clear understanding of what it was and was not achieving through this provision.

It was through the school's partnership with UWE that a possible way forward was identified. Both parties had a vested interest in finding answers to the type of challenging questions that were now beginning to surface. The agreed approach dovetailed perfectly with the tradition that was being established at the school, whereby course 'homework' and end of course assignments required participants to investigate their own practice. In this instance, staff from both the university and the school would be involved in a collaborative research project looking at the impact of the professional development programme on pupils' learning. Specifically, a sample of staff who had attended one of the courses (Improving Behaviour for Learning) had been selected and asked to complete a questionnaire designed by the two institutions. Several teachers had been involved in agreeing the research methods and designing the questionnaire. These teachers were in the latter stages of their Masters programme. Most were in the process of completing a taught course on research methodology.

Following the questionnaire returns a series of staff interviews were arranged to acquire more detailed insights into the reasons why staff were responding to professional development opportunities and what they perceived to be the benefits. The third step in this research programme has yet to be undertaken but will involve the identification of groups of pupils taught by the identified teachers. These pupils will be interviewed about their learning experiences to ascertain if there have been any discernible changes in the teacher's classroom management, subject delivery and the pupils' ability to make progress.

What then does the future hold? Ideally the momentum generated in these first few years of collaboration with the university will continue. On both sides there is a willingness to explore further possibilities. Such possibilities revolve around promoting a distinct philosophy of the school as a centre of learning and that all who work within it are 'continual learners'. There can be no better advertisement for the value of education than that of a school's staff actively demonstrating their commitment to their own education. In this context it is, of course, ultimately also a commitment to the quality of education and support provided for the school's pupils.

The immediate step to be taken is to develop a portfolio system for non-teaching staff. Whilst many have elected to attend the courses, they as yet do not have access to the accreditation arrangement, which requires a first degree. If they are to be exposed to the same experiences and provided with opportunities for further development and training then a similar route to improved qualifications to that enjoyed by the teaching staff must be provided. The school and university are collaboratively investigating ways to make this possible.

If the vision is widened still further, the possibilities are truly exciting. There is no reason why the school should be content with providing for its working community alone. If the school is serious about being a Centre of Learning then the learning opportunities it offers should be there for parents and the wider community. This is a long-term project but one which deserves attention. What better way is there to create an accessible route within education for post-school learners than to continue to provide relevant courses on the school site. Such courses could be jointly provided by the school and university and create a nonthreatening introduction to higher education for some learners.

The first step to realising this goal has already been taken. Brislington School is currently piloting a Masters Degree sponsored by the City of Bristol, a degree which, in its initial stages is not dissimilar to other modular degrees but has the potential to be flexible enough to meet the educational needs of a wide community of learners. Its conception has arisen through the partnership between UWE and the new City of Bristol unitary authority.

It is evident that the concept has drawn on the successful model which developed over several years at Brislington and it represents a natural progression that the school should be asked to pilot this initiative. There are advantages for all three partners, but for Brislington it means that the school remains at the forefront of an initiative which encapsulates what it has been attempting to achieve within its own sphere of operation. Yet to realise all that it sets out to achieve, this exercise in providing tailored courses for Bristol's teachers will eventually need to expand to include its other employees and residents. With this 'total' provision will come the access to a range of courses leading to a degree level qualification, for non-teaching colleagues in schools and members of the local community. The division between those who are educators and those who are recipients, or outside of the educative process altogether, will then start to be removed. In its place will emerge the reality of a community of learners, each taking a different pathway towards realising their potential both personally and professionally.

CHAPTER ELEVEN

Getting it Right: A Case study of a School-based Response to Teacher Development in SEN

Jim Moon

This chapter describes an approach to developing teacher-skills in managing those pupils who are regarded as having behavioural difficulties, or EBD, in one comprehensive school. It is an account of the evolution of a working approach by classroom teachers rather than a theoretical commentary. The context in which the school found itself two years ago is described, as is the detailed content of one of a range of CPD courses delivered in partnership with the University of the West of England, Bristol (UWE). The natural evolution of peer support for teachers working with pupils with perceived behavioural difficulties is outlined as a welcome informal development arising from the increasing number of staff in possession of objective and systematic skills in improving behaviour for learning.

Context

The school described in this case study is an eleven to eighteen comprehensive of some 1700 pupils, situated on the eastern fringe of Bristol. The pupils have a wide variety of achievement levels and socio-economic backgrounds. The school originally occupied two sites. The main school site was the base for Years 7 to 9 and the GCE students in Years 10 and 11. CSE and non-examination students in Years 10 and 11 were based at the 'Annexe', over a mile away from the main school. Each subject area was located within a separate department within the main school site. In addition to the subject departments, there was the Department for Special Education (DSE) which maintained a Special Class in each of Years 7, 8 and 9 and a joint Special Class for Years 10 and 11. There were two additional 'remedial' classes in Year 7. Pupils placed in DSE classes were taught English, mathematics and the humanities in small groups by the same teacher. There was little evidence of interchange or integration in these subjects between DSE pupils and their peers. The school also hosted a Special Unit funded by the LEA and designated for pupils exhibiting emotional and/or behavioural difficulties (EBD). The Unit was staffed by three full-time teachers, specialising in EBD, who worked with around fifty pupils. The Unit's Management Panel included the school's headteacher, educational psychologist, educational welfare officer, school nurse, child guidance social worker, a consultant child psychiatrist and the staff of the Unit. It acted as both an admissions panel and as a consultative group overseeing all aspects of the work of the Unit. The author was originally appointed as Head of the Unit.

Three main waves of reform since the period described have changed the structure and delivery of SEN support. The first of these arose from a change in prevailing educational philosophy. The segregation of pupils with SEN was increasingly recognised as a divisive barrier to a genuine 'comprehensive' education. LEAs began to reduce the number of pupils placed in special schools, increasingly offering statemented and supported 'mainstream' school placements for identified pupils. There was a similar drive towards integration within comprehensive schools, which resulted in the widespread reorganisation of monolithic, segregated, special education or 'remedial' departments into smaller, more flexible internal agencies pursuing a policy of maximum in-class support and minimum withdrawal. This led inexorably to increasing pressure on that part of LEA budgets which financed provision required by SEN statements.

The introduction of the National Curriculum increased review pressures on the remaining 'segregationist' departments. Statutory requirements that all pupils should follow the National Curriculum in full (unless modified or disapplied within tight constraints) made it very difficult for comprehensive schools to retain a segregated approach for pupils with SEN, hastening integrationist reforms. The maintenance of on-site EBD support units also became increasingly difficult. For example, in the (then) Avon LEA, the secondary units were charged with the responsibility for ensuring the education of pupils within a comprehensive context, who would otherwise have been placed in special schools for pupils regarded as having EBD. Most units achieved this through a combination of close liaison with parents or guardians, support and strategy-formulation for staff teaching identified pupils, and withdrawal from lessons for individual curriculum support work, groupwork to develop and maintain social skills, counselling and often *ad hoc*, additional withdrawal to defuse developing crises or for post-crisis rebuilding of the pupil's educational milieu. Pupil-centred withdrawal became virtually untenable following the advent of the National Curriculum, since withdrawal from lessons had to be demonstrated to be necessary within the defined parameters of the law, as well as the wider educational interests of the child. Because of this there was a need to enhance the skills of classroom teachers who were increasingly expected to meet the needs of identified EBD pupils rather than referring them elsewhere for specialist input.

The introduction of the CoP, following the 1993 Education Act was welcomed as timely, providing a framework which supported the school's accountability to pupils, parents and LEA. The Code provided teachers and managers with clear guidelines for the identification, assessment and appropriate provision for pupils with SEN. It also, however, further constrained the short-term flexibility which is essential in meeting the immediate needs of pupils with EBD. This placed further demands on the professional abilities of subject teachers who were required to respond more fully to the educational and emotional needs of pupils over an extended time in the classroom. As was remarked at the time, 'It's Rolls-Royce legislation on a 2CV budget.'

By this time, the 'Annexe' at Brislington School had been closed in response to planned reductions in pupil numbers, returning a significant number of 'less able' and 'disaffected' pupils to the main school site. The school had reorganised into Faculties and the Department for SEN no longer existed. This had by then been replaced by a cross-faculty support agency consisting of one Special Class in each of Years 7, 8 and 9, together with in-class support for identified pupils with learning difficulties. This again placed further demands on the professional skills of classroom teachers.

Pressure on the LEA's budget for statementing pupils led to the closure of the majority of the secondary on-site EBD support units within the authority. Since the 1981 Education Act, Unit Management Panels had accepted suitable referrals and then sought LEA funding through the statements procedure to protect the long-term interests of referred pupils. Statutory assessment was often declined by the LEA on the grounds that pupils were already receiving appropriate support. The formal statementing process was administratively unnecessary and financially wasteful. The primary reason given for withdrawal of LEA funding (in this LEA's units at least) was that they were failing to address the needs of enough statemented pupils.

Following such an intense period of internal and external reforms, it was clear that the school had to review and redefine its responses to pupils identified as SEN. In order to consolidate and build upon the rather loose cross-faculty structure of in-class support, the school established a faculty specifically dedicated to meeting individual pupil needs. In supporting pupils with learning difficulties, this entailed the development of clearly targeted support for learning: two Year 7 Special Classes are now maintained in parallel with the mainstream curriculum, allowing considerable flexibility and interchange for subject-specific groups. There is a six-week rolling programme of half-hour withdrawal on a daily basis, when identified pupils are provided with intensive tuition on literacy and/or numeracy skills.

The school has secured statements of SEN for identified pupils which has helped finance an extensive programme of in-class support from SEN teachers and general assistants, organised centrally by the ' Individual Pupil Needs' faculty. All of these initiatives are under constant review and development to ensure the best match of provision to need.

The position for children identified as having learning difficulties associated with EBD is somewhat different. Those with Statements are entitled to the in-class support, withdrawal support and other inputs as specified in their

Statements. For the those placed on the SEN register at Stages 1, 2 and 3 of the CoP, the situation was less clear. The school's residual provision could not realistically meet the demands of the number of pupils involved. This was clearly a gap in the school's provision and one where there were inadequate resources to meet pupil-need.

First response

As the school could not afford to employ additional specialist staff to meet the demands of EBD pupils at Stages 1 to 3 of the CoP whilst also providing greater supported integration opportunities for those at Stages 4 and 5, it was imperative that subject specialists should develop and refine skills to enable them to deal more confidently and effectively with such pupils.

Extensive discussions within the school and with colleagues from the University of the West of England, Bristol (UWE) led to the development of specific professional development courses on 'Improving Behaviour for Learning', which could be offered to colleagues at the end of the school day. The primary idea was to offer colleagues a chance to reflect upon, review and deploy a range of assessment and intervention strategies which could build on their current classroom practices to enable more confident and purposeful approaches to 'difficult behaviour' in the classroom. The course was accredited by UWE as a module within its CPD programme for which teachers within the school could accumulate credit towards a range of awards, including the degree of MEd. This enhanced its attraction to many colleagues.

Improving behaviour for learning

The course comprises ten two-hour sessions, with a further notional seventy five hours working on individual action research, addressing related issues at classroom level. The course outline is detailed below, with notes indicating participant responses and leader observations.

Rationale

The course represents a response to identified staff development needs. It seeks to improve the quality of pupils' learning and respond to recent changes in legislation and LEA provision.

Intentions

By the end of the course, participants would be equipped to:

- identify pupils' behavioural needs using criterion-referenced observation and survey techniques and objective recording methods;
- assess and interpret behavioural patterns for a wide range of perceived behavioural needs;
- determine appropriate behaviour strategies from a wide range of possibilities;
- formulate subject-specific Action Plans;
- review such Action Plans;
- evaluate the effectiveness of Action Plans and the progress made by the child;
- compare and contrast recent theoretical models for improving behaviour;
- assess and interpret their own values and behaviours and the effects these have on pupil engagement;
- locate all the above in the context of the CoP for Identification and Assessment of SEN, the LEA (Avon) Matrix of SEN provision and the Children's Act 1989.

Professional relevance

The course seeks to offer a purposeful increase in the range of skills and techniques available to subject teachers and tutors at the school, to enrich the skill-base of the school as a whole, to offer relevant individual professional development and to offer accreditation for UWE programmes of study for teachers.

Mode of delivery

The programme has been delivered through a wide range of teaching styles, including didactic learning, OHP presentations, worksheets and prepared notes, video/audio-tape sequences, interactive discussion, supported self-study and participant-led discussion.

Session 1

The programme was introduced through active learning techniques/exercises designed to focus on participants' own values and behaviour in the classroom and to consider the effects these have on pupil behaviours.

'People have a series of hopeful exploratory conversations, which coalesce into the forming of a group. Everyone already knows at least one other person. Everyone has chosen to be there' (Houston, 1987). The first session was all about forming such a cohesive working group. Participants were required to consider in some detail their motivation for entering the teaching profession – and to review their reasons for working at the school. They had a few minutes to address this issue individually, then shared their responses in pairs. Each partner highlighted those aspects of the other's response to the question to which they could relate. Common (or uncommon) areas were then discussed, first in pairs and then as a whole group. The exercise elicited a shared set of values which underpinned the staff's commitment to teaching in general and to Brislington School in particular. As might be expected, some of the initial responses were cynically dismissive: 'It pays the mortgage' and 'I couldn't get a proper job', but the words 'enjoyment', 'rewarding', 'valuable' and 'fulfilling' all featured in the majority of responses. A second exercise based around the most often praised and most often reprimanded classroom behaviours built upon this, confirming a shared set of core values.

Session 2
The second session introduced a theoretical framework and strategies for effective classroom observation and survey techniques were explored. Following the session, teachers were required to apply some of these strategies in their own work-setting, prior to attending the third session.

Although it was felt important not to become too involved in behaviour theory at this stage, a number of important matters were covered. The 'antecedent-behaviour-consequence' model was introduced as a working theoretical base for the group. Behaviour survey records were discussed, ranging from the admirably clear suggestions from the (then) County of Avon Education Department, via the Bristol Social Adjustment Guide, in-school pupil self-assessment cards and the 'Behaviour Survey Checklist' (MacNamara and Jolly, 1991). The majority of participants, as classroom teachers, had hitherto seen such survey mechanisms as the preserve of the educational psychologist or SENCo. Most were encouraged by the knowledge that they were less complex to operate than they first thought and gladly undertook the first independent exercise. This consisted of choosing one of the schemes discussed as a medium for surveying behavioural patterns of an individual or small group which caused concern to them either as subject teacher or tutor. The positive influence of the group-building activities undertaken in the initial session soon became evident, not least in the way that participants readily agreed to undertake mutual peer observation of target pupils or groups at this early stage in the course. This suggested that the primary objective – encouraging and empowering classroom teachers to work together confidently in seeking solutions to behavioural difficulties in their classes – was being achieved.

Session 3
This session focused on identifying behavioural patterns and taking control of behaviour antecedents. The importance of assembling systematic and meaningful data before overreacting was also emphasised. Using previously completed examples of both individual and group surveys, participants were taken through the process of analysing the data obtained to determine the underlying patterns of behaviour exhibited by the pupil(s). Wherever possible,

the triggering antecedents were identified and possible changes to them discussed. Much of the discussion in this session tended to centre on the surprised realisation of the number of behavioural triggers which can be eliminated by the teacher in the guise of 'classroom manager'. It also reversed a commonly held notion that disruptive behaviour is a stimulus (or 'challenge') presented by the disrupter to the teacher: the session highlighted the fact that most disruptive behaviour is itself a response to stimuli present (or absent) in the classroom environment.

Session 4

The next session took the form of a seminar in which participants discussed in detail their responses to the task set at the end of the second session. Particular attention was paid to the in-class behaviour observations and patterns recording.

Participants arrived at the session with their own completed surveys. These typically included classroom observation of individuals and groups, and tended to draw on a wide range of the assessment and survey techniques introduced in the earlier session. Discussion built upon the start made during the third session, the essential difference being the sense of 'ownership' by participants of their work. The session developed awareness of the application of the various techniques available as well as extending participants' professional confidence in obtaining and responding to behavioural data. Some early and very informal action plans were generated at this point.

Sessions 5 and 6

The main focus of these sessions was that of determining appropriate strategies to support colleagues in deciding how best to respond and intervene, now that they had the necessary skills to identify and observe the behavioural pattern. Examination of theoretical and practical indicators for the deployment of a range of strategies to meet the assessed behavioural needs of pupils (from the withdrawn, anxious and isolated to the overreactive, overconfident and aggressive) were described and discussed. In conclusion, participants were requested to identify and implement a suitable behavioural strategy for a pupil and to note the outcome. This was then the focus of a subsequent session. By this stage in the course, the group had become mutually supportive and clearly focused on working together. The emphasis on discussion and cooperative work in the first few sessions had a 'snowballing' effect in sharing and celebrating individual teachers' expertise in recognising and responding to behavioural difficulties presented in a variety of contexts. The group was, by this time, very ready and highly motivated to learn, and as a consequence, the two sessions were densely packed with consideration of practical ways of either initiating behavioural change or responding to a wide range of behaviours presented by pupils.

The initial focus was that of the teacher. The significance of the use of voice was examined carefully in terms of both tone and projection and some considerable time (and fun) was devoted to the non-verbal cues projected by the teacher and how these can be used purposefully in effective learning management. Pupil self-esteem and how to build it was discussed in detail, linking this very clearly with successful learning. The importance of recognising and rewarding individual achievement as opposed to criticising perceived non- or under-achievement was highlighted repeatedly. By the second of these two sessions, some of the group members had already tried independently to improve their praise/criticism ratio and were able spontaneously to report back the immediate positive effects on learning-related behaviour in their own classroom, validating and thus reinforcing this vital message for the group as a whole.

Having 'unpacked' a wide range of teacher-based strategies, the focus changed to the handling of interactions with pupils whose behaviour impedes learning – either their own or that of the class. Several simple techniques are suggested to enable the teacher to retain control of the agenda in any situation of conflict or challenge. Rogers (1992) has some very effective advice here. More systematic ways of working with persistent difficulties were discussed, including in-house behaviour improvement schemes, the materials offered by MacNamara and Jolly (1991) and the invaluable advice of Gordon (1974) on effective positive discussion with pupils.

During the two sessions, each participant decided upon his or her own approach to improving the learning behaviours of an individual or group taught and undertook a short but clearly focused initial strategy to follow, with the intention of discussing this at a later date.

Session 7

The main thrust of this session was that of 'Action Planning' for pupils exhibiting behavioural difficulties. This included Action Plan formulation, implementation, review and evaluation. Current practices and provision within the LEA were also considered, as well as national guidelines/expectations, with particular reference to the CoP. The group was also introduced to the procedures and steps leading to multi-disciplinary assessment and statementing.

There followed an uncomplicated overview of the school's behaviour policy and strategies, the CoP and the local context in which the teachers work. A few participants, working as tutors, already had some knowledge of Action Planning, especially at Stage 1 of the identification procedure of the CoP. For the majority, the session demystified the process of assessment, planning, implementation and review, enabling class teachers to feel much more clear-sighted about their aims in meeting behavioural needs in their own classes.

Session 8

This session concentrated on theoretical models for behavioural improvement, encompassing a review of current thinking with particular reference to the now substantial literature on 'pupils with problems', as they are currently termed.

Underpinning the practical elements of this programme with sound theoretical considerations was regarded as imperative. The precise timing of such an input however, was seen as significant. Busy teachers, volunteering their time to attend the course at the end of a busy school day – throughout the school term – needed to appreciate the direct value of such an investment and, at the same time, have developed a sense of trust, before such an intervention could be contemplated.

By the eighth week there was a cohesive group, members of which readily shared their successes and failures in implementing the planned interventions, and discussed what had been found to be effective systematic assessment and planning techniques. This provided a context within which a theoretical session could be held.

The group was introduced to a range of alternative views regarding the management of behaviour in school settings. The intention was twofold (a) to encourage participants to widen their own reading from authoritative sources and thus enhance their understanding of behaviour management theory and (b) to clarify the links between effective teaching (Gordon, 1974), good classroom management (Waterhouse, 1990), explicit expectations and staged responses to both appropriate and inappropriate behaviours (Canter and Canter, 1992) and high-quality learning opportunities (Smith, 1996). 'Behaviour' and its effective management was presented not as an isolated issue but as one aspect of the complex process of learning, much of which is easily within the control of the teacher.

Session 9

The penultimate session took the form of a seminar which enabled participants to draw on the outcomes of the task set at the end of the sixth session, when they were asked to evaluate the way in which they determined what interventions might be appropriate, how these were delivered and how effective they proved to be.

This was an invaluable session. Participants rapidly took control of the discussion which tended to focus on the relative effectiveness of their own short-term strategies for improving behaviour for learning in their classrooms. All had perceived some degree of success during their initial attempt and were committed to continuing to refine their strategies. In several cases, colleagues had forged new ideas for cooperating to meet the behavioural needs of their pupils during shared teaching sessions. This approach was subsequently extended to form small circles of teachers eager to consult and work with each other across faculties and classrooms as and when necessary. This has been one of the most exciting and productive outcomes of the course. The comparison of approaches and classroom change has been illuminating – one participant said: 'It's really enlightening to see how other people handle the kids I struggle with. I feel much better just knowing that I'm not on my own.'

Equally encouraging was the growing realisation amongst teachers that the task of managing and improving the behaviour of pupils in order to maximise learning is not the exclusive preserve of Heads of Year, psychologists or other 'specialists'. Rather, it is something that every classroom teacher can undertake in a way that suits his or her own teaching style.

Session 10

The final session addressed the parameters and logistical limitations of legislative and local influences as well as their implications for teachers. It was important that this session drew together the entire course and that in conclusion, it reinforced the many positive developments achieved over the previous nine weeks.

To this end, the final session revisited the areas covered and reviewed the learning which had taken place. Time was also spent in acknowledging and celebrating the new strategies that participants had acquired as well as clarifying how these might best be deployed in classrooms in support of policies advocated by the school, the LEA and the CoP.

Getting it right?

Essentially, what this chapter has attempted to do is describe an approach to *mentoring* – whether for ITE, NQT or more experienced colleagues. Those involved identified a need for support in their work with pupils experiencing one aspect of SEN – that of EBD. The intention from the outset was to refresh and refine staff skills in managing and reducing the daily challenges presented by pupils exhibiting difficulties.

The CPD course described above is a mechanism which after two years, has resulted in a core group of over a quarter of the school's teachers collaboratively engaging in active learning experiences aimed at enhancing the learning opportunities and experiences of its pupils through addressing the challenges posed by pupils exhibiting behavioural difficulties in the classroom. The deployment of objective behaviour surveys by classroom teachers, the growth of voluntary peer observation of shared groups and the development of classroom-based behavioural improvement initiatives has resulted in many more of the teaching establishment within the school requesting membership of future programmes on this issue. Those who have attended the programme have enjoyed further opportunities to share their developed skills with colleagues – both formally in Year and Faculty meetings and informally in staffroom discussion. This has resulted in an effective culture of 'peer mentoring'.

The political pressure that teachers have experienced over recent years has recently subsided somewhat. This has enabled the school and its staff to find time and energy to define its own agenda which has focused on addressing pupil needs. The CPD programme which has developed as a result of a partnership between the school and UWE has taken the opportunity to build upon the skills of existing staff.

The careful development of the Individual Pupil Needs Faculty responses to identified learning difficulties at Stages 3, 4 and 5 of the CoP have resulted in systematic and effective support programmes for pupils. The emergence of informal peer support amongst staff with a view to improving the quality of pupil behaviour and encouraging more effective learning in the classroom is only one aspect of the school's success.

It is important to note that the school did not set out to introduce another initiative, scheme or policy. Its priority was rather to establish an effective way to meet the CPD needs as defined by practising teachers, as a result of which developed an informal yet effective mentoring system. Whilst the SEN support staff at the school continue to provide effective support for pupils at Stages 3, 4 and 5 of the CoP, the school's ability to provide more effective support for pupils at Stages 1 and 2 has been significantly enhanced as a result of more subject specialists and tutors refining their skills in analysing, evaluating and responding to challenging behaviours presented by pupils in ways which also support the necessary evidence for successive stages of the CoP, should this prove necessary.

The process and outcomes described above are rooted in the school's strong commitment to purposeful and need-related staff development. Like most schools, Brislington has suffered from 'initiative overload' over recent years. A conscious and shared decision was arrived at to work towards a coherent system for pupil support that is appropriate for the school. The convergence of the development of support structures for pupils at Stages 3, 4 and 5 of the CoP, together with the establishment of a coherent CPD programme in supporting teachers in their work with pupil across the entire spectrum of educational need has been formative, productive and beneficial to pupils and teachers alike. As far as mentoring is concerned, 'getting it right' has involved developing the practice, from which a formal policy may emerge at a later point.

References

Canter, I. and Canter, C. (1992) *Assertive Discipline*. Santa Monica: Lee Canter and Associates.

DfEE (1994) *Code of Practice on the Identification and Assessment of Special Educational Needs*. London: DfEE.

Gordon, T. (1974) *Teacher Effectiveness Training*. New York: David McKay.

Houston, G. (1987) *The Red Book of Groups*. London: The Rochester Foundation.

MacNamara, E. and Jolly, D. (1991) *Towards Better Behaviour*. Ormskirk: TBB.

Rogers, W. (1992) 'Students who want the last word', *Support for Learning*, 7 (4).

Smith, A. (1996) *Accelerated Learning in the Classroom*. London: NEP.

Waterhouse, P. (1990) *Classroom Management*. London: NEP.

CHAPTER TWELVE

A Bermuda Triangle for Training:
The Case of Severe Learning Difficulties

Viv Hinchcliffe

Introduction

In this chapter I present a vision for the CPD of teachers with particular reference to those working in schools for children with SLD, although some of the points raised may be more generally relevant to the professional needs of teachers in other settings. 'School-driven' professional development refers to schools' increasing interest and responsibility for their own teachers' CPD, usually within their plans for school improvement. I choose to use the term 'school-driven' in preference to 'school-based' CPD because the former seems to sum up more accurately the increasing desire of schools to have accountability for the CPD of their own teachers and for the funds associated with it. The major thrust for teachers' CPD should always come from the individual: a teacher has got to *want* to refine his or her practice in order for professional development to take place. However, recent initiatives in education, particularly the new school inspection arrangements, together with the demise of HEI-based ITE in SLD, will mean that *schools* will take more responsibility for managing their teachers' CPD. Subsequent to an OFSTED inspection, schools are required to prepare action plans for school improvement, and within this the CPD of teachers is seen as a major vehicle for school improvement. Increasingly, therefore, schools will have a vested interest in pointing their staff towards good quality, 'needs-led' CPD, which has clear outcomes both for individual teachers and the whole school. It is likely that schools will be given more money direct from the TTA to achieve this.

Historically, the agenda for teachers' CPD has been set by forces outside schools: one example of such an external influence was HEI provision of CPD programmes as part of award-bearing courses. Previously, teachers have been relatively autonomous in making choices concerning such CPD courses. With many teachers attending 'twilight' (late afternoon–early evening) courses at HEIs and paying their own fees, it is understandable that schools have not felt it appropriate to place conditions on a teacher's registration for such courses, or to make demands for teachers to share what they are learning. Equally, it could be that, because many schools have traditionally not invested in their own teachers' CPD, and some even debate the relevance of some of these activities, they are likely to have low expectations about what they can achieve. Regrettably, this situation can lead to teachers' CPD becoming rather isolated from the real world of the classroom and from the needs of the school as a whole. If this happens there will obviously be wasted opportunities, and schools will find it hard to demonstrate that those who have gained specialist diplomas, degrees or other certification, have become more effective teachers in meeting the SEN of children. The point is that, in the past, schools have tended not to make it their business to find out in detail about the range and level of provision for CPD, nor about the content of courses followed by their own teachers. I think that this will change in future years, when schools will have to demonstrate clear outcomes from their teachers' CPD, both in order to secure funding for these activities and to fulfil an important aspect of OFSTED inspection criteria.

Even in the most flexible courses in HEIs, such as modular programmes or distance learning courses, teachers have had little control over the content of their programmes of study. Some quickly find that what is offered fails to address important issues in their areas of interest, at least as they see them. Even worse, with the demise of generic SLD courses offered by HEIs, many teachers may find themselves on courses which have limited application to the very specialist world of teaching and learning in schools for pupils with SLD. What are needed, therefore, are mechanisms which enable schools and teachers to have more control over the content and coherence of CPD provision, in order to meet identified needs. In a word, there is a need for more 'school-driven' CPD.

In the coming years, schools will increasingly set the agenda for the CPD of their staff, as illustrated by Fidler's chapter elsewhere in this book. If, as a result, they are given increased funds to manage the CPD of these teachers as an integral part of their plans for school improvement, they will not only become more accountable for the CPD they provide, but will look more towards resources already existing in schools (or consortia of schools) to deliver it. 'School-driven' CPD is unlikely to be effective if schools act in isolation; successful CPD comes from the partnership and vision of consortia of special schools which respond to the identified needs of their own staff. The Secretary of State, in her official response to the SENTC (1996) report, states that schools will have the 'freedom to take decisions about SEN training priorities based on an *informed* [original emphasis] assessment of their needs'. She indicates that the TTA will assess the efficacy of in-house priorities for teachers' CPD by examining links between schools' SEN policies, school development plans, teacher appraisal, inspection and 'other monitoring'. Moreover, it seems likely that the TTA will provide increased funding directly to those schools, or consortia of schools, which achieve given criteria for the successful organisation, management and delivery of school-driven CPD.

It is possible that schools will bid for TTA funding in the same way as many currently do under the GEST format, the major difference being that arrangements will be made direct with the TTA, not through the LEAs. In her response to the SENTC report, the Secretary of State additionally stated that substantial funding for teachers' professional development in SEN will continue to be available to LEAs through GEST. However, most schools realise that this money is insufficient to make any significant headway towards school improvement and, by axiom, towards meeting the professional development needs of individual teachers. Additional monies for the CPD of teachers may, in future, come directly from the TTA to those schools which fulfil given criteria.

HEIs will still play an important role in validating 'school-driven' CPD programmes. Teachers will collect credits for assessed school-based work, including individual study programmes, and these will contribute towards diplomas and Masters degrees awarded by the HEI by a process of credit-exemption. This will call for the adoption of far more flexible interpretations of 'accreditation of prior learning' (whether academic, professional or experiential) by HEIs, and there are signs that this is beginning to happen, as student numbers on traditional HEI-based CPD begin to dwindle. Consortia of schools will also 'buy in' education consultants to run short courses in specialist areas and these may be university staff with specialist knowledge of SLD, although such personnel are now few and far between. Consultants will, in addition, play a more supportive role in the classroom, which will increasingly become the focal point of teachers' CPD. It is also likely that schools will look to their own staff to act in a similar supportive role, functioning as 'critical friends', so that their expertise and experience may be shared with other teachers. These kinds of peer support systems in schools will play an important part in this aspect of CPD, a matter to which reference will be made later in this chapter.

Consortia of special schools already exist at county or regional levels in England and Wales (Norwich *et al.*, 1994). Within such arrangements, schools might pool their devolved GEST monies to organise conferences and staff development activities in response to both the individual and collective needs of participating schools. Providing pathways for their school staff to utilise these courses and private study as accredited learning towards an HEI qualification is a logical extension of this kind of strategic provision. At least one county has pooled its GEST funding, for example, in order to initiate an award bearing course for its teachers. In this, five schools for children with SLD in East Sussex developed a school-based SLD diploma course, validated by the University of Brighton (Edwards *et al.*, 1995).

The reasons why schools are likely to take a more active role in organising, managing and delivering school-driven CPD are twofold: first, central government favours school-based training; second, HEI courses in SLD are fast disappearing. In the case of the former, over the last few years, central government has actively promoted school-based training, an approach which has been particularly apparent in ITE, as contributions elsewhere in this book will testify. The notion of 'school partnership' has been introduced, encouraging schools to play a greater role in teacher education and forcing HEIs to devolve a proportion of their HEFC funding to schools. The 'licensed teacher' scheme is one illustration of central government's wish to promote school-based training. At the time of writing, schools can bid for up to £5000 per licensed teacher from the TTA. Some schools have been quick to take the opportunity (for two years) to pay their licensed teachers much less (as they are placed on the salary scale of an unqualified teacher) for doing the same job as their more traditionally qualified peers.

The second major factor which supports school-based CPD is the demise of specialist courses in HEIs. In 1988 there were twenty six institutions offering specialist courses in the education of children with SLD. In 1996 there are only seven. This situation has come about for a number of reasons. The first relates to the demise of the two-year optional SLD strand in ITE. The ACSET report (1984) led to the phasing out of the SLD option in all BEd teacher education courses by 1988. This meant that specialist tutors in HEIs had to turn their attention to CPD courses for serving teachers, an initiative which has largely failed to develop because of low student numbers, lack of government funding and the difficulties and cost faced by schools of finding supply cover for their teachers. The numbers of specialist SLD staff remaining in HEIs quickly became depleted as did the numbers of viable CPD courses. It is ironic that the ACSET report, whose contents became official government policy, confidently predicted that 'any recruits to undergraduate specialist courses in 1984 or 1985 will be leaving college at the end of the decade with a qualification of very limited market value' (ACSET, 1984, p.15). In the 1990s those involved in SLD work are more aware of the reality – that teachers with a specialist qualification in teaching children with SLD are valued like gold-dust and eagerly welcomed by heads of SLD schools throughout the country. The ACSET report seriously undermined the status of special education, and the demise of SLD courses within ITE continues to contribute to the widespread shortage of specialist teachers in schools for pupils with SLD. In 1990 a survey by thirteen leading training institutions revealed that only a third of teachers in schools for pupils with SLD had a relevant specialist qualification. Porter (1996) reports that, more recently, DfEE figures reveal that half the teachers in SLD schools have had specialist training (DfEE, 1995). My recent experiences lead me to think that such an assessment is fanciful.

The ACSET recommendation, that there should be an expansion of in-service courses in special education, never materialised. Lack of subsequent funding of any substantial nature has meant fewer opportunities for teachers to embark on specialist courses. Full-time secondments to SLD courses have become increasingly rare, even extinct: in 1989 there were ninety six teachers on full-time one-year courses; in 1994 there were only three (Porter, 1996). There was an increase in part-time study, but this began to diminish as GEST funding was reduced and, in consequence, teachers were expected to pay their own course-fees. Specialist courses began to close and teachers found twilight study and travel too demanding, coming as they did on top of a lengthy school-day complete with its post-1988 demands. HEI courses in SLD, taught by lecturers and tutors on HEI campuses, will thus become a thing of the past.

Teachers as teacher-educators

Do teachers have the expertise to be teacher-educators? This is a critical question for, if they don't, 'school-driven' CPD will be unworkable. As discussed earlier, central government clearly thinks that school teachers do have the necessary skills to function effectively as teacher-educators. But I would suggest that we cannot realistically answer this question until we are more clear about what the teaching profession expects from CPD. In relation to the education of pupils with SLD, this is an easier question for the profession to address on a local or regional level when consortia of special schools assume the main responsibility for their staffs' CPD. A head teacher of an SLD school may have both a general and a specific picture of the CPD needs of his/her school. On a general level, the school development plan may point to a number of staff training needs which can be addressed 'in house'. For example, an audit of the school's curriculum planning may reveal some weaknesses within the school in relation to assessment, recording and reporting (ARR). The school's own coordinator for ARR may address this by leading some INSET related to this, using examples of good practice currently within the school. Other consortia schools may contribute to this activity. On a more specific level, in response to the changing school context, the school's appraisal system may have highlighted an individual's need for professional development which can only be addressed outside school, for example by a teacher attending a course dealing with bereavement counselling. A school's OFSTED Action Plan may also indicate a number of general and specific needs. 'School-driven' CPD, with the appropriate financial backing, allows schools to meet these identified needs by either using existing resources inside schools (or consortia of schools) or by finding appropriate provision elsewhere.

The essential feature of successful 'school-driven' focused INSET activity is that such events need to be short, practical and relevant, with clear pointers for further enquiry and independent study (the 'theory to practice' link, as it has become known). Such INSET also needs to be flexible in terms of responding to an unpredictable or an urgent need. For example, a family with a child with Cornelia de Lange Syndrome may move into a special school's catchment area and the child may be admitted at very short notice. It is widely accepted that children with this rare syndrome have a predisposition to engage in severe self-injurious behaviour and the school may need to respond by providing its staff with training on this aspect of challenging behaviour. In this example, the school development plan would not reflect this need in terms of finance and resource considerations, so flexibility and adequate funding is crucial.

As stated earlier, a school's CPD needs will vary according to its complement of staff at any one time. However, there are some important matters relating to the CPD of teachers, including some specific to those working with pupils with SLD, which need to be considered. It should firstly be acknowledged that CPD never stops. Teachers continually need to investigate and reflect upon their practice in order to 'refine, alter or improve it' (Fish *et al.*,

1991). It seems misguided to think that at the end of any period of training (for example, an ITE course) individuals suddenly become 'trained' teachers. Any form of teacher education should be regarded as a learning process which continues throughout a person's professional life – an initiation process to a life-time process of acquiring knowledge about children, and about improving approaches to teaching and learning.

Secondly, professional knowledge in the field of teaching pupils with SLD is still in its infancy: state SLD schools have only been in existence for twenty five years. Teachers involvement in 'action research', or what Robson (1993) calls 'real world enquiry', is a necessary forerunner to curriculum development and will always be an important part of teachers' CPD.

Recognition needs also to be given to the fact that there are no all-embracing formulas for successful teaching. Individual differences amongst SLD children are vast and daily teaching of such pupils demonstrates the complexity of their learning difficulties.

It should be acknowledged, fourthly, that working with pupils with SLD is often unpredictable. Teachers are continually coping with the unexpected, thinking on their feet, improvising and reading the situation – what Schön (1983) calls 'reflection in action'. A teacher may be clear about where she is going, but she often has to change direction in order to get there. Schön writes about the problems of 'real-world practice', stating that problems do not present themselves to practitioners as 'well-formed structures' and tend not to present themselves as problems at all but as 'messy, indeterminate situations'. Nowhere is recognition of this fact more important than in SLD teaching.

Fifthly, a crisis of confidence in 'professional knowledge', as Schön calls it, leads him to regard teaching as a practical art. Schön's 'professional artistry' model stresses understanding and improvisation (in preference to technical skills), where teachers view knowledge as 'temporary, dynamic and problematic rather than absolute and permanent' (Fish *et al.*, 1991). As part of this process of reflection there must be a commitment on the part of teachers to acknowledge and investigate their own private assumptions, values and ideologies. Teachers' beliefs, theories and attitudes about fundamental issues in special education such as 'equal opportunities', 'age-appropriateness', 'a right to life', 'normalisation' and so on have a profound effect upon their day-to-day classroom practice. School-driven CPD can provide a context in which teachers can begin to open up their 'personal theories' – their own private, individual construct of how and why things are as they are (Fish, *op. cit.*), and possibly revise them in the light of new evidence.

School-driven CPD which addresses teachers' 'personal theory' seems far removed from a competency model of teacher *training*. The competencies required by teachers of pupils with severe learning difficulties as perceived by SENTC are more aligned with what Schön calls the 'technical-rational' model of professional practice. In this paradigm, Schon states that practitioners are expected to 'solve well-formed instrumental problems by applying theory and technique derived from systematic, preferably scientific knowledge'. Robson

Part One (30 minutes)
Please work with a partner on this short activity. Please read through all of this sheet together. One of you is going to do most of the talking; the other will do most of the listening (and a little note-taking). Decide on who will do what.

- The talkers are going to describe a brief classroom event/ incident in which you were involved and which is memorable in some way. Things may have turned out rather differently than expected, or you may have been puzzled about something, things might have gone very wrong, or very right.

- The listeners should listen carefully and take a few notes.

- Both talkers and listeners are now going to refer to different sheets for further instructions.

Talkers' Sheet
- For the next 15 minutes, talk to your partner about this event using the guidelines 1–3 below. Spend about 5 minutes on each. The listener knows that you will be talking about the incident in three different ways. Please make it clear to the listener when you move from 1) to 2) to 3).

1) Please give an objective, factual account of the event/ incident to your partner, i.e., 'replay' the sequence of events as it happened. Be factual, don't provide any opinions, interpretation, etc.

2) Now, pick out the 'critical incidents', or key moments of the event. This time, I want you to express your opinions, interpretation and feelings. Explain to your partner a) what you think was happening, e.g., why you think children / adults behaved in the way that they did; b) why you acted in the way you did; and c) how you felt both during and after the event.

3) Finally, talk about how these events/ actions might have appeared from the child's perspective. Why did the child

Figure 12.1   *An 'in-house' introductory session on peer support*

act in the way he or she did? What were the child's intentions and how do you think the child was feeling?

Listeners' sheet

● Please listen carefully to how your partner describes the event. Divide your sheet into three sections (horizontally). Your partner has been asked to relate the episode to you in three different ways and she should tell you when she is switching from one to the next. In the relevant three sections, please write down some notes when the speaker:

1) makes an assumption (warranted or unwarranted) about why a person (child or adult) acts in the way he/she does;

2) says something about people's feelings, or states of mind;

3) seems to be uncertain about something, and when he or she seems to be very confident about something.

Part Two (30 minutes)

● In this part, the 'listeners' must now get more involved. Both of you can read this sheet. Please discuss the following:

1) 'Listeners', what was different about the three ways in which the 'talkers' spoke to you about the event?
2) 'Talkers', what made you choose the event/ incident that you did?
3) 'Listeners', did the way in which the 'talkers' described the event (including the words that he/she used) tell you anything about what he or she considers to be important?
4) 'Talkers', if your beliefs and values affect your actions, in the event you described, what do your actions tell you about your beliefs?
5) 'Listeners', from what the talkers said, and perhaps from the way in which things were said, were you able to identify any of the talkers' beliefs, values, assumptions or theories? If so, what may they have been?
6) 'Talkers', be honest, how did you feel when you were talking to your partner about this event? 'Listeners', how did you feel?
7) Is there any value in doing this type of exercise?

(1993) states that there should be flexibility in the use of specialised techniques, and a 'percolation of their use into the general approach to teaching, amounting in some cases to a change in attitude about the nature of the task'. The SLD competencies included in the 1996 report all need to be addressed by CPD. However, just as important (and arguably more difficult to provide) are the essential support systems for teachers, who on a daily basis are dealing with the stress and unpredictability of teaching children with SLD and PMLD. The 'messy, indeterminate situations' alluded to earlier, in which teachers need to 'think on their feet', frequently lead to decisions and actions which are tentative, uncertain and unsatisfactory. In segregated special education, more than in any other school context, teaching can become a very insular and isolate activity. Special schools typically have poor systems of support and offer few opportunities for teachers to share their experiences. Sharing problematic experiences with a 'critical friend' is a way of opening up private assumptions and practices and there is great security in finding out about how a colleague would have acted in a similar situation. Figure 12.1 shows a CPD exercise which I have used in my own school to introduce the notion of 'personal theory' and sharing problematic classroom experience, and is an example of an approach which should be integral to CPD activity in SLD.

Conclusion

Returning to the question raised earlier about whether teachers have the expertise to be teacher educators, I would suggest that many do, and consortia of schools would do well to look to the skills and abilities of their own staff for developing teachers' professional practice. A 'school-driven' model of CPD offers schools the freedom to use resources already existing inside schools, including the pupils themselves. Some of the best curriculum-based CPD I have seen has been school-based, examining video-recording of lessons, where teachers evaluate the quality of teaching and learning, the pupils' perspectives, and so on. 'School-driven' CPD can give higher status to peer support systems, involving mentors or 'coaches', the latter being a term used by Schön (*op. cit.*) which suggests a less 'superior' role than that of mentor.

Historically, HEIs have been the most influential provider of CPD for teachers working with children with SLD. The demise of specialist university courses in this field will inevitably mean that schools, or consortia of schools, will assume greater responsibility for the planning and management of their own teachers' professional development needs. But the greatest impetus behind the 'school-driven' model is the increasing accountability which an individual school has for the CPD of its teachers, which is linked, as indicated throughout this chapter, to its plans for school improvement. If the TTA does delegate increased training funds directly to schools, this funding will be proportional to how efficiently and effectively the TTA perceives schools to be managing 'needs-led' CPD issues. To attract funding, schools will need to show clear links between their priorities for teachers' CPD and their school development plan. They will also need to demonstrate outputs and value for money from in-service training and these will be measured by the TTA against performance indicators like appraisal and inspection. Whether special schools, after several years of inertia concerning professional development for SLD teachers, can respond to these challenges remains to be seen.

References

ACSET (Advisory Committee on the Supply and Education of Teachers) (1984) *Teacher Training and Special Educational Needs*. London: HMSO.

DfEE (1995) 'Survey of LEAs' use of GEST Grant 12 (Training for Special Educational Needs) in 1994–5', unpublished.

Edwards, C., Hassell, J. and Yearly, S. (1995) 'The diploma in applied professional studies SEN (Severe Learning Difficulties)', *The SLD Experience*, **13**, 11.

Fish, D., Twinn, S. and Purr, B. (1991) *Promoting Reflection: improving the supervision of practice in health visiting and Initial Teacher Training*. Twickenham: West London Institute Press.

Norwich, B., Evans, J., Lunt, I., Steedman, J. and Wedell, K. (1994) 'Clusters: inter-school collaboration in meeting special educational needs in ordinary schools', *British Educational Research Journal*, **20** (3), 261–278.

Porter, J. (1996) 'Issues in teacher training', in B. Carpenter, R. Ashdown and K. Bovair (eds.) *Enabling Access*. London: David Fulton.

Robson, C. (1993) *Real World Research*. Oxford: Blackwell.

Schön, D. (1983) *The Reflective Practitioner*. New York: Basic Books.

SENTC (1996) *Professional Development to Meet Special Educational Needs: Report to the DfEE*. Stafford: SENTC.

CHAPTER THIRTEEN

Subject-based Study and Professional Development in Special Needs: The Appliance of Sciences

Juliet Edmonds

'For today's science lesson I want you to turn to page 12 and to copy the labelled diagram of the flower and to write a paragraph about the conditions needed for growth.'

The children faithfully started to carry out the teacher's instructions. It was painful watching some children struggle with unfamiliar language, writing without a purpose or audience. In talking to the teacher I discovered that she had little science education herself and that she believed the National Curriculum for Science was a 'flash in the pan'. She expressed the view that science was not important for children with SEN who just needed lots of writing practice.

Seven years on, the Science National Curriculum is still with us and the teacher has long since retired. The National Curriculum Evaluation Study reports that teachers of children with SEN feel that science, especially practical science, has an important part to play in the development of all children. The study, which looked at both special and mainstream schools, found that 80% of the teachers in Key Stage 2 classrooms also reported they had children with SEN in their classes (CRIPSAT, 1994). Therefore, the challenge of providing relevant, accessible and differentiated science for children exists for the majority of teachers in the primary phase. As in the case of the teacher above, the majority have little background knowledge in science. This lack of scientific knowledge affects their choice of teaching strategies and confidence in teaching science, whereas a better understanding of the subject matter would enable them to differentiate the work and provide access for children with SEN.

In this chapter I shall argue for the importance of a thorough subject knowledge for teachers with an emphasis on understanding the links between concepts and scientific domains. I believe that this knowledge is essential for teachers working with children with SEN, as only through a clear subject understanding can teachers be aware of children's progression in conceptual development and make the links between topics explicit for children. I shall also suggest those features and areas of content in CPD which I believe could go some way to helping teachers improve their subject knowledge and subject application.

The case for subject knowledge

OFSTED has identified a lack of teachers' subject knowledge as a problem in the primary phase for a number of years (HMI 1988; 1991). Kruger *et al.* (1990) supported these findings. In talking to teachers about their understanding of science concepts, Kruger *et al.* found many 'alternative frameworks', models and explanations that the teachers used to explain their physical world that did not necessarily resemble the currently held scientific models and explanations. This pattern repeated itself across the science domains. The researchers were concerned that these ideas were possibly being passed on to the next generation.

The work of the Leverhulme project looked at ITE students' attitudes towards science, as well as subject knowledge at the beginning of their initial ITE courses and at the end of their course (Carre, 1993). They were alarmed to find a very small increase in the test scores for subject knowledge in science at the end of the course, indicating little growth in understanding. They found little change in the students' attitudes to science, but a small change in their preferred teaching model towards a 'practical problem solving approach based on a constructivist view of learning' (Carre, 1993, p.34).

In recognising that there is a problem with the level of subject knowledge and understanding in primary phase teachers and ITE students, it is important to analyse whether subject knowledge is a significant factor in teaching science and development of children with SEN in mainstream and special schools.

Effective subject teaching

The debate on what makes an effective teacher in a particular subject has existed since the beginning of teaching. The DfE's list of competencies to be demonstrated before achieving QTS is a long list of skills and subject understanding all of which a student could achieve without being a good teacher (DfE, 1993).

Ellis (1995) brought together some of the thinking on the knowledge, skills and attitudes needed for effective subject teaching at primary level, drawing on the work of authors such as Shulman. He synthesised their work to present a model in which he identified the following subject specific elements:

- *Content knowledge* which consists of substantive knowledge, syntactic knowledge, beliefs about the status and role of the subject in society, controversial issues around the subject as well as the features that make the subject distinctive from other subjects.

- *Pedagogical content knowledge*, which consists of the skills and the knowledge that allow teachers to adapt the subject knowledge into an accessible form for the audience.

Within content knowledge he defines substantive knowledge as not only the facts and concepts, but also the organisational framework of the subject; Syntactic knowledge, he argues is knowledge of the process in a subject area, that which makes its process of validating knowledge scientific.

This provides a useful model of the elements of subject study that need to be addressed to develop effective subject teachers. This model can also be used to identify these elements of a professional development course in primary science.

Primary science courses often address the facts and concepts of subject knowledge without making the organisational framework of the subject explicit. The National Curriculum document for science fails to identify which are the main scientific themes and which are the resulting peripheral ideas in its layout (DfE, 1995). I believe this leaves the teacher with a piecemeal, compartmentalised view of science subject knowledge with pockets of topic knowledge such as 'forces' or 'ourselves'. There is consequently little understanding of some cross-topic and sometimes cross-domain themes which share similar conceptual models. This compartmentalised kind of knowledge may also cause problems when children ask questions in an attempt to organise their own understanding and receive 'woolly' answers based on the teacher's partial understanding of interlinking concepts

Subject application

Teachers' lack of subject knowledge can have an effect on the types and range of teaching strategy they draw upon to teach a subject. In a study of exemplary practice in primary science education, Tobin and Fraser (1990) found that when otherwise good teachers taught in areas where their subject knowledge was shaky there was evidence that they were unable to focus the children's thinking or give appropriate feedback and avoided discussions on the science content. Confirming this, Lee (1995) noted that teachers who had a lack of subject knowledge in science relied on didactic, textbook work with the emphasis on factual information. Such an approach does not seem far removed from the example of the teacher at the beginning of this chapter.

The relationship between a teacher's subject knowledge and the strategies used to teach that knowledge seems to be close. If this pattern holds true, it has implications for the type of science being taught to children by teachers with little background knowledge. The use of didactic teaching methods, possibly relying on textbooks, can only further disadvantage those children with SEN who have problems with language. A limited range of teaching methods will deny access to the science curriculum to many and can portray science as a body of facts rather than a way of working.

Attitudes to science for children with special educational needs

Ellis (1995) identified teachers' attitudes to a subject and their views of its relevance to the children as being an important element of the effectiveness of subject teachers. Teachers in the Primary phase reported that although they agreed with the principle of access for all children to the 1990 National Curriculum for Science, the curriculum demands at Key Stages 2 and 3 made the provision of differentiated work for children of differing abilities difficult. They felt there were huge conceptual and procedural jumps between the key stage levels which did not help the planning of small curricular steps to address the learning needs of some children. Other teachers reported a 'conflict between coverage and the quality of learning' (CRIPSAT, 1994, p.18). The teachers felt a need to revisit areas of the curriculum for reinforcement, but then worried that there might not be enough time to cover the next topic in enough detail.

The 1995 National Curriculum's reduced content and 'best fit' level descriptions will hopefully go some way to addressing some of these concerns although the problem of a curriculum for those working towards Level One still exists in the 1995 science document.

Opportunities for professional development in primary science

As a result of LMS, LEAs have passed over the majority of the CPD budget to schools. LEAs, which in my area of London tend to serve a small number of schools as a result of the demise of the Inner London Education Authority, try to provide CPD through a 'buy-back' package. (Schools pay a set amount each year for the LEA courses.) The buy back packages tend to contain generic courses, for example, one middle management course, one headship course and perhaps a course addressing a local or national concern like 'Handling Bullying'. This leaves no provision for more specialist courses for SEN in primary science. One teacher I talked to found that LEA courses in SEN tended to lump teachers from mainstream schools with teachers from special schools an approach which she felt did not address the specific needs of either group of teachers.

Another option open to teachers are the GEST twenty-day, ten-day and seven-day primary science courses. Areas of study for these courses have been prescribed by the DfE to cover topics where teachers have a lack of understanding, such as 'forces' and 'electricity'. Many of these course are modularised and accredited by local HEIs and can lead to further study and qualifications.These GEST courses are of a length that allow teachers to get to grips with the subject matter as well as learn some strategies for subject application.

I talked to two teachers, Laura and Keri, concerning the extent to which GEST courses had prepared them for teaching children with SEN within the classroom. Both teachers had taken part in ten-day primary science courses based at universities in the London area. Although both were science coordinators they had little experience of studying science beyond GCSE biology. Laura worked in a special school and Keri in a primary school with a high proportion of children with SEN. Both teachers felt that LEA courses on science and/or SEN had done little to address their needs in providing differentiated science work for the children in their care.

The teachers highlighted the importance of the focus on subject knowledge within the course. Keri felt this gave her confidence in teaching science within the classroom as well as in helping her colleagues. Laura stated the importance of a deeper subject knowledge for planning progression for the children. She discussed the way that a clear subject knowledge understanding had given her a clear overview of topics within the science curriculum and helped her to understand the child's level of conceptual understanding and to identify concepts they needed to tackle next. She had been able to create a scheme of work for her school that planned for continuity and progression in the children's learning as a result. She felt it had also enabled her to identify a science programme of study for the children who were working below the level prescribed by the science curriculum.

Keri indicated that she would have liked some of the subject knowledge sessions blocked together. This was a view supported by Laura, who said that it took five sessions for the structure and framework of the science curriculum to actually fall into place for her. She felt it would have been easier to have made links between domains and concepts if the course had been blocked into a five-day unit to look at science subject knowledge.

However, both teachers felt that they now had a better understanding of investigative work in science. In understanding its components they were able to differentiate investigative work for children by altering the planning demands, the type of measuring equipment, the context and conceptual burden. Keri found it useful to consider the range of vocabulary and terms to use with children of different ages within each subject domain. Laura, meanwhile, had used a constructivist approach to science conceptual understanding since she had studied it on the course. She found this was an approach that was exceptionally useful with all children. She had used the SPACE research (1990), and the Nuffield scheme (1993) which draws on it, to help her identify children's ideas about conceptual areas. She used these to plan experiences to help the children challenge their ideas. The two teachers also stated that they had extended their range of teaching strategies within science and had gained in confidence.

Both teachers identified subject knowledge as the single most vital feature of the courses which had helped them address the needs of more children in their classrooms. Subject application was mentioned with reference to particular understandings of process and teaching strategies which provide greater access to children with SEN.

The main challenges in the professional development of teachers of science for children with SEN are:

1. to build in structures and content which help teachers understand the organisation as well as framework and content of science;
2. to develop a greater understanding of processes in science to enable teachers to differentiate activities to meet the needs of all children;
3. to develop teaching strategies that start from the child;
4. to understand and share clear learning goals and encourage children to evaluate their achievements against these goals so that they can define their own future needs.

Tools for developing subject knowledge for teachers of children with special educational needs

Ritchie (1996) has stated that 'Those with SEN often exhibit a more irregular profile of concepts that may never link up. The challenge for the "constructivist" teacher is to support the learner as he or she builds up a cognitive map of "scientific" ideas that get progressively closer to the accepted scientific ideas' (Ritchie, 1996). It would seem logical that the first step in helping children make links *between* concepts is to ensure that teachers have a clear cognitive map of the relationship between the various concepts within science and an understanding of what the key concepts are and which concepts result from the key ideas in the National Curriculum for Science document. Courses which are organised along the lines of topics in the National Curriculum for Science Programmes of Study, should be explicit about the links between different areas like 'light' and 'sound', or the links between energy systems in machines as well as within plants and animals (DfE,1995). Teachers also need to be aware of the overall organisational framework of science and its relationship to other subject areas such as geography, in particular meteorology. CPD facilitators could model concept mapping as a strategy for helping children to make links and to build understandings between domains, as well as helping teachers to do the same.

In my conversation with Laura, she had suggested that subject knowledge sessions could be blocked together over a few days, making it easier to identify and reinforce the conceptual links. This would also give participants a sustained period of study without the continual adjustment back to the 'hurley-burley' of the classroom on a one day a week course.

An alternative strategy for helping teachers develop their subject knowledge could be intermittent blocks of sessions spread across the year, with specific subject-led tasks to be completed in the classroom with the children. This model would certainly support Joyce and Showers' (1982) work on the effective methods of changing practice in the classroom which suggests that teachers need to practice new skills within their real work setting (ideally with in-class instruction) and support to effect change in practice and attitudes. This approach is also supported by research which suggests the process of teaching a subject area actually helps to reinforce and clarify understanding for the teacher taking the class. Thus, Smith and Neale (1989) found that teachers' understanding of the concepts within a topic area improved after they researched, planned and taught the subject to their classes. The approach of setting teachers a teaching task to carry out with their class in a particular conceptual area could prove to be a useful tool in developing their understanding.Teaching strategies and problems encountered could be shared by the group when they meet afterwards.

An analysis of children's progress in scientific conceptual understanding could be a useful activity for those having to plan for children with SEN. I believe that this is particularly useful as there is a common belief that the development of conceptual understanding is a linear process, with a logical line of increasingly complex ideas that a child must travel along (Duerden *et al.*, 1992). Such an interpretation flies in the face of the National Curriculum for Science Evaluation which reported the view of teachers of children with SEN that 'Most felt that pupils' learning did not follow any generalised pattern' (CRIPSAT, 1994).

Investigations for children with special needs

Practical work in science is cited by many teachers as being important for children with SEN. The hands-on element provides work that is often stimulating and motivational. It provides opportunities for spoken language development and its lack of emphasis on written language allows certain children a greater chance of success within the subject. Interestingly, both Keri and Laura identified a clearer understanding of the nature of investigative, illustrative, observational and basic skill work as a result of their ten-day courses.

The understanding of investigative and illustrative work as whole processes is important. After seven years of a National Curriculum for Science, many teachers I talk with are still unaware that a difference existed between these two forms of experimental work. It is an understanding of the constituent parts of these processes which seems to give teachers the key to be able to differentiate work and to build on the skills and understanding of children. An understanding of the effect of context on children's achievements, the number and nature of variables, if any, the type and units of measurement, the methods of recording and communicating as well as the conceptual burden of the activity is vital. Teachers with this understanding of the constituent parts were able to plan investigative work that was partially open-ended, with perhaps a prescribed number and nature of variables but with the child identifying the method of recording and communicating. Purists might argue this would not be an investigation if the variables were already prescribed, but I feel that if we are to let children experience the whole process of experimental science as well as help them to develop certain skills within that process, investigation and illustration can only be seen as different ends of a continuum.

Subject application for children with special needs

Alongside the challenge of developing teachers' subject knowledge in science, subject application is a second important area. A variety of teaching strategies can be used to help children with SEN.

Professional development courses often suggest a range of activities for teachers to draw on to deliver topics in the National Curriculum, but give little emphasis to the skills necessary to mediate the subject knowledge the teacher possesses to ensure access for all children across the primary phase. A course that models strategies for mediating subject knowledge, as well as looking at the advantages and disadvantages of the use of analogies to aid children's understanding, could be helpful for teachers with children having problems understanding concepts. Wragg (1993) recognises the importance of explanation, but on ITE course and CPD courses this can often be assumed to be an inherent skill that teachers possess.

The skills involved in sharing our teaching goals and in encouraging children to evaluate their own performance against these goals is a vital area to develop in all primary teachers, but especially for those teaching children with SEN.

In our own research at Brunel University (Edmonds *et al.*, 1997) we questioned children in a Year 6 class about what was involved in science and what they felt they were trying to achieve. Our early analysis indicates that not one child demonstrated a full understanding of the structure of the various science domains and, unsurprisingly, identified a list of science topics with little indication of any relationship between them. The children also stated that to be 'good' at primary science you need to know a lot of facts and be good at drawing graphs. It seems that, as teachers, we are failing to communicate our curriculum intentions or making explicit the links between various topic areas for children.

Richardson (1993) argues that, if children with SEN learn more slowly than others, they need to be much more autonomous. They also need to be aware of their own learning strategies, which they can draw upon to aid them when the help of a teacher is not at hand. In sharing our learning goals and helping children to evaluate their own learning through self-evaluation and meta-cognition, we can give them some of the tools to help themselves. Helping teachers to communicate their intentions and discussing strategies to help children evaluate their learning in science would in consequence be a positive feature of any professional development course.

Conclusion

Much of what has been discussed here in relation to the development of teachers in science for children with SEN in the primary phase is representative of good practice for educating all teachers. A simple analogy illustrates the thrust of my argument in this chapter. In wind surfing, you use the same techniques to sail in strong winds as you do in gentler winds. But, in strong winds, your technique has to be more practised and precise or you end up in the water. In the same way, teachers of children with SEN need to have an even clearer understanding of subject knowledge in science, as well as access to a range of effective teaching strategies and the confidence to use them, if they are to address the needs of *all* children in the primary phase.

Since the introduction of the National Curriculum for Science there has been much thought, design and redesign of courses to help teachers meet the needs of the children in their care. The debate must continue if we are to prepare more effective teachers of science who are able to address the educational needs of those children who have learning difficulties in our schools.

References

Carre, C. (1993) 'Performance in subject matter knowledge in science' in N. Bennett, and C. Carre, (eds.) *Learning to Teach.* London: Routledge.

CRIPSAT (1994) *Evaluation of the Implementation of Science in the National Curriculum at Key Stages 1, 2, and 3, Volume 3: Differentiation.* London: SCAA.

Department for Education (1993) *The Initial Training of Primary School Teachers: new criteria for courses* (Circular 14/93). London: DfE.

Department for Education (1995) *National Curriculum for Science.* London: HMSO.

Duerden, B., Fortune, D. and Johnson, M. (1992) 'Access and progress in science', *British Journal of Special Education,* **19** (2), 59–62.

Edmonds, J., Emery, A. and Summerfield, J. (1997) *Self-assessment in Primary Science Project.* Twickenham: Brunel University.

Ellis, B. (1995) 'Rethinking the nature of subject studies in primary initial teacher education', *British Journal of Educational Studies,* XXXXIII (2), 146–161.

HMI (1988) *The New Teacher in School.* HMSO: London.

HMI (1991) *The Professional Training of Primary School Teachers.* HMSO: London.

Joyce, B. and Showers, B. (1982) 'Improving in service training: the messages of research', *Educational Leadership,* **37** (5), 379–385.

Kruger, C., Summers, M. and Palacio, D. (1990) 'INSET for primary science in the National Curriculum in England and Wales: are the real needs of teachers perceived?', *Journal of Education in Teaching,* **16** (2), 133–146.

Lee, O. (1995) 'Subject matter knowledge, classroom management, and instructional practices in middle school science classrooms', *Journal of Research in Science Teaching,* **32** (4), 423–440.

Nuffield-Chelsea (1993) *Nuffield Primary Science: teachers' guides.* London: Collins Educational.

Richardson, H. (1993) 'Opening up access to science', *British Journal of Special*

Education, **20** (3), 95–96.

Ritchie, R. (1996) 'Science' in B. Carpenter, R. Ashdown, and Bovair K. *Enabling Access*. London: David Fulton.

Smith, D. and Neale, D. (1989) 'The construction of subject matter knowledge in primary science teaching', *Teaching and Teacher Education*, **3** (1), 1–20.

SPACE Reports (1990–1994) Liverpool: Liverpool University Press.

Tobin, K. and Fraser, B. (1990) 'What does it mean to be an exemplary science teacher?', *Journal of Research in Science Teaching*, **27** (1), 3–25.

Wragg, E. (1993) *Primary Teaching Skills*. London: Routledge.

CHAPTER FOURTEEN

Dramatic Liaisons: Collaboration between Special and Mainstream Schools

Jane Tarr

Introduction

This chapter is an account of a school-focused, action research model of CPD initiated by the Faculty of Education at the University of the West of England, Bristol. It involved teachers and pupils from special and mainstream schools working together with ITE students and a theatre company on a performing arts project. The project aimed to:

- encourage schools in the process of inter-school liaison;
- develop teachers' professional skills, particularly in the area of SEN;
- extend teachers' specific curriculum expertise;
- increase participation of parents and governors in school activities.

This project attempted to bring pupils and teachers from mainstream and special schools together to work in the performing arts. Mainstream and special schools were paired at the outset, and the process was stimulated through the participation of a local theatre company who started off the project in each of the paired schools. Student teachers were placed in the schools on a weekly basis.

The project took place during the spring term over a period of three years. Groups of pupils and their teachers from mainstream and special schools worked together each week, participating in drama, music, dance and costume design activities. This project culminated in a grand performance when nine pairs of schools came to the University to perform the prepared piece of music-theatre. This provided pupils with an opportunity to demonstrate their work to their parents and the general public. Press coverage in the local paper gave the event an enhanced significance for all those concerned.

The visit of the theatre group to the schools was a positive aspect of the project and pupils enjoyed working with adults outside the normal schooling context. Throughout the performing arts sessions pupils were encouraged to develop a broad range of communication strategies: speech, mime, gesture, facial expression, physical interaction and visual communication. The sessions alternated between schools so that teachers and pupils became familiar with different school settings and educational regimes.

Teachers were supported through a CPD course organised at the university. This was designed to aid the process of liaison, provide participants with opportunities to reflect upon the work and to consider the wider benefits and implications of working in partnership. The concept of reflective practice for professional development can address both personal and institutional perspectives, as Elliott (1990) writes: 'Reflexive practice necessarily implies both self-critique and institutional critique. One cannot have one without the other' (p.23).

At the end of the project participants were encouraged to write a reflective account of their experiences which could then be submitted for credit within the university's Modular Programme for CPD. ITE students took a leading part in the practical sessions in schools, since the performing arts were closely linked to their university-based course. The fact that this was partly undertaken in special school settings enriched and extended their programme of study.

Whilst the project described in this chapter focused upon the performing arts, a similar initiative took place in science education and it is quite feasible for this form of collaborative intervention to take place within any curriculum area.

For mainstream teachers and schools, this process also held many potential advantages. The Code of Practice (DfEE, 1994) requires schools to provide explicit information on:

- the school's arrangements for SEN inservice training;
- use made of teachers and facilities from outside the school, including support services;
- arrangements for partnership with parents;
- links with other mainstream schools and special schools, including arrangements when pupils change schools or leave school (p.8).

The project fulfilled a number of these requirements. It provided participating mainstream schools with an opportunity to build relationships with special schools. It enabled teachers to deepen their understanding of pupils with SEN through close and sustained involvement through the expressive arts. It highlighted the importance of collaboration with a wide range of outside agencies (in this case the local theatre company). And the final performance at the end of the project helped to extend relationships between the schools and parents.

By initiating and supporting the project, the university benefited by extending its partnership arrangements with the schools involved. Schools were able to directly experience the university as an active agent in the education of pupils – as well as ITE students. On a more pragmatic level, teachers from a number of schools registered for a higher degree at the university. Finally, but significantly, ITE students experienced a valuable and stimulating school placement.

The project

Identification of schools and teachers who would participate in the project took place during the autumn term and headteachers were initially approached to secure their commitment. Relationships between several of the schools were already well established. For others this was their first experience of formal collaboration with another school. Some special schools chose to work with primary-age pupils. Others preferred to take the opportunity to develop closer working relationships with a local comprehensive school.

The identification of project coordinators in mainstream schools tended to be more problematic, however, and took some time to resolve. Teachers involved in inter-school collaborative activities should ideally possess specific professional qualities (Jowett, 1988). There is a view that teachers 'need good organisational and interpersonal skills and should have the ability to work flexibly and establish rapport with colleagues in different work settings' (Jowett, *op. cit.*).

Most schools identified a teacher who had a particular interest in the performing arts. In secondary schools this was often the head of drama or music. In others it was a teacher who had responsibility for pupils with SEN or for external liaisons. The broad variety of teachers' roles and their expertise were highly beneficial to the programme. Both enhanced the quality of professional development they experienced and provided them with an extended network of contacts.

Care was taken to stress the importance of whole-school involvement at an early stage. Where several teachers in a school were involved in the project the whole school tended to support the work. In many of the special schools, classroom assistants, together with parents and governors, were encouraged to become actively involved. The active involvement of members of senior management teams was a further contributory factor to success.

The university-based element of the programme started with a meeting at the end of the autumn term, when the organisational issues were outlined and discussed. Teachers agreed the workshop dates and it was also agreed that the first meeting for the pupils would coincide with a visit by the theatre company. Subsequent sessions were to be led by teachers from each of the participating schools – thereby recognising the importance of school-based CPD.

The structure of the university-based course allowed participants the opportunity to reflect upon existing and past practice and to consider implications for future developments. The course was designed to help develop professional liaison between teachers and pupils. This aim informed the input provided at the university. It was also acknowledged that participants could learn much from each other and all of the teachers involved were encouraged to share their experiences, skills and understandings. One way in which this was accomplished was the maintenance of a journal throughout the duration of the project. This journal formed the basis of the written assignment which could later be submitted for assessment as part of a higher degree or diploma.

The theatre company *Actiontrack* works with pupils and teachers in schools to devise music-theatre performances. Member of the company were introduced to teachers from the participating schools during the first session. They use improvisation techniques in drama and music through group games to stimulate pupils' ideas. The guiding principle of their work is the creation of a strong feeling of unity between participants by activities such as 'circle games' and shared group activities. *Actiontrack* led a practical session with the teachers during which a title for the performance was arrived at. This was a very simple theme, such as 'Home and Away' or 'Together Again'. Each pair of schools decided on an aspect of the title which they would later develop. For example, in 'Home and Away', schools took topics such as domestic appliances, pen-friends, returning from a wonderful holiday to discover a burglary, and time travel. After the practical session *Actiontrack* discussed with the teachers ways in which they might subsequently develop the idea in their schools and helped to plan the initial session.

Teachers and pupils then worked on their topics for the remainder of the term, each school producing a short sketch and a song. *Actiontrack* visited each pair of schools towards the end of the term, at which time they taught the pupils a song which helped to link the work together.

The university-based course took place alongside the practical work in school and enabled teachers to explore the challenges and successes of their work. A variety of different models of teaching and learning were examined and the benefits for collaborative ventures considered. Wood (1988) outlines the work of Vygotsky when he writes:

> I believe the development of certain ways of reasoning and learning about things is a direct product of both spontaneous and contrived social interactions between the developing child and more mature members of his community. (p.15)

Vygotsky (1934) proposed that *developmental* processes in children do not align directly with *learning* processes but rather lag behind, the result being what he called the 'zone of proximal development'. In consequence he suggested that it would be far more useful and accurate to investigate the abilities of children under adult supervision, or in collaboration with more capable peers, to ascertain their potential development. This was particularly pertinent when teacher discussed the achievements of pupils at different levels engaged in the project described here. The recording of pupils' achievements became an important aspect of the reflective journal and informed teachers' processes of assessment.

Working in small groups was a vital element of the practical work in the schools and managing this way of learning was a frequent topic for discussion amongst the participating teachers. For example, the communicative abilities/aptitudes of the pupils had to be ascertained and decisions made about who could best work with whom. The result of these discussions was that the composition of groups varied throughout the project to enable pupils to explore a range of communication strategies. Many schools used the groupwork activities as an opportunity to involve parents and governors alongside teachers, students and classroom assistants, to support children's learning. The principle of varying group membership enabled every pupil and adult to inter-relate in the process and added an important dimension to the exercise.

Team teaching was another aspect which stimulated considerable thought and discussion amongst the teachers involved in the project. Within each school pairing, there were teachers who felt confident about working collaboratively in certain situations, but less so in others. They were encouraged to identify their own strengths and their weaknesses and through shared planning, were able to negotiate aspects of the work which they felt most comfortable with. The organisation and planning of team/paired teaching situations was seen to be crucial to the success of the work, and the parallels with much SEN work in schools can immediately be noted.

The location and the environment for the practical sessions was considered in terms of its accessibility and its suitability for the nature of the practical work. The latter is vital in supporting the success of learning outcomes. The Plowden Report (1965) and the Bullock Report (1975), for example, both recommended a learning environment designed to encourage interaction and communication between pupils. In the project, discussion about the location of the work led to the development of activities for pupils during break- and lunch-times on those occasions when they were visiting each other's schools. Teachers played a supportive role during these times, encouraging pupils to share refreshments, play games, show pupils around their school and meet new friends.

Performance

At the end of the spring term all participants in the project (teachers, students, pupils and others) met at the university to rehearse and perform their work to a public audience. This event provided a further dimension for the work and enabled parents, friends, colleagues, as well as other ITE students and university staff to witness the culmination of the project. The local press provided considerable publicity, thus increasing the participants' sense of achievement – an issue which is a fundamental concern for many teachers working with children with SEN.

Evaluation

This project enabled both schools and the university to develop a broader perspective on the educational provision in the locality. By bringing together groups of teachers from primary, secondary and special schools over an extended period of time, a greater understanding of the work going on in unfamilar settings was made possible and resulted in an enhanced professional discourse about a range of SEN matters. Schools, particularly special schools, can often be isolated institutions and, in the current restrictive climate, it is not easy for teachers to find the time to visit other schools in order to observe a range of alternative teaching and learning practices. This project provided them with such an opportunity which formed the basis for subsequent liaison and collaborative professional development.

The pupils involved in the project generally enjoyed the interaction it initiated and, in many cases, spoke of their new friends. Several pupils from special schools were, at the time of the project, attending a mainstream school for part of the week. These pupils were pleased to be able to share the experience with their peers in both settings. One girl who was a pupil at a participating mainstream school was able, for the first time – as a result of the project – to work with her brother who attended a special school. This proved to be an enlightening process for the childrens' teachers and a positive delight for their parents who attended the final performance. All of the pupils were proud of their involvement in the project, as evidenced by their enthusiasm and commitment to the work.

Most schools performed their contribution to the show several times – during a whole school assembly and in both school locations. Some pupils in one mainstream school began to learn the basic principles of British Sign Language to enable them to communicate with their peers who communicated solely in this way in their own special school. Several pupils spoke of their new understanding about children from special schools and how their initial fears and prejudices had been reduced as a result of participating in this exercise. Their involvement in a public performance at the university as a part of a large 'theatre company' was an experience that many pupils said they would never forget.

The teachers found that the major benefit for them was the enhanced communication with colleagues from different schools. Through this process a sense of joint ownership developed which enabled teachers to relate easily and build close professional relationships. Many teachers found that working collaboratively on a specific curriculum area increased their expertise, the shared ideas and approaches informing their professional practice. One example of this was the case of a secondary school teacher of GCSE Art. As a result of the project, she encouraged several pupils from her partner special school to attend her classes and enter for the GCSE Art examination. This practice has continued since the conclusion of the project. Another drama teacher from a secondary school was already involved in touring local primary schools with theatre performances and workshops as part of her school's regular activities. The contacts that she made as a result of participating in the project extended this work to include local special schools. The involvement of *Actiontrack* in the school-based work allowed non-specialist teachers to develop useful strategies and new ideas for their subsequent work, from the work of the theatre company. The availability of accreditation for the work completed by teachers attending the university course was a further benefit.

Schools can work together in a variety of ways and for a variety of reasons. The positive outcomes of this project for pupils, students and teachers encouraged schools to consider ways in which they could instigate further collaborative ventures. Recent research on behalf of the DfEE (Tarr and Thomas, 1997) into the monitoring and evaluation of schools' SEN policies found that where schools had worked together in clusters on the writing of the policy they were generally more appropriate to the needs and of a much higher standard. The commitment to joint activity contributes considerably to the success of liaisons between schools. Where schools took a whole-school approach to the project and involved several members of staff in particular senior management, the liaison was most successful. A secondary school, wishing to ensure that the project reached a large number of pupils, placed the focus within the Personal and Social Education (PSE) aspect of its curriculum. This fostered discussions around disability and discrimination and work experience programmes to be set up in the future to ensure continued contact between pupils.

The university benefited from the profile that the project gave it within participating schools. This served to develop and extend existing partnership arrangements. The process of involving student teachers in the project served to support the work of teachers in the schools whilst enhancing the school experience of the students. The project has also resulted in the development of placements for ITE students in special schools thus providing further opportunities to introduce more students to a sector of education which is often overlooked in ITE.

Lessons for the future

The dramatic liaisons which occurred between the schools involved in this project have been successful, and more schools have become involved in subsequent versions of the project. On some occasions, two performances have had to be organised to house all the pupils comfortably. There are several issues which need to be considered when embarking upon such a project to ensure that pupils, teachers, students and schools benefit from the venture:
1. the aim of the project is clearly outlined to everyone concerned before the onset of the work;
2. the whole school is committed to the work, informed of the project and senior management are involved in the process;
3. the support of the wider school community – parents and governors – is sought to enhance the development of understandings and relationships within the local community;
4. HEIs can work in partnership with their LEAs to provide elements of professional development for teachers;
5. an element of continuity is planned into the project to enable contacts formed to progress and develop at the culmination of the project.

It is hoped that this project will stimulate others in special and mainstream schools to work collaboratively, so that such practice may become an integral part of ITE and CPD programmes. This process has particular benefits for enhancing professional expertise in the area of providing a rich and varied education for all pupils in an inclusive setting.

References

Department of Education and Science (1967) *Children and their Primary Schools* (The Plowden Report). London: HMSO.

Department of Education and Science (1975) *A Language for Life* (The Bullock Report). London: HMSO.

DfEE (1994) *The Code of Practice on the Identification and Assessment of Special Educational Needs*. London: HMSO.

Elliott, J. (1990) 'Teachers as researchers: implications for supervision and for teacher education', *Teaching and Teacher Education*, **6** (1), 1–26.

Jowett, S. (1988) *Joining Forces*. Windsor: NFER Nelson.

Lunt, I., Evans, J., Norwich, B. and Wedell, K. (1994) *Working Together: inter-school collaboration for special needs*. London: David Fulton.

Tarr, J. and Thomas, G. (1997) 'The Quality of SEN Policies: Time for Review' *Support for Learning*. **12** (1) 10–14.

Vygotsky, L. 1934 (1989 edition) *Thought and Language*. Boston: MIT Press.

Wood, D. (1988) *How Children Think and Learn*. Lewes: Falmer Press.

CHAPTER FIFTEEN

The Role of Local Education Authorities in Continuing Professional Development

Morag Bowden

Fullan and Steigelbauer (1991) argue that staff development must view the personal and professional lives of teachers in holistic terms. According to them, CPD should become the sum total of formal and informal learning experiences accumulated across individual careers. They also believe that effective schools incorporate the attributes of successful CPD into everyday activities in order to encourage acceptance of the principle of *continuous* learning.

CPD is intended to bring about change, although this is often difficult to measure, particularly as it happens over a period of time. Nevertheless, there are a number of general conditions which are required for change via CPD to take place (Loucks-Horsley *et al.*, 1987). Of these, I have found the most significant to be:

- a supportive environment with the involvement of colleagues;
- an element of personal motivation e.g. accreditation, career enhancement;
- relevance to the school/work situation.

On a more practical level, the factors for planning and running a successful course have been identified by Wallace (1988) and include:

- collaborative planning between course leaders and former or prospective participants;
- a clear focus upon participants' current and future needs;
- careful preparatory briefing for participants ahead of the course, with opportunity for pre-course work;
- a programme which is structured but flexible enough to allow modifications in the light of formative evaluation;
- a programme oriented towards experience, practice and action and using as appropriate, methods such as action learning, action research, performance feedback and 'on the job' assistance;
- 'sandwich' timetable including course-based and job-based experiences to facilitate this approach;
- careful debriefing after the course with sustained support.

Local Education Authorities, since the Education Reform Act of 1988, have had to alter their way of working significantly, whilst at the same time seeking to accommodate the kinds of principles outlined by Loucks-Horsley (*op. cit.*).

The role of LEAs in providing CPD has changed particularly since the introduction of LMS. The relationship with schools is now much more 'arms length' in nature, and schools can choose to purchase LEA services, including all or parts of its professional development programme. Much of the funding for professional development currently comes through LEA bids to the DfEE under the GEST programme. There are other areas from which the LEA may receive money for professional development (for example, through single regeneration bids) but currently GEST grants are the major source.

These grants have a legal basis in the Education (Grants and Awards) Act, 1984, and the Education Act, 1993, and can be used only within given parameters designated by the DfEE. They have to be matched or supported by LEA funding. The grants therefore indicate government priorities on an annual basis. LEAs, in turn, are obliged to delegate the monies out to schools according to the terms of the grant. Although schools have a high degree of autonomy under LMS, LEAs have a responsibility to monitor the use of GEST funding.

The annual cycle of events is that the DfEE circular advising LEAs of the coming year's GEST programme, the administrative arrangements and the areas of individual grants is sent to LEAs in July each year. LEA bids are to be returned by early October of the same year. Usually an LEA has a named officer responsible for coordinating CPD or INSET provision and administration, who allocates responsibility for writing individual bids to designated subject-personnel within the LEA. These might include inspectors, advisors, heads of Learning Support Teams and Specialist Service Teams. By December in the year of GEST application the LEA is advised whether or not its bid has been successful, and it must confirm acceptance no later than the following month. Next, the LEA advises schools of their individual share of the total LEA GEST budget. Funding is available for expenditure from April onwards. The timetable is therefore tight, especially given that LEAs then have to advertise and recruit to their available courses.

The above schedule illustrates some of the pressures and constraints experienced by LEAs. Following confirmation of successful bids, the INSET programme has to be published and distributed to schools in time for the new financial year. The constraint of annual budgets also has implications for planning, especially when partnership involves other institutions, whose accounting system may operate on the *academic* rather than the *financial* year, or when planning long courses which may run over two financial years.

CPD is important to LEAs, as it is an area where it can make a positive impact on the performance of its schools, disseminate LEA policy and act as an 'agent of change' in areas of concern. However, the delegation of budgets to schools, together with increasing school autonomy and their resulting confidence in their own ability to make independent arrangements for CPD, has meant that schools do not necessarily purchase or use LEA provision. In fact, there has been an increasing tendency for schools to respond to approaches and advertisements from external providers of CPD programmes in an attempt to gain independence from traditional LEA provision. This has led to the development of a privatised market in professional development (Harland *et al.*, 1993).

For many years LEAs have had a culture of long-term planning but they now face the additional pressure of having to take a strategic view of CPD against a background of the annual round of grant applications and often a lack of information concerning the precise nature of the priority areas for training. In addition, schools themselves are also being encouraged to have long-term 'Institutional Development Plans', which include an outline of their intentions regarding staff development. The latter are, sensibly, based on the school's assessment of its CPD needs, which may not concur with GEST priorities. Moreover, long-term planning is made difficult because schools are only made aware of the parameters surrounding the use of GEST money on an annual basis.

Schools' approaches to CPD have become increasingly discriminating since LMS was introduced and since the influential DES report (1989), in which HMI raised concerns about the management of INSET. Delegation of financial management now means that schools have access to considerable professional development budgets, for which they must have a rationale and also be accountable to the LEA. Moreover, as much CPD provision is now school-based and more attention is being given to relatively new professional development activities such as job shadowing, coaching, mentoring and job rotation. This reorientation requires an attendant shift in thinking on the part of the LEA.

Within the CPD budget, schools have to cater not only for the ongoing maintenance of the staff development essential for the efficient running of the school (e.g. professional meetings and networking initiatives with other schools) but also those school initiatives which are either likely to be short-term, one-off activities, such as the introduction of *Circle Time* or which concern the personal professional development of individuals (for example, their attendance on a specialist course, leading to certification). On occasions the focus of these varied demands may be concomitant, but they are just as likely to be different. It is worth noting that one effect of teacher appraisal has been to raise the expectations of teachers concerning the likely availability of professional development opportunities. This, of course, has implications for CPD budgets in schools, and also for staff morale, both positively and negatively.

In SEN the spate of recent legislation, particularly that relating to the Code of Practice and to so-called 'pupils with problems', has undoubtedly had an impact on both institutional and individual perception of need. To organise and provide effective and relevant CPD in these changing and challenging times, it is necessary for the LEA and its officers to respond to market forces. The current market requires good business practice, involving knowing one's own strengths and weaknesses, surveying the field and competition, and knowledge of the client base. In addition, future markets and trends must be anticipated in order to keep ahead of the competition.

An LEA response

The example provided here is illustrative of the response by LEAs to post-1988 changes in education, to which I have made reference in the opening section of this chapter. It is indicative of the constraints facing many LEAs in ensuring that they meet the CPD requirements of teachers whilst demonstrating the value of locally based approaches, rooted in local knowledge and contexts.

The LEA in question adopted a pragmatic approach to the changing times by recognising a number of underpinning principles:

- that the climate had changed and was unlikely to return to the traditional pattern of CPD, and its level of financial resourcing, due to the clear and consistent direction provided by central government, and the increasing acceptance by schools of these new arrangements.
- that a new, privatised market for CPD was developing and that the LEA had to change the way it operated if it was to be part of it. There was an acceptance that schools were no longer a captive audience and that the LEA had ceased to have a monopoly as a CPD provider – competition had arrived.
- that the current and potential market for CPD in SEN had to be identified. This now included both Grant Maintained and independent schools as well as LEA-supported schools, together with those schools and teachers from neighbouring LEAs, and other, specialist SEN organisations.
- that more clarity and precision was now required in identifying CPD needs in SEN by use of an annual audit of client needs.
- that the LEA should recognise its own strengths and weaknesses in providing for CPD and identify appropriate procedures to obtain additional CPD providers to help bridge the short-fall.
- that the LEA should develop ways of meeting market demand by formulating a business strategy for CPD in SEN.

Based upon these principles of operation the LEA adopted a clearly defined strategy for CPD in SEN. The first element of this was a resolution to provide a comprehensive range of course types. These included introductory through to high-level accredited and specialist SEN courses, specific specialist topic-based CPD alongside more general SEN issue-based courses, short courses through to one year courses, consideration of single issues to on-going 'maintenance' and improvement courses. Each of these could be presented as either customised, school-focused CPD provision or as courses with an LEA or nationally based emphasis.

At the same time the LEA resolved to promote other types of CPD, including the development of client partnerships for mutual support and discussion. An important element of this approach was the encouragement of cluster groups of schools and professional networks of teachers, in which common issues could be explored and examples of good practice shared.

In addition, the LEA was aware that all of these initiatives needed to be monitored for their effectiveness in meeting the CPD requirements of teachers by regular course evaluation alongside the annual audit of need, referred to earlier. This was not simply an end in itself but was used as the basis for follow-up support and consultancy. The development of partnerships between the LEA and a range of providers, including HEIs, was used as a way of adding alternative perspectives and variety to the delivery and content of the CPD programmes. The following examples illustrate the range of approaches taken by one LEA.

Provider partnership

This was a long (one-year), accredited course in supporting pupils with special educational needs, delivered in conjunction with a local Further Education (FE) institute and a professional organisation (City and Guilds). The FE links with The City and Guilds made this an ideal partnership for the LEA to offer a nationally accredited course for classroom assistants. The partnership involved a wide range of individual providers alongside the input from LEA staff, each of whom had considerable expertise in a given aspect of SEN. This gave the course credibility whilst also allowing the LEA perspective to be expressed. It also proved to be the most cost effective way of delivering such a course. The course accreditation opened a number of career possibilities for the participants whilst at the same time providing the LEA with effective, well qualified personnel. Demand for places was high, indicating that the LEA's assessment of CPD need was accurate.

Schools as providers

This was a medium length (one-term) course aimed at mainstream primary and secondary schoolteachers. It was intended to develop greater understanding of the range of special needs and to utilise the knowledge and experience of special schools and units in delivering a programme of CPD. The use of special schools in this programme raised the prospect of them being used to provide ongoing outreach support to mainstream schools. The sessions were based on visits to the special schools and units, so that the course participants could see specialist facilities, gain an understanding of the objectives of the school/unit, discuss the type of differentiated curriculum on offer with colleagues who delivered it, and critically examine the implications of a particular SEN for curriculum planning. It successfully changed the participants' perceptions of SEN and enabled them to see special schools as a resource upon which mainstream teachers could draw. The providers themselves gained insights into the organisation and logistics of delivering a CPD programme together with the prospect of far closer collaboration with their mainstream colleagues than had hitherto been the case.

Providing a national and LEA perspective to a range of clients

This example comprised a conference plus follow-up session, delivered to the school 'triad partnership' of SEN governor, headteacher and SENCo, to introduce the Code of Practice and communicate information concerning the various levels of responsibility which the Code outlined. In certain circumstances this assortment of clients, each group of which could have had a different agenda, may have inhibited free discussion and debate. However, the shared responsibilities for the implementation of the Code made this an eminently suitable course for joint participation, giving opportunity for structured discussions and agreed approaches whilst disseminating both national and LEA perspectives on the Code. The interdependence of their roles within the legislative framework gave a common understanding and encouraged a feeling of mutual support and shared responsibility between the governors, heads and SENCos.

Encouraging client partnerships for mutual support and discussion

This innovative approach to a potential problem came about through meetings with the local Downs Syndrome Association, who perceived a need for CPD in specific areas. A weekend conference was arranged, which enabled both teachers and parents to attend. Many of those attending already belonged to flourishing teacher–parent partnerships. The conference helped forge a closer link between teachers and parents, between home and school (and LEA) and served to develop a greater understanding of ways of developing effective home–school support. The conference was extremely well supported.

Developing school cluster groups for CPD

This came about when a group of schools expressed a wish to develop a cost effective way of addressing a number of common concerns which the SENCos were experiencing and on which they wanted an LEA perspective. It proved to be a very useful and effective way for the group to work, with the SENCos themselves providing a customised agenda. From the LEA perspective, this method ensured that policy and practice developments fitted comfortably with LEA requirements and it also served to generate additional CPD work with a number of individual schools who expressed a wish for a very specific school-based SEN concern to be addressed.

Follow-up support and consultancy in CPD

The requirements of the Code of Practice were delivered through a number of LEA courses and seminars. However, schools appreciated the offer of individual support/consultancy to finalise their arrangements concerning the Code, or to deal with a very specific, SEN-related problem. Feedback suggested that this kind of involvement by the LEA, on a follow-up basis, was highly valued by the schools. Likewise, following an OFSTED inspection, some schools requested support or consultancy in relation to the development of their Action Plan. Again, a number of schools considered it useful to have a familiar person, with whom a relationship had been established and who had an understanding and appreciation of the local context.

The attributes for successful CPD, which have been identified by Wallace (1988) and outlined earlier in this chapter, are illustrated in the following case study.

Meeting special needs in primary schools

This course arose out of an LEA response to a GEST grant for developing expertise in SEN in mainstream schools. In the light of the trend for schools to involve professionals from outside the LEA in CPD courses, and in view of the LEA's intention to make the course an accredited one (in keeping with the market-orientation in CPD), it was decided to run the course in conjunction with an HEI. This was an additional cost to the course and, in order to ensure financial viability and to involve a sufficient number of participants, it was decided to collaborate with a neighbouring LEA in the venture. The course was targeted at primary school teachers who were either working, or aspired to work, as a school SENCo.

Course aims

As a general aim for the schools represented on the course, the crucial need identified was to 'consider and develop policies and practice for meeting SEN'. For individual participants the course aimed to develop an awareness of current trends, policies and provision and to develop the confidence, skills and approaches for working effectively with colleagues.

Scheduling

The course level and content indicated that the delivery time would be substantial, accumulating to 60 hours, in order to cover the syllabus and meet the requirements of accreditation. The GEST grant allowed for an element to pay for supply cover for participants, which is understandably popular with headteachers, and it was consequently decided to schedule the course partly in school time and partly in personal time, between 13.30 to 18.00 hours amounting to 12 sessions of 4 hours (with a half-hour break). This was felt to be a good compromise, as benefits could be seen from both the schools' perspective (in gaining better trained/qualified staff) and by the individual (who, at the conclusion of the course, would receive a recognised and 'portable' qualification).

Nevertheless, the course demanded a substantial commitment from both the schools and their participating teacher(s). An initial twilight presentation was made to headteachers in March prior to the commencement of the course in order to brief interested schools and advise them of the formal selection procedure. It was also decided that each course participant should undertake to involve all colleagues in their school, so that information could be disseminated. A detailed application form was sent to all interested schools, as a way of determining the most suitable and motivated applicants. Included in this were requests for schools to identify their current situation with regard to SEN and the approaches which they were using to meet the needs of SEN children. We also wanted information on how the application related to the school's IDP and how the course could help the school to realise its content. Finally, we were anxious to discover the level of support that participants were likely to get, how the rest of the staff in the school were to be involved in the project and some indication of the focus of the individual, school-based project which was integral to the course.

Because of the time-scale for GEST fund authorisation, the earliest start for the course would be the summer term, 1992. Although this did not seem to be a sensible time to start a major CPD initiative it was decided to capitalise on an early start date in July with an opening one-day session to give participants both an introduction to the course and a number of 'items for consideration', together with some activities to undertake, during the summer break. These included an action plan and time-line for the main course project. The period also provided course-participants with opportunities to encourage whole-school involvement. In order to emphasise the support and involvement of senior management teams in the schools, headteachers were requested to attend this introductory session. The substantive part of the course resumed in September, with weekly 'twilight' sessions for the participants.

Location

This can be an underestimated aspect of CPD course attendance. At a time when CPD providers are actively having to attract course-participants, its importance should not be overlooked. A number of issues need to be taken into account, with course location requiring:

- geographical convenience for participants;

- removal from competing pressures of school/home;
- opportunities to meet other teaching staff outside class time;
- availability of teaching resources;
- access to parking and refreshment facilities;
- cost-effectiveness of accommodation;
- a welcoming and comfortable environment;
- proximity to shopping and other amenities.

Decisions made in the light of these locational factors meant that the course was held in a number of venues: the initial one-day session was based in the Teachers' Centre of the participating LEA and the main part of the course, comprising 'twilight' sessions, was conducted in the regional Teachers' Centre. A final day, which consisted of a 'project presentation' was organised in a hotel, which helped bestow a sense of occasion and achievement on the proceedings.

Content

The syllabus for the course comprised four principal themes (or modules), which could be delivered in any order and whose specific content could be modified. This built-in flexibility was intended to encourage ownership of the course and to ensure its relevance to the schools. The four modules were:
1. The concept of SEN;
2. National Curriculum and Assessment;
3. Developing Practice;
4. Classroom Management and Practice.

The 'project' part of the course was seen as a key task if full, whole-school involvement of schools was to be subsequently obtained. The initial choice of project by the participant required that it be relevant to the school's IDP; throughout the course LEA personnel would visit the schools in order to provide support to both the course participant and to their colleagues.

Presentation

The providers were to be principally the LEA advisors and an HEI lecturer who, together, had planned the course. They were to be supported by a number of external speakers. A variety of styles of presentation were to be used, including lectures, discussions, school visits, workshop and simulation activities. In addition, each participant would be required to make a presentation concerning their work to the course membership. The inclusion of external CPD providers gave the course the added advantage of being able to draw upon a range of experience in different fields of SEN. In addition, this strategy ensured inclusion of:
- national and international perspectives of SEN;
- knowledge of current research;

- a needs identification survey on INSET carried out in one LEA;
- the various in-house evaluations of INSET of which were available to the two participating LEAs.

Evaluation

The form of evaluation was threefold: oral feedback from both participants and headteachers, written feedback from participants and submission of the project work.

The course was oversubscribed in its first year, and, with the availability of further GEST funding, it ran for a second year. Evaluations from course participants and their headteachers indicated a high degree of satisfaction with the course and that the 'project' in particular had helped to bring about a reorientation in that area of SEN. The most positive feedback concerned the legislative and practical aspects of the course and the provision of opportunities to discuss and network with other participants. The project work, although regarded as satisfactory overall, did vary somewhat in quality and it was clear that the undertaking had proved daunting to some participants. A number had required in-depth, on-going support.

There was some debate as to whether the course had promoted a genuinely whole-school approach. The course team reviewed this in an attempt to determine what strategies could be adopted to obtain a more collegiate approach in the schools and thus to encourage a higher degree of 'whole-school involvement' and change. It was clear, though, that the course was occurring at a time when the whole educational climate was changing. Changes include:

- the new Code of Practice, emphasising that all teachers were involved in SEN and class teachers' growing awareness of their training needs;
- new exclusion legislation (Circular 10/94);
- improved IDP planning, which meant that schools were less willing to take on major whole-school projects unless they were high priorities in the IDP;
- increasing costs of providing CDP courses based on this model.

These factors and the attendant need to attract new course members, indicated that it was time to develop a new course with a possible new HEI partner. Such a new course would have to meet the requirements of the GEST grant, as outlined earlier.

In consequence, an annual audit to determine the CPD needs of schools in SEN was carried out, the findings of which formed the basis of the LEA's forthcoming CPD programme. The audit highlighted schools' concerns in managing pupils with behaviour difficulties. This evidence suggested a possible focus for the new course and suggested that the HEI partner should be a specialist in the field of behaviour difficulties, thus providing additional credibility whilst at the same time ensuring that the course was developing and keeping abreast of trends. This change in direction was indicative of the need to retain flexibility in CPD provision, and of the LEA's view that even well-attended and apparently successful courses needed constant revision and update.

CPD and LEAs: the future

LMS has now been in place for several years and one effect of this has been a distancing of some schools from LEAs. Recently, however, it has been possible to detect a changing perspective on the role of LEAs, as increasing governmental concern is shown concerning the outcomes of OFSTED inspections, National Curriculum assessment results, and so on. In consequence, I believe that there has been a shift towards a partnership, with LEAs working more closely once again with all schools to promote quality in all aspects of practice, coordinating school networks, and assisting in the implementation of national initiatives (DfEE, 1996). Collaborative involvement in CPD is one area in which LEAs and schools can be productively involved.

Nor should it be forgotten that the majority of schools, although having had the opportunity to become far more independent from their LEA, have chosen not to do so. Whilst their new relationship with the LEA, which offers both distance and greater choice, has been welcomed, many schools have sought to retain links with the LEAs. This is reassuring but LEAs need to guard against complacency. The 'privatised market' in CPD activities remains very influential.

LEAs, however, have a number of advantages over other CPD providers and these can be capitalised, whilst still providing a good, cost effective service to schools. They have a detailed knowledge and understanding of the local educational, social and economic context and are thus able to offer customised CPD provision in which the economy of scale makes for cost-effectiveness. LEAs have established good working relationships with schools over a long period, and are able to use a wide range of experienced CPD providers, who can provide cross-phase or interdisciplinary perspectives, rooted in local conditions and issues.

The implicit message coming from schools appears to be 'we want you, but, we also want more, and we want to be free to import new ideas'. In this respect the range of accreditation procedures and the variety of methods by which a teacher can gain additional qualifications and training need to be recognised and incorporated within the LEA's strategy for CPD in SEN. The flexibility offered by modular, accredited courses in collaboration with HEIs is a particularly attractive option. It raises the status of the LEA's own CPD programme, whilst accommodating the constraints of annual funding and annual priorities referred to elsewhere in this chapter. The introduction of transportable credit accumulation has made this option even more attractive, as teachers were previously reluctant to undertake a long course if there was a possibility of a move to another part of the country.

Current buzz words or phrases – such as inclusive education, school improvement, self-evaluating schools, effective schools, and so on – are, I suggest, the key words for future CPD. In SEN in particular, the demand for inclusive approaches is gaining momentum and this obviously has implications for both schools and LEAs. A sustained and high level of CPD will be required if schools are to understand the concept and to develop appropriate strategies and procedures to ensure that all pupils receive an 'entitlement curriculum', with equality of access in order to develop their abilities. Inclusive education will also have major implications for CPD budgets, both for the school and for the LEA, and this will call for a high degree of strategic planning. The provision of specialist CPD for teachers working in specific areas of SEN (for example, SLD, VI or PMLD) is likely to remain problematical due to the cost, length of training and the low numbers of staff involved. These areas of practice, commonly referred to as 'low-incidence SEN', have been a matter of concern for some time within both the various professional organisations and SENTC (see elsewhere in this book). It is an area where there is undoubtedly a need for an increased level of collaborative work between HEIs, other specialist providers and the LEAs themselves, particularly in the light of the relative scarcity of experienced trainers in these fields.

In other areas of SEN, for example Autism or Hearing Impairment, where there are too few potential CPD clients, it will remain difficult for an LEA to provide a level of ongoing professional support which is financially viable and sufficiently stimulating for participants. In such situations, the further extension of collaboration between neighbouring LEAs or professional organisations is a possible option. Moreover, if this approach is able to maintain some sort of consistency by, and between, the various providers, it could promote networks and allow professional relationships to develop, thus assisting in the future planning of CPD events to become established.

The Code of Practice emphasises the need for partnership between Education, Health and Social services. These partnerships can prove elusive and time consuming for individual schools to forge. LEAs will have an important role to play in this and will be able to draw upon their traditional interdisciplinary expertise and contacts, making this aspect of future development in CPD a unique opportunity for them to establish an important and lasting contribution to SEN provision.

CPD in SEN also needs to meet both the teacher's need to acquire or develop new skills or competencies, whilst at the same time giving them opportunities for critical reflection. A major factor in the success of the course described in this chapter was the practical, action research activities undertaken in the workplace by the course participants, together with the opportunity for professional reflection and discussion. There has been, of course, much debate concerning the efficacy of CPD based on a competency framework, as opposed to one that is driven by critical reflection. LEAs, therefore, will have to balance both approaches very finely, and incorporate elements of each within their CPD provision.

References

Department for Education and Employment (1996) *Self-Government for Schools*. London: HMSO.

Department of Education and Science (1989) *The Implementation of the Local Authority Training Grants Scheme: report on the first year of the scheme 1987–88*. Report by HM Inspectors. London: HMSO.

Fullan, M. and Steigelbauer, S. (1991) *The New Meaning of Educational Change*. London: Cassell.

Harland, J., Kinder, K. and Keys, W. (1993) *Restructuring INSET: privatisation and its alternatives*. Slough: NFER.

Loucks-Horsley, S., Harding, C., Arbuckle, M., Murray, L., Dubea, C. and Williams, M. (1987) *Continuing to Learn: a guidebook for teacher development*. Andover, MA: Regional Laboratory for Educational Improvement of the Northeast and Islands and National Staff Development Council.

Nixon, J. (1989) 'Determining in-service needs within specific contexts', *British Journal of In-service Education*, **15**, 150–155.

Wallace, M. (1988) *Towards Effective Management Training Provision*. Bristol: Bristol University School of Education.

CHAPTER SIXTEEN

Professional Development to Meet Special Educational Needs: The Role of the Special Educational Needs Training Consortium (SENTC)

Olga Miller and Malcolm Garner

Background

The report of the Special Educational Needs Training Consortium – *Professional Development to Meet Special Educational Needs* – was submitted to the Secretary of State for Education in February, 1996. The SENTC working party which produced the Report incorporated representatives from a wide range of organisations and agencies concerned with the education of pupils with SEN. This was the first report of its kind, focusing on the professional development needs of all teachers working with pupils with SEN and students undertaking ITE courses.

This chapter addresses three discrete aims. Firstly, it describes the context in which the SENTC evolved; then it provides a brief outline of the Consortium's report, together with its conclusions and recommendations. Finally, it considers the responses made to the SENTC Report by the Secretary of State.

Context

The 1993 Education Act drew on the recommendations of the Warnock Report (1978) and emphasised the importance of clearly identifying and responding to the SEN of children. For some, this might best be met through the drafting of a Statement of need, whilst others would receive support from the school's existing resources. After the 1981 Act, funding for the professional development of mainstream teachers in the area of SEN was earmarked and the DES Circular (3/83) outlined the criteria and arrangements for such training opportunities. Further resources were secured for enhancing the existing arrangements for the training of specialist teachers of pupils with more severe needs.

The advice of ACSET in 1984 however, resulted in the cessation of ITE programmes for those who wished to work with pupils who had SLD. It had been anticipated that increased post-experience opportunities for professional development would compensate for this. Unfortunately the expected increase in such opportunities did not materialise and by 1986 the recruitment of teachers to full-time specialist courses in SLD, for example, had declined by two thirds.

The devolution of funding from the then DES to schools, bypassing the LEAs, as defined in the 1988 Education Act, had a further significant impact on provision of training and support for teachers working with pupils with SEN. There was a dramatic reduction in full-time training and an increase in part-time modular professional development programmes and distance learning initiatives. Whilst greater diversity in training routes was welcomed, regrettably, these did not compensate for the demise of more traditional full-time opportunities. Between 1989 and 1996, there was, for example, a reduction of nearly 50% in the number of teachers for the deaf trained each year (see Table 16.1).

Even in the early 1990s no nationally recognised programmes of training existed for SENCos in mainstream schools, and opportunities varied widely between LEAs. The 1993 Education Act and the Code of Practice in particular, echoed the significance which the Warnock Report had placed on the role of the teacher with responsibility for SEN in mainstream schools. The Code of Practice clarified the part that schools were to play in identifying, assessing and responding to a wide range of educational needs It also reaffirmed the role of parents as partners in this process as well as recognising the expectation held by parents that children with SEN should have appropriate support from teachers appropriately skilled and knowledgeable in this area. Also in 1993, the recently established TTA assumed the responsibility previously held by CATE in restructuring ITE, so that schools assumed greater responsibility in that process.

By late 1993 widespread concern was being expressed about the training of

Table 16.1   *Number qualifying as teachers of the deaf – 1989 to 1996.*

Year	Full-time courses	Secondment	Part-time courses	Total qualifying
1989	130	89	23	153
1990	126	90	20	146
1991	118	79	32	150
1992	68	54	33	101
1993	66	44	58	124
1994	41	29	63	104
1995	28	14	73	101
1996	23	12.5	60	83

teachers in the area of SEN. Responsibility for quality assurance in this area was unclear and, whilst HMI had traditionally monitored the quality of teacher training, their future role was under review and there was no mutually agreed guidance in relation to SEN training.

Whilst a diversity of training routes was available, both at ITE and CPD levels, no obvious progression existed between the different aspects of training and SEN. NQTs in particular were expressing concern regarding their preparation for teaching pupils who were underachieving and for managing pupils with EBD. At the same time, teachers working with pupils with SLD were faced with managing the increased complexities of the needs of such pupils, yet their professional development opportunities had diminished dramatically. In this and other areas of SEN there was an increasing demand for teachers with additional skills and knowledge, yet few had access to appropriate post-experience training.

Monitoring groups

Following earlier concerns regarding the changing patterns of CPD and the reduction in the numbers of teachers registering for courses in the specialist areas of SLD, VI and HI, a number of 'Monitoring Groups' were established. These groups drew together both purchasers and providers of training, together with representatives from the voluntary sector and teacher organisations. They were concerned not only with the numbers of trainees, but also with monitoring the quality of specialist courses nationally and trying to ensure their consistency.

The Monitoring Groups increasingly recognised the need to work more closely together and to collaborate with others representing the wider field of SEN. Thus it was that in 1993 they agreed to form a consortium, under the aegis of the Council for Disabled Children, which is itself an umbrella body for parents, professionals and others working on behalf of children with SEN. Where no Monitoring Groups had previously existed (e.g. in Autism and Physical Disability), new groups were established and the Consortium's Steering Group invited observers from relevant statutory and other bodies to reflect the breadth of interest and responsibility in the area of teacher development and SEN.

This widely representative group, which became known as the Special Educational Needs Training Consortium (SENTC), assumed the following aims:

- to collect and disseminate information on the provision of training for those concerned in meeting SEN;
- to promote the development of strategic planning to provide and fund appropriate training and professional development opportunities to meet staffing requirements for special education provision;
- to support trainers in the various areas of SEN in establishing generally

accepted standards for the professional development of those involved;

- to encourage the promotion of equal opportunities in access to training, in order to provide an appropriate range of teachers and lecturers for those who have SEN;
- to provide a forum for communication and collaboration amongst all involved with the training of those concerned in the education of children and young people with SEN;
- to collate information on the staffing needs for all forms of provision for those with SEN and to encourage the planning of adequate staffing levels.

SENTC did not replace the individual Monitoring Groups, which continued to meet separately. Rather, it sought to provide a forum for these groups to meet collectively. In this way the information gathered by the individual groups could be shared and a national overview of the professional development of teachers in the area of SEN facilitated.

Models of competence

One of the most significant features of the work of the Monitoring Groups was the formulation of competency documents for each of the training areas represented. The move towards the use of models of competencies has been apparent in ITE during the last five or six years and a number of official circulars (notably 9/92 and 14/93) has meant that such an approach has now become commonplace in ITE (Reynolds and Salter, 1995). For teachers working in the more specialist, lower incidence areas of SEN, the debate concerning competencies was particularly significant. Not only did Monitoring Groups see the production of competency documents as a way of safeguarding the quality of the outcomes of training but also as a way of informing employers and parents of the extent of additional skills and knowledge which should be expected of teachers working with children with less common forms of SEN. This aspect of the work of the monitoring groups forms a significant part of the SENTC Report, which includes lists of the suggested competencies in an appendix.

The SENTC working party

Following approaches by SENTC, and in recognition of the gravity of the situation regarding teacher supply in SEN, the DfEE agreed to make funding available in February 1995 to establish a Working Party. Its agreed terms of reference for the were to:

- review the systems currently in place for the training of teachers of pupils with SEN;
- make recommendations on how these systems might be improved to make more efficient and/or effective use of resources in the light of the

respective roles and responsibilities of those involved in the provision of SEN teacher training.

It was decided at the outset that a set of principles should be agreed so that any proposed recommendations generated by the Working Party could be set within a context of shared aims and objectives. These were based:

firstly, on the rights and needs of pupils with special educational needs to be taught by teachers who are appropriately trained to meet those responsibilities and, secondly, on the entitlement of teachers to have opportunities to update their knowledge, skills and understanding in response to changing needs and provision. (SENTC,1996, p.3)

The Working Party approached its task by considering four main areas. These were:

- ITE;
- Induction Training for NQTs;
- CPD for specialist teachers;
- Funding mechanisms.

Each area was considered in detail and extensive consultation carried out to ensure that as far as possible, the wider views of consumers, professionals and others involved were incorporated. A series of recommendations were produced, based on this consultation process.

Initial Teacher Education and newly qualified teachers

In relation to the provision of an effective SEN element for students and new teachers, the dilemmas posed by the changing structure of ITE in general are considerable. There are competing pressures between the need to design courses which fit the new partnership arrangements between schools and HEIs, which result in new teachers demonstrating specific competencies, and the demands made by the National Curriculum. The time available in such courses for specific training in SEN is minimal and inevitably much now depends on the expertise and motivation of mentors within the partnership schools. This can by no means be guaranteed since many SENCos already find themselves under considerable pressure to fulfil the duties with which they are charged as a result of the Code of Practice, as well as a range of associated professional responsibilities. Many NQTs enter the profession unfamiliar with their formal responsibilities for SEN and are not equipped, at the start of their careers, with a sufficient repertoire of teaching strategies to meet the wide range of SEN they will encounter. These issues are dealt with in greater detail in the introductory chapter of this book, and remain a constant theme throughout this volume.

In response to this reality, the SENTC Report highlights what are considered to be core areas of competency for teaching pupils with SEN. These ITE Core Competencies are grouped under the headings of:

- Context;
- Curriculum Design;
- Access and Delivery;
- Managing Professional Responsibility.

Recognition is given to the need for NQTs, during their induction, to build on the knowledge and skills they have acquired during their ITE course. The Report also acknowledges the importance of opportunities during the induction phase for NQTs to observe and experience a variety of educational settings and be encouraged to develop a thorough knowledge of the school's SEN policy and its implementation through the Code of Practice.

The Report recognises the fact that the abolition of the 'probationary period' has meant that a formal opportunity to monitor how successfully new teachers are trained in meeting the range of SEN they regularly meet in mainstream classrooms has been lost. It therefore highlights the increased importance of the role of mentor for the NQT in ensuring that sufficient access to expertise in SEN is assured. In so doing it is recognised that additional pressure may be placed on the SENCo who may be required to monitor this process. There is, therefore, a clear need to ensure that the NQT 'profile' supports further professional development in the area of SEN and that appropriate resources are available to implement this.

Continuing professional development

The SENTC Report describes the identification of teachers' needs as a process which can be achieved through several existing procedures, including school development planning, appraisal and inspection. Subsequent decision making rests with a combination of the individual teacher, the school and a range of external agencies whilst implementation is dependent upon the necessary funding being available. Over recent years, funding has been provided by central government through GEST, or by the Funding Agency for Schools in the case of schools with GMS status. However, it is unfortunate that, all too frequently, funding shortages still dictate the priorities which LEAs and schools set for staff development, and individual needs may take lower priority if appropriate training proves too expensive. In addition, the practice of short-term funding makes long-term planning for staff development extremely difficult.

The SENTC Report stresses the importance of teachers receiving guidance in planning their professional development. This guidance can help ensure that skills, knowledge and experience gained during ITE and Induction can be built upon subsequently.

The Report recognises that, when choosing a focus for their professional development, teachers new to designated roles in SEN may not yet have sufficient knowledge of the possible demands made by these roles. A case in point is that of the SENCo, where, in the absence of an agreed framework, their role may differ between individual schools in terms of demands and status, leading to very different training requirements.

Low-incidence areas of SEN

For teachers working with pupils who have low-incidence SEN (for example, VI and HI) the Report supports the concept of mandatory training but also emphasises the importance of such specialist training being widely available. Access to appropriate training in these areas is considered equally important in both the mainstream context and support services, just as it is within specialist provision. The Report therefore recommends the extension of mandatory training to include these areas. It also highlights a worrying increase in the age profile of teachers training in the specialist areas, following the abolition of the ITE routes and suggests that there is a need for incentives to encourage younger teachers to enter these specialist fields.

Finally, given the low incidence of some types of SEN, and the consequent difficulty in addressing training needs at local levels, the Report also emphasises the need for planning of this training at a national level.

Funding

Three types of professional development have been identified for which funding is necessary. These reflect the variety of roles undertaken by teachers in relation to pupils with SEN and include:
- teachers in mainstream schools;
- teachers with designated responsibilities for pupils with SEN in ordinary schools;
- specialist teachers working in special schools and units, and in support services.

Central government funding is currently used to finance training in respect to all these areas, but the absence of a national overview has led to problems in funding arrangements. Some of these difficulties have been identified through a recent TTA survey of CPD (TTA, 1995):
- money which is in school budgets and intended for CPD is sometimes used for other purposes;
- there are no nationally agreed criteria to ensure that funding is targeted at the right teachers or made available to them at the right time in their careers;
- there is a lack of accountability for the deployment of resources on CPD at national, local and school levels;
- there is a considerable feeling that the annual GEST cycle does not allow for medium- or long-term planning.

Both the TTA review and the SENTC Report point to the need for clarity in determining how responsibilities should be allocated at the school, the LEA and the national levels. The SENTC Report illustrates how this dilemma causes problems in planning by identifying the following issues:

- a persistent shortage of teachers with additional qualifications in particular areas of SEN (for example, SLD);
- a tendency for GEST SEN funding to be directed at short programmes of limited training, leaving insufficient funds for the longer training required to qualify teachers of pupils with more severe and complex needs;
- the difficulty found by teachers working in support services, in non-maintained/independent special schools, in gaining access to GEST funding, even for mandatory for SEN training;
- a lack of data on how funds are used, and how far this is effective for ensuring that pupils' SEN are met;
- an indication from the rising age profile of specialist teachers that funds are not being invested for the best return in length of quality service;
- variability in the earmarking of GEST funds from year to year, which makes it difficult to maintain training policies and provision.

Conclusions

The Report reaches a number of conclusions which stress the need for a more coherent approach to teacher education in SENs at every level. These range from the need of individual teachers who may require additional support to feel fully confident in their classroom practice, to the decisions about future planning in relation to SEN made at whole-school and LEA levels. In particular, the Report highlights the following:

- Since every teacher is a teacher of pupils with special educational needs, it also follows that a systematic plan of staff development must reach all teachers. This should begin with a carefully planned special needs element in ITE, continue through the induction process and then develop into a range of opportunities for continuing staff development which will enable all teachers to meet the needs of all children.
- Planning and funding of staff development has to take place at a variety of levels – the DfEE, the TTA, LEAs and individual schools and teachers. There has to be full consultation with the relevant professional and voluntary organisations and clear lines of responsibility and accountability between all agencies.

In all, the Report makes thirty two recommendations of which the following are highlighted to illustrate the range of coverage:

R2.1 The Secretary of State's competencies for ITE should be revised in the light of the TTA's work on standards for NQTs. These standards should take account of the Code of Practice and other recent developments in legislation and professional practice.

R2.6 The role of SENCos should include the SEN training and induction of NQTs and, in schools involved in partnership arrangements in ITE, also with trainee teachers. Governors need to ensure that they, and any other staff involved in this work, are given time and staff development support to enable them to make an informed and effective contribution to this work.

R2.8 The Career Entry Profile of NQTs should include reference to SEN experience and competencies acquired during ITE.

R3.2 The DfEE in collaboration with the TTA, LEAs, schools and HEIs should be responsible for identifying the overall need for a sufficient supply of appropriately trained specialist teachers.

R3.4 The mandatory qualification for teachers working with hearing or visually impaired pupils should be retained and extended to specialist teachers working with hearing and visually impaired pupils in mainstream settings and in support services, including those with pre-school children and their families.

R3.6 Consideration should be given to means of enabling and encouraging younger teachers to undertake training in specialist areas of SEN. This should include consideration of opportunities for training immediately or soon after acquisition of QTS and/or the provision of training grant specifically for younger, experienced teachers. Similar consideration should be given to encourage teachers who are themselves disabled to undertake further training in SEN.

R4.1 Responsibility for formulating a coherent and continuing policy to fund CPD for SEN should be clearly located with a national body with the aim, over a specified period, of ensuring that all teachers are effectively trained and qualified to meet the continuum of pupils' SEN.

R4.3 A Special Educational Needs Training Advisory Group (SENTAG) should be set up, to support policy formulation by the body or bodies designated in R4.1 (above).

In view of the importance of the proposed SENTAG, the Working Party also indicated what they considered should be the remit of the Training Advisory Group:

- provision of an overview of SEN training in order to ensure a range of training opportunities in a variety of modes, delivery and locations;
- provision of advice on funding priorities in specialist lower incidence areas, including those covered by mandatory requirements;
- data collection (in collaboration with TTA and DfEE) on the supply, demand, distribution (including age, gender and ethnic profile) and changing needs of teachers in designated SEN posts;
- establishment of training priorities using the data collected, in order to assist the government in providing and maintaining an adequate supply of specialist teachers;
- identification of national priorities in the area of CPD and SEN;
- provision of a forum for liaison between SEN organisations, and lobby groups representing the continuum of SEN;

- dissemination of information on appropriate training and qualifications of teachers in designated posts in order to inform employers and the teachers' pay review body;
- consideration of alternative funding possibilities/training arrangements to encourage younger teachers to train for designated SEN posts;
- examination of access for teachers with disabilities to specialist training courses.

Response to the SENTC Report from the Secretary of State for Education

The Secretary of State for Education responded to the recommendations of the SENTC Report in August, 1996. She made it clear that the TTA would be the key agency involved in the process of taking recommendations forward and agreed the following measures:

- the DfEE will revise its criteria for ITE and update the SEN references;
- the TTA will encourage innovative initial training courses with an SEN focus and use these courses to promote good practice;
- new teachers will be required to understand the SEN Code of Practice and this will be noted in their Career Entry Profile;
- the TTA will ensure that new employment based routes into teaching will also be available through special schools;
- the TTA's work on induction for new teachers and on developing national teaching standards will reflect the issues teachers need to understand in teaching children with SEN. The TTA will take account of the recommendations in the SENTC Report in taking this work forward;
- the TTA will in addition bring together a focus group to advise it on SEN issues.

Although considerable further discussion will be undertaken both with the TTA and the DfEE on the detail and implications of these measures, and these comments represent an early analysis, it is immediately clear that the response represents a mixed bag and some major recommendations of the Report have either been ignored or not accepted.

In general terms, the recommendations which relate to ITE and the Induction of NQTs have been accepted and it is pleasing to note that greater emphasis will be given to new teachers and those in training gaining a fuller understanding of the Code of Practice and the need of pupils with SEN in their classes. Also pleasing is the assurance that TTA will draw up national standards for SENCos and that they will consult widely in this development.

Conversely, the proposal that 'new employment-based' routes into teaching will be available through special schools (which was not a recommendation of the Report) leaves many questions unanswered. For example, it gives no indication of how, or indeed whether, trainees in a special school will be required to demonstrate the competencies presently required by those training in mainstream settings. It also appears to ignore the emphasis throughout the Report on the importance of progression in SEN training and the need for teachers to build on experience gained through ITE. It may also be seen to be paving the way for a further reduction in the involvement of HEIs in specialist training.

The willingness of the TTA to consider innovative ITE courses with a focus on SEN should also be viewed with some caution. In discussion with representatives from the DfEE following receipt of the response from the Secretary of State, there was agreement that the existing framework for initial training already leaves insufficient time for SEN issues to be adequately or consistently addressed. The only way therefore, that this focus could realistically be strengthened would be to extend the duration of ITE courses. However, no suggestions have been made as to how such an extension would be funded. It is therefore important to guard against any attempt to try and 'squeeze a quart into a pint pot' to the detriment of the quality of existing training.

If, however, course extensions could be funded, from additional grants to individual teachers for example, this may not only enhance the quality of SEN experience gained but also be an effective means of attracting younger teachers into areas of SEN where there is a shortage of qualified staff.

Neither this, nor the proposal discussed in the preceding paragraph seem to fit with the existing requirements for teachers to have mainstream experience before training to work in the special sector. Removal of this requirement would be controversial. Although most support the logic behind it, in practice, since its introduction it has contributed to the considerable increase in the age profile of teachers entering the SEN field. However, in our experience, there has never been a significant correlation between whether a good teacher in special education did or did not have previous experience in a mainstream setting and as such, a properly structured combined ITE course may have benefits and complement the existing postgraduate training routes.

It is pleasing to note that the need for what the response describes as a national 'SEN Focus Group' has been accepted. The fact that the 'Focus Group' is to be lodged within the TTA seems appropriate and should ensure the work of the agency is monitored from an SEN point of view. Conversely, however, it means that it will not have a direct influence on the allocation of GEST funding by the DfEE. This is a concern as the Working Party was clear in its view that more informed decisions were needed in making these allocations. DfEE representatives acknowledged this in their meetings with SENTC and agreed that 'more public consultation' may well be helpful in this process.

The most disappointing part of the response relates to CPD, and especially training in the more specialised areas of SEN. The Working Party's recommendations in this area have not yet been accepted. Subsequent discussions with DfEE representatives suggest that there are two main reasons for this. Firstly, there is confusion regarding the use of the term 'shortage'. For example, LEAs have apparently reported that there is no shortage of staff in the field of SLD. However, DfEE surveys consistently show that the real shortage is of teachers with specialist training and indicate that in the SLD field nearly 50% of teachers are not additionally qualified in the given area of specialism. This is a different kind of shortage but is nonetheless of considerable concern to parents and others who believe that pupils educated in this sector should receive teaching from professionals who have enhanced knowledge and skills in the field.

The second reason for not accepting the recommendations is that the DfEE is apparently not convinced that specialist training makes any difference. It claims that schools with very different resources in terms of additionally trained staff produce similar results in terms of pupil outcomes, thereby indicating that possession of specialist qualifications is not a significant factor. Without this being proven, they are reluctant to further extend the scope or availability of specialist training. This view represents a challenge for the SEN profession. We all know that this is a qualitative matter and that there are poor teachers who are qualified as specialists, just as there are some remarkably good teachers who are not yet specially trained. Yet, most in the field would agree that the best teachers are those who are good teachers and who also have training and experience in their specialist field.

How then, can those in authority be persuaded that investment in specialist training is both necessary and cost effective? There is an urgent need for research into this subject. This however, will take time and, in the short term, it is important that parents, consumer groups and others continue to monitor the situation and put pressure on the appropriate authorities. Only in this way can the entitlement of pupils with SEN to be taught by appropriately qualified and possessing the skills, knowledge and expertise be secured.

In her response, the Secretary of State for Education said: 'My Department, working closely with the TTA, will take a long hard look at the training needs of those teachers who teach children with more significant needs'. This could so easily be an avoidance strategy. Care needs to be taken to ensure that this 'hard look' is taken sooner rather than later and that the widely held views of the value of additional training, based on the competencies outlined in the appendices of the SENTC Report, are given full and urgent consideration.

Although the SENTC has provided, and continues to provide, a platform for cooperation and joint action, it remains vital that the individual Monitoring Groups and other agencies are pro-active in ensuring that the impetus generated by the publication of the SENTC Report is not lost. They should continue to press for improvements in the training of teachers in SEN so as to ensure that, in the recent words of Gillian Sheppard 'all children get a better deal from education'.

We strongly share this desire and are convinced that it is only with concerted action from all those representing what will always be a minority of pupils, that it will be achieved. As such, the production of the SENTC Report should only be viewed as a beginning and there remains much to be done if children with SEN are to receive their educational entitlement.

References

DES (1978) *Report of the Committee of Enquiry into the Education of Handicapped Children and Young People* (The Warnock Report). London: HMSO.

DES (1983) Circular 3/83. London: DES.

Department for Education (1992) *The Initial Training of Secondary School Teachers: new criteria for courses* (Circular 14/92). London: DfE.

Department for Education (1993) *The Initial Training of Primary School Teachers: new criteria for courses* (Circular 14/93). London: DfE.

Reynolds, M. and Salter, M. (1995) 'Models of competence and teacher training', *Cambridge Journal of Education*, **25** (3).

Special Educational Needs Training Consortium (1996) *Professional Development to Meet Special Educational Needs*, Report to the SENTC Working Party. Stafford: SENTC.

Teacher Training Agency (1995) Letter from Sir Geoffrey Parker to Secretary of State for Education, 26.7.95 (Annex A: the Continuing Professional Development of Teachers).

CHAPTER SEVENTEEN

A Blueprint for the Future: Special Educational Needs and Teacher Education in the 21st Century

Gary Thomas

Blueprints, recipes and visions

I was asked to write a 'blueprint for the future' for this chapter. There are distinctions to be drawn here amongst recipes, blueprints and visions. Academic educationists are wary of giving recipes, yet of the three phenomena – recipes, blueprints, visions – recipes are probably the most innocuous. They are sets of instructions, to be followed or adapted according to the predilections of the cook. Blueprints, however, are miniature representations, to be complied with in the minutest detail by the builder. A vision is an apparition seen by someone with a thought disorder or religious faith (or both).

Since I share a reticence to provide recipes, I am doubly convinced of the impossibility and undesirability of providing blueprints. Perhaps a vision is the best I can do, aware as I am of the unflattering comparisons which might be made. Despite those comparisons, a vision is appealing since it gives me the excuse to be hopelessly optimistic and gloriously unrealistic about the likely funds with which to resource the system of the future. Before sharing that vision, though, I want to discuss some of the hopes of teacher education in the twenty years or so since the Warnock Report (DES, 1978), and the reasons why those hopes have turned to confusion.

The background to today's thinking

Special education over the last century has concerned itself with the separation of specific groups of children who, after they had been separated, would be taught differently. The assumption has been that children who had experienced problems at school were qualitatively different from other children – that they had learning difficulties.

This assumption about learning difficulty, though it has been expressed in different ways (children have been called idiots, morons, ESN and now SEN), has pervaded our thought in this century about the way children who experience difficulty at school should be treated. Indeed, it is enshrined in legislation: the 1981 Education Act and subsequent legislation make it clear that children with any sort of difficulty at school – from sensory disability to physical disability to 'challenging' behaviour – all have learning difficulties.

This is the assumption on which the edifice of twentieth century special education has rested, and it is not peculiar to the UK. In the USA, the assumption is that children who experience difficulties at school have learning disabilities. This goes one step further, imputing some medical or physiological cause for the child's difficulties. Whilst to British readers this appears alien, it is perhaps a more honest articulation of the world-view which is taken by the educational establishment; the assumption is that there is something wrong within the child which has to be remedied.

More recently, that is within the last twenty years or so of this century, there has been a reaction against this predominant world-view. Commentators on the special education system have suggested that when children experience difficulties at school, it is not necessarily the fault of the children. It is, the received opinion has come to say, the fault of the education system. The problem has been that the system has failed adequately to educate all children. It has concentrated on the education of those with higher attainments and more acceptable social attributes and has failed to address the needs of those with learning difficulties. Critical commentary about special education has usually seen the failings of the special education system resting in social and political factors rather than in inappropriate models of learning. Such commentary has thus stressed the maintenance of the special system by people with vested interests, the alienation of children from it, and its inherent unfairness. Children's failure has been reconceptualised as a failure of the school system.

But alongside this reconceptualisation the assumption has still been that a substantial minority of children (one in five, if the Warnock Report is to be believed) have learning difficulties. This is a bit like having one's cake and eating it. The view which has emerged in the last quarter of the century has been that there are no (or, at least, very few) 'within-child' difficulties as was once assumed to be the case, but the notion of learning difficulties is still unashamedly retained.

It is the fact that we continue to retain the notion of learning difficulties which causes policy and practice within SEN to be confronted with so many dilemmas. At one and the same time, there are a) no children with specific problems (there are only schools which haven't catered adequately for all children), and b) there are children (20% of the school population) with learning difficulties. The tacit assumption is that some children have problems (which, one assumes, are located somewhere in their brains) which are causing them to have difficulty at school.

Because this contradiction is maintained – there are no children with difficulties, and there are 20% of children with difficulties – huge problems are created for the education system. The system has to reconcile the modern doctrine that the difficulties children experience at school are the cause and the responsibility of the school with the deeply held (and legally reinforced) view that some children have problems which are rooted in some organic deficiency. The result of this contradiction is that the system creaks and strains with pressures it cannot contain.

It is this contradiction which gives rise to a situation in which LEAs have to be seen to be developing and operating policies of integration and inclusion, whilst at the same time maintaining an establishment of special schools essentially unchanged for forty years. It is the same contradiction which gives rise to a situation in which schools publicly espouse inclusive education whilst referring increasing numbers of children for special education and excluding record numbers of children for unacceptable behaviour.

There are of course many reasons for the current unhappy state of the special system and it would be an over-simplification to suggest that they are all located in this contradiction. However, it is by confronting this contradiction that I shall base a vision for the future of teacher education in SEN.

Teacher education – the recent past

Particularly over the last few years, the education of teachers in the field of SEN has reflected this contradiction. In the mid-1980s, courses which trained teachers for specific 'categories' of disability (for example, children with SLD) were closed, on the assumption that these children would become the responsibility of all teachers. Therefore in-service education or CPD would be more appropriate than ITE.

It was not only specialist courses which were to be subject to this logic. Following the ACSET report (DES, 1984), many courses of ITE changed direction in such a way that targeted modules which focused on SEN were withdrawn. Their input was to be delivered instead in a 'permeating' way – that is, it would be the responsibility of individual module leaders (in maths, English or whatever) to address SEN as part of the module. Whilst this was fine in theory and certainly meshed with the integrationist climate, in practice the privately expressed fear of many practitioners was that the topic of SEN would not be as comprehensively covered as previously.

Parallel to these developments, the National Curriculum was being introduced and its eventual establishment resulted in a rewriting of all courses of ITE. The heavy emphasis on curriculum subjects in the new courses further squeezed the time available for special needs to be covered adequately.

Another organisational development was the change in the pattern of in-service education for all teachers over the period since the late 1980s. Prior to this there had existed a system of funding teachers' attendance on long courses, some of which were in SEN. Subsequently, this system has disappeared and in-service education is now provided in a more heterogeneous range of courses both within and outside HEIs.

There is a further development which is likely to exaggerate these trends and that is the 'academicisation' of CPD. Where once teachers would go on certificate or diploma courses to learn about how to teach children who were experiencing difficulties at school, there is now the understandable temptation to take – instead of a post-graduate certificate in SEN – one of the many Masters courses in education, with SEN as a specialisation. These courses provide excellent grounding in research methodology and encourage critical and reflective thinking, often with the opportunity for in-depth analysis of a particular topic; they thereby contribute significantly to an experienced professional's understanding and approach. However, these courses are usually academic and, if they concentrate at all on nuts and bolts, it is on the nuts and bolts of research methodology and design rather than the practicalities of teaching, classroom planning or organisation. Certificate and diploma courses still exist, of course, and continue to recruit healthily but there can be no doubt that the widespread introduction of Masters courses (and now EdD courses) has reduced somewhat the appeal of the more practically orientated courses.

Perhaps the most major changes, however, came from the shift in thought about appropriate pedagogy for special needs and the influence which this brought to the content of courses. These shifts, and their influences on teacher education in INSET, are summarised well by Rouse and Balshaw (1991). They outline the 'traditional' outlook to INSET and the 'new' outlook:

Table 17.1 *The view of traditional and new perspectives on INSET, as seen by Rouse and Balshaw*

Traditional	New
– disability perspective	– educational perspective
– narrow curriculum focus	– wide curriculum perspective
– testing	– observation, assessment and recording
– individual development only	– individual and institutional development
– skills	– process
– passive receivers	– active participants
– content prescribed	– content negotiated
– 'training up' experts	– developing staff collaboration and reflective practitioners

The differences of course reflect the integrationist spirit of the times. The moves are of focus: from segregation to integration; from emphasis on specific problems which children may experience to stress upon the whole curriculum and ways of making it meaningful to all; from a view which sees special education as doing something remedial to children, to a view which assumes that good teaching is good for all children.

This optimistic view is one that has been almost wholly supported and policy has slowly but surely moved to provision which has stressed the CPD (as opposed to initial education) of teachers specialising in SEN. Whilst this change of emphasis has been laudable, there have been problems associated with it.

First, the change in thinking has coincided with a serious decline in resources, exemplified in the atrophy of one-year courses on SEN, in such a way that the amount of training provided has proved inadequate to the task of skilling very large numbers of teachers (in an ideal world, all teachers should be skilled-up) to meet SEN in their classrooms.

Second, though, there is the major problem of the mismatch of the two essentially incompatible mindsets I introduced at the outset, and this problem is perhaps even more intractable than the problem of resources.

To recap, those mindsets are, first: the doctrine that the difficulties children experience at school are the cause and the responsibility of the school, and, second: the view that some children have problems which are rooted in some organic deficiency or developmental delay. The problem has been that the system has assimilated the first of these views with regard to teacher education and has changed systems very widely, as I have just indicated. At the same time it continues (tacitly, of course) to hold the second set of views. These latter are far more difficult to shift in the real world of schools and classrooms, where teachers are faced with children's day-to-day problems. It is one thing to be told that there is a curricular or whole-school solution to a child's serious learning difficulties or disruptive behaviour. It is another to translate that well-meaning advice to action on Monday morning. It is small surprise then that the shift to integrative education has been so much slower than the architects of the 1981 Education Act assumed that it would be.

This situation seems likely to continue, since the clash of mindsets is insoluble as long as resources are not forthcoming to provide adequate quality and amount of support for children with difficulties in mainstream schools. Furthermore, the attenuation of specialist training in SEN is likely to be exaggerated as further emphasis is placed on within-school education of teachers in partnership arrangements.

The future

If this clash of mindsets is indeed a real one and has impeded change to more inclusive education, what should be done? Perhaps it should be recognised first that with the willingness in many schools to translate inclusive policies into practice, there is every opportunity to make inclusion happen. Many school managements and individual classteachers have the will to accommodate and educate children with serious disabilities in their classes but are overwhelmed by the prospect of not being able to cope or not knowing the right thing to do. Faced with this, is the logical solution to admit defeat for the integrative, whole-school emphasis (outlined in Table 17.1) of teacher education of the last fifteen years or so? To admit such defeat would augur a return to specialist training – and one should be clear about the consequences, were this to happen. A return to specialised training for teachers would be to acquiesce in the view that there is a very special set of methods and pedagogies which are needed for teaching children who experience difficulties at school. The consequence is that movement to an inclusive education system will be further impeded, as Skrtic (1991) has warned. Skrtic's views are discussed further below.

This vision, then, attempts to make sense of the contradictory mindsets I have referred to and offers some possible avenues to follow. Before tackling these specific issues, I wish to set down three important principles on which the professional education of teachers must be based in coming years.

The first is that professional development cannot be seen as the preserve of teachers and neither can it be assumed that a special set of skills are needed for teaching certain children. Skrtic (*op. cit.*) has suggested that it is because of what he calls the 'professional-bureaucracy' of schools, with its assumptions about expertise, that progress towards inclusion is so slow. It is because of the assumptions about professional and special expertise that so many initiatives towards a more integrated education system in the USA have failed. He asserts that 'mainstreaming simply reproduced the special education problems of the 1960s in the 1980s' (p.156). This failure – this reproduction of problems – remained because people were unwilling to confront the uncomfortable political reality that skills acquired under one ideology were not appropriate under the newer integrative or inclusive philosophies. Neither are they appropriate in a consultatory context with the mainstream teacher – because, he implies, they are worthless. The continuing maintenance of the facade of consultation and collaboration with the devolution of special skills from consultant to non-specialist maintains the very divisions which mainstreaming sought to eliminate. Whilst Skrtic's ideas are controversial, they are powerfully and logically argued and demand close attention by the teaching profession and all those concerned with the professional development of teachers.

One consequence of Skrtic's argument is that there should be less sententiousness about the potential contribution of learning support assistants (LSAs) *vis-à-vis* 'properly qualified' teachers; my own work (Thomas, 1992) suggests that LSAs may in certain circumstances provide a better alternative to a trained teacher in the support role. Learning support assistants are taking an increasingly important role in most classrooms, especially for children with statements and especially in SLD schools. However, LSAs need to feel comfortable with their role and they need certain basic competencies to fulfil that role adequately.

The second principle is that professional education must be geared towards providing inclusive education. All our education should be directed towards enabling changes in practice and attitude in school systems in such a way that all children can be educated together. This has implications for the way teaching is organised; Porter (1995) distinguishes the implications of an inclusive philosophy from an integrative one (see Table 17.2). These distinctions are relevant for teacher education, since they de-emphasise the special skills of specialists and emphasise the importance of more all-purpose support in the classroom, in line with the ideas and advice of Skrtic.

Table 17.2 *Porter's (1995) comparison of traditional and inclusionary approaches*

Traditional approach (which may include integration)	Inclusionary approach
Focus on student	Focus on classroom
Assessment of student by specialist	Examine teaching/learning factors
Diagnostic/prescriptive outcomes	Collaborative problem-solving
Student programme	Strategies for teachers
Placement in appropriate programme	Adaptive and supportive regular classroom environment

The third principle is that people with disabilities must in future be included fully in the education of teachers and LSAs. Rieser and Mason (1992) make a powerful and irrefutable case for this involvement.

Using these principles as a vehicle with which to proceed, I suggest a pattern of provision which emphasises five main elements:

- specific short courses on needs associated with particular disabling conditions – so-called 'low-incidence' SEN;
- training for all LSAs;
- an expansion in CPD (including distance and open learning) for those coordinating SEN provision in schools;
- professional masters degrees and EdD programmes dedicated to inclusive education;
- specific provision for SEN in ITE.

To take these one by one . . .

Specific short courses on needs associated with particular disabling conditions

Some of the children now entering mainstream schools have recognised disabling conditions, such as cerebral palsy. It would be wrong to stereotype the difficulties which are associated with these disabling conditions, since the 'condition' covers a huge range of potential difficulties when a child is faced with the average classroom – some very minor and some very significant. However, it may be the case that there is advice which can usefully be offered relating to difficulties which often arise with particular conditions: for instance in autism, sensory impairment, physical disability. This is the assumption of the SENTC (1996), which suggests that there is a range of competencies needed by those specialising in particular areas, such as those just outlined, and including competencies for SENCos and 'Learning Support Teachers'.

This advice is welcome, though it is difficult reconciling it with Skrtic's analysis and his emphasis on despecialisation. Reconciliation probably can be effected in examining closely the extent to which individuals are trained. The range of competencies needed to manage the rather varied collection of shared characteristics which will be needed by any one group is limited. And if the assumption that there is a special set of teaching methods applicable for particular groups of children is disposed of, then the remaining set of skills to be covered in CPD will concern aspects of familiarisation and organisation which can be covered without great expense of time. Children, for instance, with Down's syndrome have been shown to progress at least as well in mainstream schools as in special schools (Buckley, 1985; Casey *et al.*, 1988; Sloper *et al.*, 1990) and this is despite the lack of specific training of the staff (teachers and support assistants) who are teaching them. Yet there is often a reluctance to accept these children into the mainstream. Perhaps this reluctance would be ameliorated by the provision of very short courses (of between two and five days) which would familiarise teacher-and-assistant teams with the main characteristics and needs of particular children. If these were offered as a guaranteed right to the teacher-and-assistant team accommodating a child with a statement into their classes it would do something to contribute to their confidence in their own capacity to succeed. Research shows (Thomas, Walker and Webb, 1997) that they do succeed, yet they rarely believe they can at the outset of an inclusive enterprise.

Training for learning support assistants

Although this strictly speaking does not fall under the ambit of teacher education, there can be little doubt that it will form one of the most important aspects of professional education in this field in the foreseeable future. The effective working of the teacher-and-assistant team is central for the success of the inclusive school and the inclusive classroom. My research (Thomas, *op. cit.*) has shown that this teamworking is difficult to effect and effort clearly needs to be invested in enabling people to work together.

The thrust of what has been said already about teacher professional development applies also to LSAs. There are few (if any) special teaching skills which are needed for teaching particular groups of children, though there will certainly be organisational skills and general teaching strategies which need to be understood. A programme of education for all LSAs therefore, perhaps on the lines of that currently offered at the Open University, is necessary.

An expansion in professional development (including distance and open learning) for those coordinating special needs provision in schools

The role of the special needs coordinator (SENCo) in schools is an enormously important and difficult one and the evidence recently emerging attests to the fact that SENCos feel under-prepared and under-resourced for the role (Lewis *et al.*, 1996). The specific demands of the SENCo's role need to be covered in short courses which enable SENCos to have a thorough understanding of the Code of Practice, which will include:

- recording;
- stages of assessment;
- writing and reviewing a policy;
- working with governors;
- liaising with colleagues and professionals;
- understanding the multifarious needs which may need to be met in classrooms;
- the resources which might be used to meet those needs;
- the more common conditions which may lead a child to be in receipt of a statement.

All SENCos need to attend short courses which cover these elements. Given the logistic problems of providing these, structured courses could be provided by regional providers, but at a distance, using open learning.

Professional masters degrees and EdD programmes dedicated to inclusive education

The newest addition to award-bearing continuing professional development is the taught doctorate in education. Its introduction has prompted some interesting discussion concerning its orientation and purpose, which is relevant for CPD generally and the development of Masters courses, which currently provide one of the main forms of accredited CPD in education. This discussion has centred on the specific professional purposes and aims of the EdD, as distinct from the essentially research aims of the more traditional PhD. Indeed, many have insisted that these courses be called professional doctorates rather than taught doctorates.

The discussion is valuable since it focuses attention on the aims and purpose of the other main kinds of credit-bearing CPD – the Master's degree – which has usually stressed the generic skills of research in the context of wider study and reflection on a particular topic or set of topics – perhaps with a particular 'pathway' followed. Most courses established have been generic and few have offered a specialist qualification (e.g. MA in SEN). The logic of non-specialisation (at least in the SEN field) rested at least in part on the need to integrate course content and course membership in the same way that integration was being effected in schools. Special education was not to be separated, 'specialised' or 'ghetto-ised'. Whilst one can understand this logic (which applied also to the 'pervasive' input of SEN in ITE) on reflection it seems unreasonable to expect that the history, research, organisation, professionalisation and pedagogy of SEN should not be studied discretely in the same way that educational management, educational psychology, further and higher education, or indeed any of the subject studies are studied discretely.

This is particularly so as the move to inclusive education gains momentum. Its thrust, as Table 17.2 showed, is towards good practice and support for effective learning and high quality teaching. It is thus not merely a replacement for the term 'integration'. It concentrates on an approach which is consistent with the de-specialisation emphasis of Skrtic and others. If CPD is to address the many issues bound up in inclusion it has to provide a vehicle which will enable participants to study both the history and research of SEN and the ethic and practice of inclusive education in sufficient depth.

Specific provision for special educational needs in ITE

I have just tried to make a case for the inclusion of specialised elements of CPD in inclusive education, and there I touched on ITE and the logic which led to SEN being taught 'pervasively'. The problem, as I indicated at the outset, was that often the pervasive elements would be lost in the pressure of subject specialists to cover the subject in a very restricted time. These pressures were intensified as students' time in schools assumed a greater proportion of the whole.

It is surely time for such elements to return, both to cover the competencies which were mentioned above in relation to specific disabling conditions, but also to cover the aspects of the teacher's role which are necessary for a move to inclusive education: working as a team with LSAs and other professionals; an accessible curriculum for all; differentiation; appropriate classroom organisation and management.

Conclusion

On reflection, the above seems more of a shopping list than a vision, and it is perhaps foolhardy to try to look more than a few years into the future, given the pace of change politically.

Perhaps the greatest controversies over the future shape of teacher education for SEN will hinge on the degree of specialisation which the system supports, the nature of that specialisation and whether it continues to stress alternative pedagogies.

References

Buckley, S. (1985) 'Attaining basic educational skills: reading writing and number', in D. Lane and B. Stratford (eds.) *Current Approaches to Down's Syndrome*. London: Holt.

Casey, W., Jones, D., Kugler, B. and Watkins, B. (1988) 'Integration of Down's syndrome children in the primary school; a longitudinal study of cognitive development and academic attainments', *British Journal of Educational Psychology*, **58**, 279–286.

DES (1978) *Report of the Committee of Enquiry into the Education of Handicapped Children and Young People* (The Warnock Report). London: HMSO.

DES (1984) *Teacher Training and Special Educational Needs: report of the Advisory Committee on the Supply and Education of Teachers*. London: HMSO.

Lewis, A., St.J. Neill, S. and Campbell, J. (1996) *The Implementation of the Code of Practice in Primary and Secondary Schools*. London: NUT.

Porter, J. (1995) 'Organization of schooling: achieving access and quality through inclusion', *Prospects*, **25** (2), 299–309.

Rieser, R. and Mason, M. (1992) *Disability Equality in the Classroom: a human rights issue*. London: Disability Equality in Education.

Rouse, M. and Balshaw, M. (1991) 'Collaborative INSET and Special Educational Needs', in G. Upton (ed.) *Staff Training and Special Educational Needs*. London: David Fulton.

SENTC (1996) *Professional Development to Meet Special Educational Needs: Report to the DfEE*. Stafford: SENTC.

Skrtic, T. (1991) 'The special education paradox: equity as the way to excellence', *Harvard Educational Review*, **61** (2), 148–206.

Sloper, P., Cunningham, C., Turner, S. and Knussen, C. (1990) 'Factors related to the academic attainments of children with Down's syndrome', *British Journal of Educational Psychology*, **60**, 284–298.

Thomas, G. (1992) *Effective Classroom Teamwork: support or intrusion*. London: Routledge.

Thomas, G., Walker, D. and Webb, J. (1997) *The Making of the Inclusive School*. London: Routledge.

CHAPTER EIGHTEEN

Teacher Education, Special Needs and Inclusive Schooling: Some Lessons from around the World

Mel Ainscow

In this chapter I address the question of what forms of teacher education are needed in order to prepare and support teachers in developing more inclusive practices. Drawing on the experience of an international research and development project which has included initiatives in over fifty countries, I will argue that if this goal is to be achieved there is a need to rethink what is involved. In this sense the chapter uses experiences from other parts of the world in order to reflect on what might be desirable in our own country. To begin this process I first offer an anecdote from the People's Republic of China.

A Chinese tale

Jiauzhan Normal College in Shandong province prepares teachers to work in primary schools. It caters for some 1,000 student teachers, all in the age range fifteen to twenty. The visitor to the school is struck first of all by the neat, orderly appearance of the campus, with its modern buildings and attractive grounds. Students, who all wear multi-coloured track suits, live in hostels nearby. Relationships between them and the staff of the school seem relaxed and friendly.

Classes are usually conducted in a formal manner, with lecture presentations given by the teacher, sometimes followed by periods of student questioning, although these are usually short. By and large Chinese students seem reluctant to ask questions during the lesson. This reluctance was explained to me by one teacher when he commented, 'we are taught that the tallest tree in the forest is usually the first one to be cut down.' Certainly to the European eye the classrooms have a somewhat regimented appearance, seeming to provide little or no opportunity for students to make individual contributions.

In the midst of this predominant style of working a small group of the teaching staff are experimenting with some alternative teaching approaches that are intended to focus much more attention on the individuality of the students.

Mr Hu, an education teacher, is a member of this group. A brief account of one of his classes gives a flavour of the approaches being used.

The purpose of the class is to explore ways of responding to pupils who may be experiencing learning difficulties during a lesson. There are fifty nine third-year student teachers, sitting in groups of about eight, around tables. In preparation for the class they have each studied a story which tells of an imaginary island where gracefulness is seen as the most important and necessary attribute for educational success. In this context it is children who are clumsy who are perceived as experiencing difficulties in school. Known as 'gawkies', these children present considerable problems to their teachers and there is much debate as to how they should be dealt with. Indeed some feel that they should either be given an adapted form of curriculum in the same school or be placed in separate types of school.

Mr Hu's class consists of a series of activities, stimulated by the story, during which the students are encouraged to reflect upon their own experiences and attitudes, and to discuss their ideas with their colleagues. Initial discussions are carried out in pairs and then this is followed by the sharing of ideas in larger working groups. Occasionally Mr Hu interrupts the discussions to take feedback from members of the class and then to refocus the discussion. Otherwise he moves around the room listening to the student conversations, sometimes joining in to help clarify a point or to introduce further questions.

The class lasts one hour. Towards the end of this time the various groups are asked to summarise their conclusions, relating these to the situation in Chinese schools. Volunteers from each group take turns to go to the front of the class and present their findings. For this purpose each group has prepared a drawing that illustrates their main ideas. One of the drawings shows a teacher lecturing to the blackboard even though there are no students in the room. Another has the teacher talking to a class that consists solely of large ears. Yet another illustrates schooling as a long narrow bridge leading to the university, with lots of students falling off into a deep valley below. All of the pictures and presentations focus on the need to reform schools in ways that encourage forms of teaching that recognise student individuality.

A remarkable feature of the presentations is the confident way in which the students express themselves. They are obviously used to addressing their classmates in this way, and they speak with expression, conviction and, occasionally, a sense of humour. During the presentations members of the class listen attentively, sometimes applauding what is said.

At one point a discussion occurs when one student expresses his disagreement with a point made by a presenter. An argument develops, during which a number of students contribute their points of view. The disagreement is about the role of assessment and whether all children should be judged against common criteria. During this debate Mr Hu stands back, allowing the argument to continue without his involvement. The smile on his face suggests that he approves of the interchange. After a while, however, he intervenes to summarise the main points and then to move the discussion forward.

During the final moments of the session Mr Hu asks the class to reflect on the activity and to write a short memo summarising what they feel they have learnt. In particular, he asks them to write about factors that inhibit children's learning and how such barriers can be overcome. Finally, at the end, he instructs the students to do further reading for the next session of the course.

Mr Hu's approach is new to teacher education in China and, as we have seen, is in sharp contrast to the usual teaching experienced by these students. A researcher from Beijing describes it as the fresh air that is coming in because 'the window has been opened'. A local official comments: 'We have been asking for reform in teacher education for years – at last we see it in action'.

Special Needs in the classroom

The materials and approaches used by Mr Hu and his student teachers were developed as part of a UNESCO teacher education project known as 'Special Needs in the Classroom'. This project began in 1988 with the aim of producing and disseminating a resource pack of materials that could be used within pre-service and in-service contexts to help teachers to respond positively to children experiencing difficulties in learning, including those who may have disabilities. Pilot materials were field tested and evaluated by a resource team in eight countries (Ainscow, 1993a; 1993b; 1994a; 1994b). Subsequently the project has expanded throughout the world, with initiatives in over fifty countries. Apart from the development of the project materials, all of this experience has thrown light on how the tasks of preparing and helping teachers to respond to pupils we describe as having special needs might be best conceptualised. Furthermore, this conceptualisation represents a major challenge to the status quo in many countries, not least our own.

Before explaining the nature of this reconceptualisation, however, it will be helpful to consider the place of teacher education with respect to special needs within the context of the education system as a whole. In particular it is important to consider the place of special needs work within the wider international discussions of 'Education for All', as stimulated by the 1990 World Conference held in Jomtien, Thailand. During the years since Jomtien, thinking in the field has moved on. The rather token mention of special needs within the early Education for All documentation is being gradually replaced by a recognition that the special needs agenda should be seen as an essential element of the whole movement. Thus, instead of an emphasis on the idea of integration, with its assumption that additional arrangements will be made to accommodate pupils seen as being special within a system of schooling that remains largely unchanged, we now see moves towards inclusive education, where the aim is to restructure schools in response to the needs of all pupils (Sebba and Ainscow, 1996).

This inclusive orientation is a strong feature of the Salamanca Statement on Principles, Policy and Practice in Special Needs Education, agreed by representatives of 92 governments and international organisations in 1994 (UNESCO, 1994). Arguably the most significant international document that has ever appeared in the special needs field, the Statement argues that regular schools with an inclusive orientation are 'the most effective means of combating discriminatory attitudes, building an inclusive society and achieving education for all'. It goes on to suggest that such schools can 'provide an effective education for the majority of children and improve the efficiency and ultimately the cost-effectiveness of the entire education system'.

Implicit in this orientation is, therefore, a paradigm shift in respect to the way we look at educational difficulties. This shift in thinking is based on the belief that methodological and organisational changes made in response to pupils experiencing difficulties can, under certain conditions, benefit all children (Ainscow, 1995). Indeed, within such a formulation those seen as having special needs come to be recognised as the stimulus that can encourage developments towards a richer overall learning environment.

The approaches to teacher education developed as a result of the research carried out within the UNESCO project are consistent with the Salamanca orientation. Specifically, they involve a move away from what I am describing as an integration perspective towards an inclusive approach. Within the project this shift came about as a result of a realisation that the ways in which earlier attempts to develop integrated arrangements had, unintentionally, undermined our efforts. As we tried to integrate pupils seen as having special needs into mainstream schools, we adopted practices derived from earlier experience in special provision. What we learned was that many of these approaches were simply not feasible in primary and secondary schools, certainly in poorer countries with their massive classes and scarce resources. Here I am thinking, in particular, of the individualised responses, based on careful assessments and systematic programmes of interventions, that have been the predominant orientation within the special needs world. For many years, of course, this was very much the orientation that shaped my own work (e.g. Ainscow and Tweddle, 1979; 1984). Gradually, however, experience has taught me that such approaches do not fit with the ways in which mainstream teachers plan and go about their work. For all sorts of sensible and understandable reasons the planning frame of such teachers has to be that of the whole class. Apart from any other considerations, the sheer numbers of children in the class and the intensity of the teacher's day makes this inevitable.

Consequently, when integration efforts are dependent upon the importing of practices from special education they seem almost certain to lead to difficulties. Indeed they are likely to lead to yet new forms of segregation, albeit within the mainstream settings (Fulcher, 1989), through the use of what Slee (1996) calls 'dividing practices'. For example, in this country we have seen the proliferation of largely untrained classroom assistants who work with some of the most vulnerable children and their individual programmes. When such support is withdrawn, teachers feel that they can no longer cope. And, of course, the formal requirement for individualised education plans laid down by the Code of

Practice is encouraging colleagues in some schools to feel that many more children will require such responses.

In summary, then, our experience within the UNESCO project led us to rethink the way in which we formulate the task of responding to special needs in the classroom. This involved a move away from responses aimed at individual pupils towards an orientation that concentrated attention on planning for the whole class. This move, apart from being much more feasible for practitioners, drew attention to possibilities for development that had previously been largely overlooked.

Studying practice

The gradual recognition that schools for all will not be achieved by transplanting special education thinking and practice into mainstream contexts has, therefore, opened my mind to many new possibilities that I had previously failed to recognise. Many of these arise from the study of practice, particularly the practice of classteachers in primary schools and subject teachers in secondary schools. As my awareness of the value of such studies has developed, so my interest in observing and trying to understand practice has grown. Put simply, I am arguing that a scrutiny of the practice of what we sometimes call 'ordinary teachers' provides the best starting point for understanding how classrooms can be made more inclusive. Some examples will give a flavour of what I have in mind.

First of all, a primary school classroom in Inner Mongolia, China. There are approximately 75 children, sitting in rows of desks packed into a long, rather bleak looking room. The teacher stands at one end of the room on a narrow stage in front of a blackboard. In the back row of the classroom there are some pupils who look older than the rest. In fact, these are children who either started school later than the rest or, in some instances, are resitting the grade having failed in the previous year. Lessons are 40 minutes long and, although each is taught by a different teacher, mostly follow a common pattern. Typically this involves a process by which the teacher talks or reads and, frequently, uses questions to stimulate choral or individual responses from the class. Throughout the lesson the pace is fast and the engagement of pupils is intense. Afterwards the teacher explains how she tries to help those who experience difficulties by directing many more questions to them and by encouraging their classmates to go over the lesson content with them during the breaktimes. They all have to learn to 'march together in step', she says. In these ways, even under the difficult conditions in which she works, she is in her own way attempting to make her lessons more inclusive.

A second example to consider is in Ghana, West Africa. It is a primary school in a rural district. Here class sizes are much more manageable than those observed in the Chinese school. Typically there are 50 or so children in each class. On the other hand, the physical resources are noticeably poorer. Many of the children arrive in the morning carrying a stool on their heads. It seems that for these children this is the equivalent of children in the West bringing a pen and a ruler from home. Apparently each evening the stools are taken home so that they can be used for domestic purposes. It may also be that some families are reluctant to leave them in school where they might be stolen, since the classrooms are open, having few walls. One of the teachers explains that his biggest problem is the lack of textbooks. In fact, for most lessons he only has one copy of the book and so frequently he has to write the text on the blackboard. A surprising feature of the lesson, certainly from an English perspective, is the presence of a couple of pupils who are noticeably disabled. Further inquiries confirm that the headteacher assumes that it is his responsibility to admit all children in the district. 'Where else would they go?', he remarks. Apparently such examples of what Miles (1989) refers to as 'casual integration' can be found in a number of so-called developing countries, particularly in rural districts. Indeed they raise the question, is it significant, in some way, that it is a rural environment? A parent in Queensland, Australia, for example, explained recently how she had found it necessary to move out of the city to find a school that would welcome her disabled daughter. Certainly it does seem that teacher attitudes is a key factor, with acceptance of diversity as a possible starting point for the development of an inclusive pedagogy.

Examples such as these, in faraway places, have been significant in drawing my attention to the potential for learning when observing the practice of regular school teachers. So much so that it has pushed me to spend much more time looking at the practice of teachers in our own country.

Recently, as part of a study I am carrying out with Tony Booth and Alan Dyson, I watched a Year 7 geography class in an urban comprehensive school (Booth *et al.*, in press). The students were seated in rows, two at a table, each with a text book in front of them. The teacher began the lesson by explaining, 'This is the first of a series of lessons about the USA'. He went on to say that before they opened their books he wanted to know what the class already knew about this subject. Immediately lots of hands went up and within minutes the blackboard was full of lots of information. Despite the fact that none of these young people from a poor city estate had ever been out of the country, their regular viewing of films and television programmes meant that their knowledge of the American way of life was extensive. Sitting on the front row was James, a student who has Down's Syndrome. Next to him was a classroom assistant who, for what use he was at this stage of the lesson, might as well have not been there. James raised his hand and, when called on by the teacher, said, 'They have yellow taxis.'

So, here the teacher was using a familiar tactic to 'warm up' his class; that of using questioning to draw on existing knowledge, prior to introducing new material. It is an approach that many teachers use. Certainly it is not 'special education' but, nevertheless, it proved to be a means of facilitating the participation of members of the class, including one who is seen as needing a permanent adult helper.

Moving on to the primary field, I have also been studying practice in another school that has made enormous progress towards the development of a pedagogy of inclusion (Ainscow, 1996). The school, which I will call Eastside, has four wings, each of which has its own suite of interconnected, open areas. The wings all have multi-disciplinary teams coordinated by a teacher who is known as the team leader. In the four years since it was established the school has gradually evolved an overall pattern that guides the work of each of these teams. This working pattern is informed by the strong emphasis placed in the school on encouraging pupil autonomy. The school's statement of aims declares that there is 'a shared vision which is one of developing relationships and a curriculum that ensures that everyone feels valued, respected and reaches a high level of achievement.'

In each area a wide variety of possible activities are prepared from which the children can choose. Materials and equipment are arranged in ways that enable children to get at them without assistance. In this way they seem to carry out their tasks with a minimum of teacher attention. This leaves staff free to observe what is happening, intervening as and when they perceive this to be necessary. Within this busy and complex environment the adults are, in fact, to be seen engaged in a continual process of instant decision-making, adapting their existing plans and, indeed, formulating new plans in the light of decisions made by pupils and unforeseen opportunities that arise. This form of what I will call 'planning in action' is, I believe, both vital and demanding. It involves a sophisticated form of improvisation whereby the teachers make what, I assume, are often intuitive judgements about how best to proceed in the light of their observations.

The evidence suggests that at Eastside the skills of the teachers in making such judgements are enhanced by the formal planning processes in which they participate. In general these formal processes address two broad areas: the nature of the curriculum experiences that are to be offered to all the pupils; and the perceived needs of each individual child, including those who are seen as having special needs. It does seem that the understanding, confidence and sensitivities that emerge as a result of these processes provide members of staff with preparation and support as they carry out necessary improvisations during the day. Such improvisations seem to be at the centre of inclusive practice and sometimes they involve a degree of risk-taking. An example will illustrate the point.

The school records indicate that Faheema is aged just six, has cerebral palsy and requires a rolator to aid her walking. It also notes that she is able to communicate, to some degree at least, in both English and Punjabi. On one occasion I watched her for some 45 minutes sitting on the floor in a very busy area of the wing doing a shape building task. Her walking frame was just behind her. For much of this period there was little direct adult involvement However, she did receive some assistance from one of the other pupils. Indeed this particular girl had some difficulties in moving away since when she tried to do so Faheema would call her back, even pulling her arm at one point to persuade her to sit down. In my field notes I commented on how I had been struck by the level of engagement sustained by Faheema, even in this context where there were so many potential distractions.

Directly after the lesson one of the teachers mentioned that Faheema had developed her ability to make choices well. Even so, she noted, just over 50% of the child's time is directed by adults. After I explained how I had observed her finish building the shape (a polyhedron) the teacher indicated that the staff would probably not have expected this of her. They would have assumed, she explained, that Faheema's fine-motor control was not sufficiently developed and that the task would not 'excite or stimulate her enough'. In this way Faheema had, it seems, overcome the limited expectations of the staff. As the teacher noted: 'There is a good lesson to learn in that and that is why it is important to allow children a level of choice. Out of that has come amazing developments in fine-motor skill and shape discrimination.' This also led her to comment that if planning is, in her words, 'too prescriptive', it may obstruct the recognition of such possibilities. Commenting on Faheema's persistence and concentration, she remarked: 'If it had been an adult chosen activity, say, at the moment, colour sorting, she would probably have done it for about thirty seconds and then had a bit of a "squawk" for thirty seconds.'

The emphasis placed on team work is also very evident in the classrooms at Eastside. This provides many incidental opportunities for staff to assist one another, share ideas and, of course, observe one another's practices. There is considerable research evidence to support the view that this type of mutual observation in the classroom can be a powerful stimulus for teacher development (e.g. Ainscow, 1995; Hopkins *et al.*, 1994; Joyce and Showers, 1988).

As can be seen, then, my interest in studying practice takes me beyond a consideration of the work of individual teachers. Much of my research over the last few years convinces me of the importance of the school context in creating a climate within which inclusive practices can be developed. The nature of such positive contexts can take many forms and, therefore, attempts at generalisations are very difficult. Nevertheless, the monitoring of developments in particular schools over time suggests certain patterns that are at least worthy of consideration (Ainscow, 1995; Ainscow *et al.*, 1994; Hopkins *et al.*, 1994). Specifically this suggests that greater collaboration between teachers is a powerful means of creating the conditions whereby more inclusive practices will develop. Much of this seems to be about creating an atmosphere that encourages teachers to reflect upon and experiment with aspects of their practice.

Developing practice

The approaches to teacher education adopted in the UNESCO project, as well as being based upon a study of mainstream classrooms, also assume a particular view of how teachers develop their practice. Specifically they assume that the development of practice occurs in the main through a largely 'trial and error' process within which teachers extend their repertoires as a result of finding out what works for them. Their previous experience as pupils themselves may be very influential in shaping this developmental process, in addition to their observations of other practitioners – including those who lecture to them in teacher education contexts. In this way, teachers create their own individual theories of teaching that guide their day-to-day practice. Such theories are largely unarticulated (Iano, 1986). They represent the 'tacit knowledge' that has been created through what seems to be a mainly intuitive process of learning from experience.

Similarly, Huberman (1993) argues that practice develops through what he calls 'tinkering', i.e. small adjustments that teachers make in their usual repertoires in response to unusual feedback from members of the class. Earlier, in my account of practices at Eastside School, I argued that skills of improvisation involved in making such adjustments may well be at the heart of the development of an inclusive pedagogy, with those pupils said to have special needs seen as sources of understanding as to how existing classroom arrangements might be improved in ways that could be to the benefit of the whole class (Ainscow, 1995).

Within the UNESCO project we attempt to work in ways that are consistent with this view of how teachers learn. Specifically we try to encourage teachers to become more confident and skilful in learning from experience through processes of reflection, in ways that we hope will stimulate further tinkering. Rather than simply leaving this to chance, we believe it is possible to create workshop contexts that enable them to recognise the value of this form of learning and to gain greater control of the processes involved.

There is, however, a rather obvious weakness in this emphasis on learning from experience. It may lead to situations where individuals are left alone to make sense of their experience and to draw whatever conclusions they can determine. It is, therefore, potentially a restricted and restricting source of learning. Consequently, within the UNESCO project we have placed considerable emphasis on the exploration of the power of collaboration in order to widen the resources available to teachers as they seek to develop aspects of their thinking and practice.

Here the aim is to encourage them to experience the value of dialogue with others in order to gain better understanding and to see further possibilities for improvements in practice. In this respect 'others' may include colleagues, pupils, parents and, of course, teacher educators. All of these are seen as sources of inspiration and support that can be used to facilitate learning. In addition they are all seen as offering alternative perspectives that can help individuals to interpret their experiences in new ways, not least by challenging taken-for-granted assumptions that may be influential in guiding their practices. Information from articles and books provide yet further resources that can be used to inform and extend this process of learning through experience.

These two ideas then, reflection and collaboration, are at the heart of the approaches that have been developed within the UNESCO project. Our experience of using them in many countries suggests that they can be influential in encouraging teacher and teacher educators to see improvement as a fundamental area of their work. We have also found that these ways of working can encourage teachers to adopt a more flexible view of the learning difficulties experienced by pupils in their classes – a view that sees such difficulties as sources of feedback on existing classroom arrangements. Indeed, as I have already argued, this feedback can be used as a stimulus for adjusting classroom arrangements in ways that may well be beneficial to the whole class. In this way, schools can be helped to provide teaching that is more effective in responding to the experience and existing knowledge of individual pupils.

Implications for teacher education

All of these arguments have major implications for teacher education in general. Put simply, they suggest that the tendency to treat the consideration of what we currently call special needs as a supplement to the core programme should be replaced by attempts to encourage teachers to develop more inclusive ways of working. Furthermore, this should be seen as an integral part of the development of the pedagogy of all teachers.

What, then, does this mean for the future of more specialised teacher education? What, if anything, should be the role of special needs training? Certainly it does seem that those in and around schools who are to take on the task of leading moves towards inclusive education have a massive agenda and will, therefore, need to draw on a wide range of expertise. Consequently it is necessary to consider what forms of professional development will be required for those who are to take on this radically reconstructed special needs role. Recently a report was prepared for the Department for Education and Employment by a working group of the Special Educational Needs Training Consortium (SENTC), addressing the professional development of teachers. The Report argues that a more planned and strategic approach is needed urgently. Unfortunately, its specific recommendations, particularly the competencies that are suggested, continue to argue for the use of the 'dividing practices' of traditional special education, based largely on what I have referred to as an individualised focus.

So, what competencies are necessary amongst teachers who are to take on leadership roles that will facilitate the development of inclusive schooling? What areas of understanding and skills are needed? Here it is important to recall the implications of the concept of inclusion referred to earlier. Whereas the idea of integration was seen as preparing children perceived as being special to fit into a school that remained largely unchanged, inclusive education starts from the assumption that all children have a right to attend their neighbourhood school. Therefore, the task becomes one of developing the work of the school in response to pupil diversity. As we have seen, this has to include a consideration of overall organisation, curriculum and classroom practice, support for learning and staff development.

Clearly this represents a very different agenda than that which has been included in the curriculum of most courses for special needs teachers. Rather than preparing them to work intensively with individuals or small groups of children, they need to acquire competencies that will enable them to take a lead in the development of schools as 'learning organisations', i.e. organisations that are continually seeking to develop and refine their responses to the challenges they meet (Singe, 1989). In this way direct links are made between difficulties in learning and the overall improvement of schooling.

It seems to me that the time is ripe for such a change. The SENTC Report has been successful in stimulating a debate as to the future shape of teacher education. We should use this opportunity to explore new possibilities, learning from both the successes and failures of previous experiences.

At the Centre for Educational Needs in the University of Manchester we are attempting to make positive moves in these directions. Starting in September 1997, there will be a new masters degree programme that will engage with the relationship between special needs and development. It is designed to prepare experienced teachers, from this country and overseas, to take on leadership roles in their school systems. The focus will be on using the stimulus of children experiencing difficulties to ask questions as to how the school can be developed. In other words, we will be asking what is wrong with the school rather than what's wrong with the child.

The course includes a module on school-based enquiry, focusing on processes for analysing and interpreting existing policy and practice. There will also be modules addressing management and organisation, curriculum, pedagogy and pastoral care. Thus the course will provide participants with the necessary skills and knowledge to coordinate a process of school review and development.

Possibly the most significant aspect of the new course, however, will be the emphasis it places on the importance of collaboration between pupils, teachers and parents as a means of developing schools for all. Here we are building on evidence that schools which are effective in responding to diversity do so through an intensification of team work, including cooperative planning and, wherever possible, partnership teaching in the classroom. It is a simple idea but one that is difficult to implement in schools that seem to have been designed to isolate teachers from their colleagues.

In order to reinforce this approach, the planning and teaching of the new modules will be undertaken by small teams of tutors, modelling the power of collaboration as a means of creating more inclusive learning environments. In this way, teacher educators will be attempting to demonstrate their belief in the principles they are promoting.

References

Ainscow, M. (1993a) 'Teacher education as a strategy for developing inclusive schools', in R. Slee (ed.) *Is There a Desk with my Name on it? The politics of integration.* London: Farmer.

Ainscow, M. (1993b) 'Teacher development and special needs: some lessons from the UNESCO project "Special Needs in the Classroom"', P. Mittler and R. Brouillette (eds.) *Special Needs Education (World Yearbook of Education).* London: Kogan Page.

Ainscow, M. (1994a) 'Supporting international innovation in teacher education', in H. Bradley, C. Conner and G. Southworth (eds.) *Developing Teachers, Developing Schools.* London: David Fulton.

Ainscow, M. (1994b) *Special Needs in the Classroom: a teacher education guide.* London: Jessica Kingsley/UNESCO.

Ainscow, M. (1995) 'Education for all: making it happen', *Support for Learning,* **10** (4),

Ainscow, M. (1996) 'The development of inclusive practices in an English primary school: constraints and influences', paper presented at the American Education Research Association Meeting, New York.

Ainscow, M. and Tweddle, D. (1979) *Preventing Classroom Failure.* London: David Fulton.

Ainscow, M. and Tweddle, D. (1984) *Early Learning Skills Analysis.* London: David Fulton.

Ainscow, M., Hopkins, D., Southworth, G. and West, M. (1994) *Creating the Conditions for School Improvement.* London: David Fulton.

Booth, T., Ainscow, M. and Dyson, A. (1997, in press) 'Understanding inclusion in competitive system', in T. Booth and M. Ainscow (eds.) *From Them To Us: international voices on inclusion in education.* London: Routledge.

Fulcher, G. (1989) *Disabling Policies? A comparative approach to education policy and disability.* London: Falmer.

Hopkins, D., Ainscow, M. and West, M. (1994) *School Improvement in an Era of Change.* London: Cassell.

Huberman, M. (1993) 'The model of the independent artisan in teachers' professional relations', in J. Little and M. McLaughlin (eds.) *Teachers' Work: individuals, colleagues and contexts.* New York: Teachers' College Press.

Iano, R. (1986) 'The study and development of teaching: with implications for the advancement of special education', *Remedial and Special Education,* **7** (5), 50–61.

Joyce, B. and Showers, B. (1988) *Student Achievement Through Staff Development.* London: Longman.

Miles, M. (1989) 'The role of special education in information based rehabilitation'. *International Journal of Special Education,* **4** (2), 111–118.

Sebba, J. and Ainscow, M. (1996) 'International developments in inclusive schooling: mapping the issues', *Cambridge Journal of Education,* **26** (1), 5–18.

SENTC (1996) *Professional Development to Meet Special Educational Needs: A Report to the Department for Education and Employment.* Stafford: SENTC.

Singe, P. (1989) *The Fifth Discipline: the art and practice of the learning organisation.* London: Century.

Slee, R. (1996) 'Inclusive schooling in Australia? Not yet', *Cambridge Journal of Education,* **1**, 19–32.

UNESCO (1994) *The Salamanca Statement and Framework for Action on Special Needs Education.* Paris: UNESCO.

Name Index

Subject Index